Public Speaking

Skills for Success

Public Speaking

Skills for Success

Thomas J. Farrell
Maureen M. Farrell

both of

Johnson & Wales University

***MIRROR PRESS*™**
IRWIN

Chicago • Bogotá • Boston • Buenos Aires • Caracas
London • Madrid • Mexico City • Sydney • Toronto

Excerpt from EFFECTIVE TELEPHONE SKILLS, Second Edition, by Thomas J. Farrell, copyright © 1994 by Harcourt Brace & Company, reprinted by permission of the publisher.

© Richard D. Irwin, a Times Mirror Higher Education Group, Inc., company, 1997

Mirror Press:	*David R. Helmstadter*
	Elizabeth R. Deck
Marketing manager:	*Carl Helwing*
Project supervisor:	*Paula M. Buschman*
Production supervisor:	*Pat Frederickson*
Assistant manager, desktop services:	*Jon Christopher*
Designer:	*Andrew Barnes/Electronic Publishing Services, Inc.*
Compositor:	*Electronic Publishing Services, Inc.*
Typeface:	*11/14 Cheltenham Light*
Printer:	*TMHEG Manufacturing Group*

Times Mirror
Higher Education Group

Library of Congress Cataloging-in-Publication Data

Farrell, Thomas J.
    Public speaking : skills for success/ Thomas J. Farrell, Maureen M. Farrell.
      p. cm.
    Includes index.
    ISBN 0-256-18701-0
    1. Business presentations. 2. Public speaking I. Farrell, Maureen M. II. Title.
HF5718.22.F37   1997
808.5'1—dc20   96–9323

Printed in the United States of America
1 2 3 4 5 6 7 8 9 0 WCB 3 2 1 0 9 8 7 6

Preface

Public Speaking: Skills for Success will give students the keys to success in a business career and in their interpersonal relationships. While the major focus of the book is on the art of public speaking, it also serves as a catalyst to explore a full range of other communication skills that are necessary to full and productive participation in society. The fundamental premise of the book is that to be successful, one must communicate effectively.

This book is organized into four parts. Part 1, "Fundamental Principles of Communication," explains the relationship between success and effective communication skills. Next, this section examines the basic concepts of intrapersonal and interpersonal communication, as well as listening and nonverbal communication. Finally, we cover the relationship between communication skills and leadership skills, a subject that attracts considerable student interest on campuses across the country.

Part 2, "Public Speaking for Business and Community," guides the reader through the preliminary steps of preparing a speech, including selecting a topic and analyzing the needs of an audience. Methods of preparing and writing speeches, along with the effective use of visual aids, are covered. Model speeches and exercises are provided at the end of each chapter.

Part 3, "Presentation and Practice," addresses the best ways to deliver a successful speech. It begins with instructions to help overcome speech anxiety. Four different types of speeches are analyzed, as well as shorter speeches for special occasions and impromptu talks. Again, models and exercises are provided to help readers sharpen their skills.

The goal of Part 4, "Applying Communication Skills in Business," is to ensure that the reader is prepared to use communication skills in real-world situations. It first presents job-search strategies, including the steps needed to create a résumé, research jobs and job fields, prepare for an interview, and interview successfully. The last chapters introduce the reader to the world of corporate communications with a look at the new technology that is changing the way communication takes place in the workplace.

Features

Unique topic coverage. This textbook goes beyond oral communication topics to cover listening skills, leadership skills, group communication, and conflict resolution. It also includes unique chapters linking communication skills to community and business environments, and emphasizes that speaking skills should be part of ongoing career growth.

Learning outcomes. Listed learning outcomes at the beginning of each chapter outline the objectives and scope of the chapter.

Questions for review and discussion. These exercises at the end of each chapter keep students involved in improving their speaking skills. Exercises review chapter content through checklists, self-assessment questionnaires, and discussion questions. Questions ask the students to review chapter content and are appropriate for in-class use or as homework.

Applications. Beginning with the first chapter, application exercises are designed to get students in front of the class, practicing their skills. Questions prompt students to react to situations with an appropriate speech to simulate real-life speaking situations.

Sample speeches. Model speeches appear at the end of most chapters to provide students with models of effective speech making. Speakers are drawn from fields of business, government, and entertainment. Topics are current and range from achieving success in work or school to leadership in the community. Discussion questions follow each speech.

Ancillaries

An Instructors' Manual containing teaching aids and exercise answers is available.

Acknowledgments

We would like to thank the following reviewers for their thoughtful contributions to this text:

Karen L. Cole, Southern Ohio College, Ohio

Beth Crawford, DuBois Business College, Pennsylvania

Phyllis T. Fox, South Hills Business School, Pennsylvania

Vincent Miskell, Bergenfield, New Jersey

Celeste Toffolo, Elmira Business Institute, New York

Melvin Wyler, Hagerstown Business College, Maryland

Contents

Part 3 *Presentation and Practice*

Public Speaking

Skills for Success

Fundamental Principles of Communication

Success and Effective Communication Skills

Learning Outcomes

After studying this chapter, you should be able to:

❶ Explain the relationship between success and effective communication skills.

❷ Understand the relationship between personality and communication style.

❸ Define the socialization process.

❹ Identify the characteristics of three types of communicators.

❺ Recognize some of your present communication strengths as well as those areas you need to improve.

INTRODUCTION

Every four years, athletes from all over the world gather together to compete in the Olympic games. The athletes' goals are to represent their countries to the best of their abilities and, if they are the best, to take home the coveted gold medal. Young men and women work hard to perfect their specialty, whether it be swimming, basketball, running, skating, or some other sport. Each has the same objective: *to succeed, to win the gold.*

As students, you are very much like those Olympic athletes. You train for two or four years with a clear objective in mind. You look forward to the day when you can, with pride, represent your family and your school in the competitive world of business. Even your goal is similar to the Olympic athlete's: *to succeed, to do the best work of which you are capable.* All your courses are geared toward helping you achieve your goal, but the course (or courses) that will help you the most is the one that focuses on improving your communication skills. It may be called "Public Speaking," "Speech," or "Communication Skills" in your curriculum. The course title is not important, but the course content is vital. Make it your specialty.

Think of this book as a training manual that provides a program to prepare you to be a winner in the competitive business world that awaits you. Listen to your instructor in the same way you would respond to the directions of a coach. Be enthusiastic; enjoy what you are doing; and take pride in your growth and development. Be confident that, with sincere effort on your part, you too can be a winner. *You can be successful!*

COMMUNICATION SKILLS IN AN INFORMATIONAL SOCIETY

It is **essential** that you understand and accept the premise that the most important factor in determining your future success is how well you communicate with others. Believe it, for it is fact. Should you need more convincing, consider the following statement:

> The Midwest College Placement Association conducted a study to determine what skills and qualities employers look for in hiring. The results were revealing. The most important skill was oral communication—83 percent ranked it as very important—and the third most important skill was the ability to build interpersonal relationships—74 percent ranked it as very important.[1]

Figure 1–1
Qualities that Count
with Employers

Figures from a Census Bureau survey of 3,000 employers nationwide, conducted in August and September of 1994.

When you consider hiring a new non-supervisory or production worker, how important are the following in your decision to hire?

(Ranked on a scale of 1 through 5, with 1 being not important or not considered, and 5 being very important.)

Factor	Rank
Attitude	4.6
Communication skills	4.2
Previous work experience	4.0
Recommendations from current employer	3.4
Recommendations from previous employer	3.4
Industry-based credentials certifying skills	3.2
Years of schooling completed	2.9
Score on tests administered as part of interview	2.5
Academic performance (grades)	2.5
Experience or reputation of applicant's school	2.4
Teacher recommendations	2.1

Source: Census Bureau.

A 1994 Census Bureau survey produced for the U.S. Department of Education questioned 3,000 employers nationwide about what qualities were important in their decision to hire new employees. The most important factor was *attitude* and the second most important was communication skills, as you can see in Figure 1–1.

Simply put, strong communication skills play a major role in your getting hired, and once you are employed, those same skills are vital to advancement and promotion. You do not have to be in public relations or marketing to need to communicate well. Throughout your working career, you will have to present yourself, your ideas, and information to others. If you aspire to positions of leadership, if you wish to have a positive impact on others, if you want to have your talents recognized and rewarded, the conclusion is inescapable. To be successful, you must strive to be an effective communicator.

Why now? To some degree, this has always been the case but, today, more than ever, it is a basic requirement in business. Along with everything else in our lives, the nature of work in our country has changed rapidly over the past forty years. In the bestseller, *Mega-trends,* John Naisbitt sketched a brief occupational history of the United States that is helpful to an understanding of our point.

Until 1956, we lived and worked in an industrial society where most people were blue-collar workers producing goods. After 1956, white-collar workers began to increasingly outnumber blue-collar workers. Industrial America began to give way to a new post-industrial society where most people work with information rather than producing goods.[2]

Today, the industrial and post-industrial societies are gone. They have been replaced by an informational society in which the need to communicate well is more critical than ever. Today, the largest job classification in our economy is clerical and the second largest is professional. In these categories people work with information as programmers, teachers, clerks, secretaries, accountants, stockbrokers, managers, insurance agents, bureaucrats, lawyers, bankers, and technicians. No matter what sector of the economy you work in, you will need excellent communication skills to be successful in the information age.

At the same time that the informational society was evolving, other social and cultural changes were occuring that affected communication. The workplace has become more humanized with better-educated workers insisting that their work be more personally satisfying and that they be treated as individuals rather than cogs in a machine. The drill sergeant model of management has passed away—even in the Army. Theory X, the management approach which supported an authoritarian type of management, has been replaced with Theory Y and other more progressive concepts of management involving employees in more participatory, democratic approaches to decision making. In this new environment, employees who are confident of their communications ability can have a greater impact than ever before.

HOW TO MAKE IT HAPPEN

The two keys to improving your communication skills are *awareness* and *change.* To start, you must evaluate your own strengths and weaknesses as communicator. What are you presently doing well? What not so well? What do you understand about your own personality and how it relates to communication? Are you knowledgeable about current theories of communication? Once this honest inventory has been taken, you are ready to begin behavioral change to improve your skills. Like the Olympic athlete in training, you can set your goals and begin working to achieve them.

SOCIALIZATION IS ONGOING—CHANGE IS POSSIBLE

It wasn't too long ago that the common belief was that our personality was fully formed by the time we finished adolescence and little fundamental change occurred after that point in our lives. That idea has now been set aside. While it is still recognized that the most significant socialization occurs during childhood and adolescence, there is now widespread agreement that change and development continue into old age. Erik Erikson and Orvill G. Brim, Jr., are two theorists who contend that substantial personality change and development do occur throughout our lifetimes.

Erikson's *Eight Stages of Human Development* (see box p. 8) suggests that, as we move through the stages of our lives, we encounter difficult challenges that need to be met and dealt with before we are able to go on to the next stage.[3] These developmental stages continue all the way to old age. If we experience difficulties or emotional hurt at one stage of our life, they can be repaired by successful coping at another stage. As a means of helping you to continue to evaluate your personality, read the description of each of Erikson's stages to see the challenges you have already met and ones you have yet to face. Keep in mind: *change is possible.*

Brim's theory stresses the differences between childhood socialization and the socialization of adults. Two of his points are of special importance to you as you prepare to learn the communication skills that are necessary to career success:

- Adult socialization is more likely to change outward behavior, whereas childhood socialization molds basic internal values.
- Adult socialization is designed to help a person gain specific skills; childhood socialization deals more with motivation.[4]

The course you are taking and this textbook you are reading are both part of *your* ongoing adult socialization process. If Brim is correct, and there is general support for his views, feel confident that you can change your present communication habits and acquire the skills that you need to accomplish your goals.

Erikson's Eight Stages of Human Development

1. *TRUST vs. MISTRUST (infancy)*

   From nursing, diaper changing, napping and cuddling, babies learn to what extent their basic needs will be met. When infants are secure enough so that they no longer feel rage or anger when their caregiver goes away, the first crisis in development has been resolved. Traces of mistrust may remain, however; resolution often is not complete.

2. *AUTONOMY vs. SHAME AND DOUBT (1–2 yrs.)*

   The child learns how to talk, learns to run without falling down, and acquires much more knowledge about the world. This is when self-assertion and defiance of authority blossom. At the same time, it is the stage in which parents usually attempt bowel training. Too many demands in this area can instill a strong sense of shame and worthlessness in the child and undermine his or her efforts to achieve autonomy and self-direction.

3. *INITIATIVE vs. GUILT (3–5 yrs.)*

   This period is one of movement, curiosity, and imagination. Rivalry and awareness of sex differences are prominent at this stage. As a result, the child experiences conflict over how far to take the initiative in asserting new abilities.

4. *INDUSTRY vs. INFERIORITY (early school yrs.)*

   Children learn to carry out individual tasks like reading books and collective tasks like classroom work projects. They form relationships with teachers and other adults. They become interested in real-life roles: fire-fighter, pilot, nurse. Their most important task, however, is to gain self-confidence and competence, since it is during this stage that children are introduced to (and act out in their fantasies) actual adult roles. Unsuccessful resolution of this crisis leaves a child feeling inferior and inadequate.

5. *IDENTITY vs. ROLE DIFFUSION (adolescence)*

   Two major events occur at this time. Physically, young people become adults with an active sex drive: they are also expected to find a niche in society. The adolescent must decide whether to go to college, find a job, and choose a mate. Failure to do so may disrupt later attempts to choose suitable jobs, partners, and friends.

6. *INTIMACY vs. ISOLATION (early adulthood)*
   Courtship, marriage, and other types of intimacy are the key objectives during this stage. The person seeks an open, trusting relationship, usually with a permanent mate; this may, however, fail and lead to separation or divorce. If the conflict between intimacy and isolation is not resolved, the person may go through a series of temporary, always-broken relationships.

7. *GENERATIVITY vs. STAGNATION (middle adulthood)*
   This stage is concerned mainly with coming to terms with work and parenting. How ambitious is the person? How early does he or she burn out in a work career? Can he or she successfully generate new members of society through birth and caring? How are failures in work and parenting coped with?

8. *INTEGRITY vs. DESPAIR (late adulthood)*
   In this phase the person sums up his or her life, grows old gracefully or bitterly, and perhaps takes on some new philosophical view of life. If the person is satisfied with his or her life, the result is a sense of integrity. If not, the outcome is despair.

PERSONALITY AND COMMUNICATION

Your effort to develop communication skills that will contribute to a successful career must start with self-evaluation. Before you go forward, you must look backward. You have already lived a significant span of your life and, in the process, formed a personality that directly influences the way you interact with others. It is necessary that you reflect for a while on just how you became the person you are and why each of you has a personality distinct from one another.

Social scientists define *personality* as a system of beliefs, attitudes, and behaviors that are the particular qualities and characteristics of a person.

There are many theories explaining how personalities develop, but it is not our purpose to present detailed explanations of these theories. That is more the function of a psychology or sociology textbook.

However, we can generalize by noting that these theories take one of two broad approaches: biological determinism or cultural determinism. Simply stated, biologically deterministic theories suggest that genetic factors have a greater impact on human behavior than was previously thought. Culturally deterministic theories claim that environment, the things we are exposed to in our lives, is the primary influence that molds our personalities. The truth probably lies somewhere between the two theories and there is still much that we have to learn. We can, however, acknowledge the biological theories and still claim that our personalities are primarily the result of the cultural stimuli we receive during the *socialization* process.

Socialization

Socialization is the way that you acquire your human personality: that is, the process in which you learn the skills, values, attitudes, and role behaviors that you use in life. For most of you, the most important influences during your socialization were your parents, the teachers in the schools you attended, your religious education, the friends you have, and, today more than ever before, television and other media that help shape your views. It might be useful at this point for you to try to connect some of your positive personality characteristics with the socializing factor you consider most responsible for each characteristic. Choose any ten of your personal qualities that you consider to be positive and write them in the spaces provided. Next to the ones that you choose, indicate whether your parents, your teachers, your religion, your peers, or television and other media have been the major factors shaping that part of your personality.

EXERCISE

1

Positive Quality or Characteristic *example:* competitive	*Major Influence* father
1. _____	_____
2. _____	_____
3. _____	_____
4. _____	_____

Positive Quality or Characteristic	*Major Influence*
5. _____	_____
6. _____	_____
7. _____	_____
8. _____	_____
9. _____	_____
10. _____	_____

When you have completed the exercise, take a few moments to think about the choices you have made. What do they tell you about your personality and how it has been formed? Clearly, your selections say a lot about your self-image, which is so vital to developing effective communication skills. You have a positive self-image when you see and evaluate yourself in terms that are consistent with the person you ideally want to be. When this occurs, you are able to present yourself to others in a manner that will lead to successful and productive communication.

The reverse is also true. Negative self-images (which may also result from the socialization process) make effective communication difficult, if not impossible. Since very few people have entirely positive (or negative) self-images, you need to identify those personality traits that are not consistent with the person you really wish to be. As before, see if you can connect each undesirable trait you write down with the major socializing influence responsible for it. For example, if you started smoking as a teenager because of peer pressure (as many teenagers do), you would list smoking as a negative personality characteristic with "friends" as the major influence.

Negative Quality or Characteristic	*Major Influence*
1. _____	_____
2. _____	_____

Negative Quality or Characteristic	*Major Influence*
3. _____	_____
4. _____	_____
5. _____	_____
6. _____	_____
7. _____	_____
8. _____	_____
9. _____	_____
10. _____	_____

Once again, think about the choices you have written down and the connections you made. What else do they tell you about your personality and how it was formed? Which of the two lists was easier to complete? How do you feel about your self-image? Positively? Negatively? Mixed? . . . Whatever the results of this initial self-evaluation, remember that your personality is the product of your socialization. It is important that you keep that in mind as we consider some new knowledge about the socialization process.

Habits: Break Bad Ones—Learn New Ones

Before you begin to consider this program of self-improvement, another insight into your personality may be helpful. Do you know that to a large extent, our everyday behaviors are patterned, and quite predictable? This is so because we are creatures of habit who tend to repeat and reinforce our behaviors until they become automatic. According to William Brown, chairman of the Sociology Department at the University of Florida, 90 percent of our behavior could be called habitual. This reliance on habit helps us cope with our everyday lives and makes life easier. Think of all the behaviors you engage in each day by habit, without thinking out each detail of what you are doing. When you drive a car or play a sport, you are acting by habit. This is all for the good.

Unfortunately, habitual behavior has its negative side. We can just as easily learn incorrect, non-productive habits as we can correct, productive ones, and we do. For example, if you are like most people, you probably are not a good listener, which means you have acquired ineffective listening habits. *All habits are difficult to break* but they can be broken and replaced with different and stronger habits. To do this you need the desire, the will, and the knowledge. That is, you have to want to change, be willing to work hard at doing so, and have access to the information necessary for change. If you have these three requirements, you can begin to identify the person you really are, develop a positive self-image, and learn how to communicate with others in ways that will lead to success.

THREE TYPES OF COMMUNICATORS

Another method of identifying the person you really are is to try to place yourself in one of the broad categories of communications types characterized below: the Cooperative Communicator, the Dominating Communicator, and the Yielding Communicator. While it is true that your behavior as communicators will vary depending on the people you are with and the situation you are in, it is probably equally true that certain patterns or habits tend to characterize our behavior *most* of the time. Whatever your own repetitive patterns are will determine which category you belong to. Next to the terms below, write "yes" after the characteristic that describes your communications behavior *most* of the time and "no" where the characteristic occurs infrequently or not at all. The category with the most "yeses" may in fact be the one to which you presently belong.

The Cooperative Communicator

- Encourages dialogue and is willing to listen to another person's point of view. _____
- Works for joint understanding and solutions to problems so that goals may be attained. _____
- Offers new ideas and suggestions willingly. _____
- Recognizes that he/she is not always right and that to be wrong is, indeed, quite human. _____
- Looks for new ways of doing things and is not reluctant to "stick one's neck out" by experimentation. _____

The Dominating Communicator

- Is strictly a one-way communicator. _____.
- Feels that his/her own ideas are best and does not listen to others. _____
- Imposes his/her own point of view on others whenever possible. _____
- Is not open to alternative approaches to accomplishing objectives. _____
- Tries to preserve the status quo and does not encourage experimentation. _____

The Yielding Communicator

- Is passive and shifts the responsibility for communication to the other person. _____
- Believes that other people have more to contribute than he/she does. (Often, it becomes clear, after the fact, that this is not the case.) _____
- Allows himself/herself to be manipulated by other people even when he/she knows what is happening. _____
- Assumes that nothing can be done to improve a situation so why bother trying. _____
- Will consider alternatives and experiments only if others are responsible for the outcome. _____

CONCLUSION

Once you have studied the three types of communicators, which of the three do you feel describes you best? Obviously, in today's "informational" society, the more "cooperative" characteristics you possess the better prepared you will be to participate in the new wave that is sweeping management-employee relations in our economy. The "dominating" communicators are still to be found but, like the dinosaurs of the Mesozoic Era, they are a vanishing breed who will soon be extinct. Finally, it is self-evident that the "yielding" communicator is one who is not going to share in the potential rewards of a successful business career. As was discussed earlier, change is possible. *Work to become a "cooperative" communicator.*

NOTES

1. Douglas Ehringer; Bruce E. Gonbeck; and Alan H. Munroe. *Principles of Speech Communication.* Glenview: Scott, Foresman and Co, 1984, p. 10.

2. John Naisbitt. *Megatrends: Ten New Directions Transforming Our Lives.* New York: Warner Books, Inc. 1982, p. 13.

3. Eric Erikson. *Childhood and Society.* New York: Norton, 1963, p. 247.

4. Orville Brim and Stanton Wheeler. *Socialization after Childhood: Two Essays.* New York: John Wiley & Sons, Inc., 1966, p. 26.

QUESTIONS FOR REVIEW AND DISCUSSION

Demonstrate that you have mastered the objectives (outcomes) of this chapter by answering the following questions.

1. How highly do employers value oral communication skills in prospective employees?

2. What does it mean to shift from an industrial society to an informational society?

3. What are the two keys to improving your communication skills?

4. How do social scientists define personality?

5. What are the most important influences on an individual during socialization?

6. Why is a positive self-image so important to effective communication skills?

7. According to Erikson, what are the eight stages of human development?

8. What are the key differences between childhood socialization and adult socialization according to Brim's theory?

9. Can negative communication habits be changed? How?

10. Describe the three types of communicators.

APPLICATION EXERCISES

1. Each student in the class should spend approximately 10 minutes jotting down on a slip of paper why they are nervous about public speaking. What are you afraid will happen? Be specific. If the instructor or a student collects these papers and reads them aloud, the class will be surprised—and probably comforted—to know that most in the class share exactly the same fears. Sharing common concerns and the common goal of working on these anxieties should lessen anxiety and provide the class with a sense of unity—you already have something in common!

2. Each student should introduce him- or herself to the rest of the class. Spend about fifteen minutes preparing a brief (two or three minutes) speech of self-introduction. To do so, try to reveal one aspect of yourself—perhaps a goal you are working toward, an event which changed your life, or a hobby which greatly interests you. In focusing on any one of these aspects, you will introduce yourself to the class in an effective, interesting way.

3. Take a few minutes to do the personal assessment test on the next page. This is a general test that will give you some understanding of your pluses and minuses as a communicator. The test should also be a starting point for you to evaluate your "communications quotient" or your communications awareness. Please keep in mind that there are no right or wrong answers. Simply answer the questions honestly. Usually the first answer that comes to mind is your best answer. The questions that follow explore various areas of communication that we will discuss throughout the book. These questions cover listening, nonverbal communication, public speaking and presentational skills, speech anxiety, intrapersonal communication, interviewing, small group communication, and interpersonal communication.

Please answer the questions as follows:

1/Always   2/Sometimes   3/Never

If you are asked the following question: "I enjoy speaking before audiences.", write the number that best fits your position. If you don't enjoy it, you would write #3. Or if the question reads: "My friends seek me out because they know I listen well." Write #2 if you believe you "sometimes" listen well.

Work carefully and alone on the questions. Do not consult with your classmates.

Please write your answer in the space provided. Write 1, 2, or 3 only.

1. _____   I know the right thing to say in all types of environments.

2. _____   I look forward to speaking before all types of audiences.

3. _____   I am sought out to represent others when they can't represent themselves.

4. _____   People recognize me as a good listener.

5. _____   I withhold evaluation while I am listening until I have heard all the facts.

6. _____   I can accept compliments without embarrassment.

7. _____   I try to write all the facts down when I'm listening to a lecturer.

8. _____   My emotions do not interfere with my ability to listen.

9. _____   I enjoy debating all types of issues.

10. _____   I look forward to the challenges of interviewing for a job.

11. _____   I enjoy interviewing people to work for me.

12. _____   I find myself reacting to ideas instead of the personality of the speaker.

13. _____   People compliment me on my smile.

EXERCISE 3

(continued)

14. _____ It is easy for me to concentrate and get rid of distractions when I am working.

15. _____ Speaking in public is something I relish.

16. _____ I know what is required of me in all communicative settings.

17. _____ I am looked upon as an extrovert.

18. _____ One of my communications strengths is my voice.

19. _____ I am considered a person who knows how to dress for the occasion.

20. _____ When participating in small groups, I like to take a primary role in directing the other group members.

21. _____ When meeting people for the first time, I never find myself at a loss for words.

22. _____ Discussing controversial topics is something I handle well.

23. _____ When speaking with others, one on one, I find myself reinforcing my messages by the use of examples and illustrations.

24. _____ When speaking with others, I maintain eye contact.

25. _____ I like to voice my opinions in groups.

26. _____ I look forward to breaking down in small groups to discuss the resolutions of problems.

27. _____ I know how to get people to do things for me with little difficulty.

28. _____ Getting along with others is easy for me.

29. _____ I would be a good salesperson because I'm a persuasive speaker.

30. _____ I am aware of the nonverbal messages others transmit.

31. _____ I like to give directions to others.

32. _____ People look upon me as a good judge of character.

33. _____ I have a strong self-image.

34. _____ I am relaxed when in a room full of strangers.

35. _____ One of the things people compliment me on is my good attitude.

36. _____ I understand social custom and the rules of etiquette.

37. _____ When I come right down to it, I consider myself a superior communicator.

38. _____ I find it easy to control my temper and emotions.

39. _____ I consider speaking before others a privilege and an important opportunity.

40. _____ I listen to others without daydreaming.

41. _____ I speak positively to myself as part of a "stage-fright" reduction technique.

42. _____ When a person smiles at me, I know it could mean many different things. Therefore, I don't jump to conclusions when interpreting messages.

43. _____ I am looked upon as an understanding and sympathetic friend.

44. _____ Before speaking, regardless of the environment, I do my research.

45. _____ A sales presentation is an exciting opportunity for me.

46. _____ When interacting with others interpersonally or one on one, I am successful.

47. _____ When I am involved with clubs or organizations I like to function in a leadership role.

48. _____ I understand the interviewing process and feel confident that I could successfully answer the questions an interviewer is likely to ask.

49. _____ When it comes to controversy or settling disputes, people seek me out as a calming influence.

50. _____ Shyness is never a barrier to my interaction.

Remember, there are no right or wrong answers.

EXERCISE 3

(continued)

Next, write the number of the questions that you answered 3, 2, or 1, and fill in below; refer to the next page for additional directions.

1—ALWAYS		2—SOMETIMES		3—NEVER	
Ques. No.	Skill	Ques. No.	Skill	Ques. No.	Skill

Now, from the chart below, fill in next to the question number the kind of skill involved in each question. The ones that crop up most frequently in column 3 are the areas in which you need the most help; column 2 suggests areas where your self-evaluation is mixed; column 1 should be your strengths.

1. Public speaking—presentational
2. Public speaking
3. Interpersonal
4. Listening
5. Listening
6. Interpersonal
7. Listening
8. Listening
9. Small Groups
10. Interviewing
11. Interviewing
12. Listening
13. Interpersonal
14. Interpersonal
15. Public Speaking
16. General
17. Intrapersonal
18. Intrapersonal
19. Intrapersonal
20. Small Groups
21. Interpersonal
22. Interpersonal
23. Interpersonal
24. Nonverbal
25. Small Groups
26. Small Groups
27. Interpersonal
28. Interpersonal
29. Interpersonal
30. Nonverbal
31. Interpersonal
32. Intrapersonal
33. Intrapersonal
34. Interpersonal
35. Intrapersonal
36. Interpersonal
37. Intrapersonal
38. Intrapersonal
39. Public Speaking
40. Listening
41. Speech Anxiety
42. Nonverbal
43. Intrapersonal
44. Public Speaking
45. Presentational
46. Interpersonal
47. Small Groups
48. Interviewing
49. Interpersonal
50. Intrapersonal

FOR ADDITIONAL READING AND DISCUSSION

AND THEN SOME
Give More, Get More, Want More from Life!

by Richard L. Weaver III

The following motivational speech was delivered by Richard L. Weaver II, Professor of Interpersonal and Public Communication, Bowling Green State University to the university's Golden Key National Honors Society on November 12, 1989. Weaver offers a useful philosophy for you to consider as you begin learning the different meanings of "success" and the extent to which your success depends on your relationships not only with society and with other people but also with your self.

A prominent salesman friend of mine summed up his success in three simple words: "and then some." He discovered at an early age, he said, that most of the difference between average people and top people could be explained in three words:

"The top people did what was expected of them—*and then some.* They were thoughtful of others; they were considerate and kind—*and then some.* They met their obligations and responsibilities fairly and squarely—*and then some.* They were good friends to their friends—*and*

Published in *Vital Speeches of the Day,* March 15, 1990. Reprinted with permission.

then some. They could be counted on in an emergency—*and then some."*

"And then some"—three little words— and those three little words could transform our society as well as your academic and personal life. It *could* become a philosophy of life—a way of living. Let me show you the power in those words.

What I want to do in this speech is show you how this "and then some" philosophy relates first to society, second to your studies, and, third, to your personal life. The unique thing about it is that it can be applied to almost everything with which you have contact! We'll apply it to society first.

Before I get into how "and then some" relates to society, however, I have a confession to make; I have a hang-up. Earlier this year I wrote about my hang-up to the *Toledo Blade.* It was published in January, 1989. Here's what I wrote there:

"As I watch people throw trash and cigarette butts out their windows, dump their ashtrays in parking lots, and leave the places they visit littered with their leftovers, I am reminded of a beautiful statement I once read: 'We live a life luxurious beyond the dreams of millions of the earth's inhabitants. We are lucky. We were born into it. The least we can do with this magnificent heritage is to preserve it and pass it along as rich and as pure as it came to us.'

"With the beginning of a new year, with the inauguration of a new President, and with the goals of renewal and enhancement, let us all resolve, in the paraphrase of an old Greek promise made more than 2,000 years ago, to transmit this country better than it was transmitted to us (*Toledo Blade,* January 30, 1989, p. 8)."

How do we "transmit [a] country better than it was transmitted to us?" The key, I think, is in those three little words: "and then some."

We are the leaders of the next generation. As far as this campus is concerned, we're the leaders of the current generation. If *we* don't take the responsibility, then who will?

The "and then some" philosophy forces us out of our complacent, self-centered, apathetic, lazy, preoccupied, busy *little* worlds and puts us in touch with a bigger reality. It's a message that says if we don't take responsibility for the world, who will? We *can* make a difference!

Now I am not suggesting you have to suddenly become involved in world affairs, American politics, or even student government—although that wouldn't be bad! I'm not even suggesting that you read a daily newspaper, a weekly news magazine, or watch the TV news—"boring stuff" according to *my* teenage daughter! What I *am* suggesting is taking some responsibility for the world *you* touch—the one with which *you* come into contact. What you will begin to notice, is that as you start using this "and then some" philosophy in small ways, it will become habitual, and you will start using it in bigger ways. Some of the little ways might include:

—leaving a room cleaner than the way *you* found it. The other day, I asked my son to straighten up the family room before coming upstairs. He quickly looked around the room and said, "None of this is mine!" (If I had thought more quickly, I would have run into the study to get this speech! I missed an opportunity

Continued on page 24

Continued from page 23

to practice it.)

Leaving a room cleaner than the way *you* found it is one of the little ways we might begin practicing the "and then some" philosophy in the world we touch. Let me list a couple more:

—not just being a critic but offering a few suggestions

—closing a door that needs closing, cleaning a table that needs cleaning, putting dishes or things back where they belong

—not just giving someone directions but drawing a map

—not just speaking to someone else but offering a handshake

—not just listening to others but actually caring

—not just giving others a smile but offering a few words

Let me share with you an example of "not just giving others a smile but offering a few words." This was a letter to Ann Landers, printed October 19, 1989:

"Last Sunday I attended an art exhibit in Michigan. I was wandering around among hundreds of people when a young woman touched my arm and said, 'You are a beautiful lady.' Ann, I was thunderstruck. I am 88 years old and never considered myself anything special to look at. But I'm healthy and happy and grateful to the good Lord for all his blessings. Maybe this is what comes through in my face.

"What a delight to be told that I am beautiful by a stranger. Every day this week I have been cheered by that lovely compliment. It gave my heart a lift.   —Mrs. E. C. W., Kalamazoo."

Do you see what we can do to go above and beyond? I'm sure you can come up with many additional ideas of your own.

So you see, even in little ways, the "and then some" philosophy can help us "transmit this country better than it was transmitted to us." But how can it help us academically?

If I were to single out the biggest problem I see with students today—based on almost twenty-five years of teaching experience—it would be that students allow floors to become ceilings. That is, they allow minimal expectations to become their maximum goals. Now, I recognize that one reason why many of you are sitting here today is that you did *not* allow this to happen, but my guess is that with an "and then some" philosophy you could do much better in this area.

As Director of the basic speech-communication course on this campus, let me share with you an often-repeated experience that occurs in my office. Disgruntled students come in with a paper that they had received a "C" or "D" on from their graduate-teaching assistant. Not only did they expect a "B" or an "A," but they tell me, "This is the first time I have *ever* received a "C" or "D" on a paper." Here is what they say as they continue, "You know," they almost always start with "you know." "You know," Dr. Weaver, "I did *everything* asked for on the assignment for the paper; I just can't understand how I could have received this grade." The first thing I ask them is whether or not they have talked to their graduate teaching assistant. In most cases they say they have; if they haven't, I send them back. If they have, then I look over the paper and read the evaluation. In most cases I find that everything they say is true: they filled all of the criteria for the paper, and they received a low grade. But, inevitably, they stopped short of the "and then some" philosophy! *You* don't need anyone else to ask these questions; you can ask them of yourself:

—What makes *my* effort outstanding or exceptional?

—How does *my* effort distinguish itself from all the others submitted that also fulfill all of the criteria? . . . and most important of all . . .

—What is it that makes *mine* a genuinely individual contribution? or phrased a bit differently . . .

—Where in this effort do *I* put *my* own, unique imprint on it?

Maybe you think this is unreasonable—an unfair request to make of students. But this is precisely what distinguishes the great from the "also ran," the "exceptional" from the "mediocre." Or, as my salesman friend would say, those who "met their obligations and responsibilities fairly and squarely" and those who did that *and then some*.

One of the pleasures I have in working with students is writing recommendations for them, and one of the things I love to be able to say in those recommendations is: "So-and-so was willing to go the extra mile." The Bible states it this way: ". . . and if any one forces you to go one mile, go with him two miles" (Matthew 5:41 R.S.V.)

Let me play teacher for just a second and plead with you right now. Don't just go the distance. You have the gift; you have the talent; you have the capacity. Now, take the responsibility. If it means becoming your own critic, then do it. Go the distance, *and then some*.

Okay, we've seen how the "and then some" philosophy can help our society, and we've seen how it can help us academically, let's see what kind of contribution it can make to us in our personal lives.

My first suggestion ties our personal lives to education. If I could make one suggestion to students today that would, at least could, make a major difference throughout their lives, it would be this: "become a sponge for knowledge." Never allow *any* opportunity to be an educational vacuum! Turned positively it says, get the most you can from *every* experience! There was a great book published a couple of years ago that escaped many people's attention. It was Sheldon Kopp's *Even A Stone Can Be A Teacher: Learning and Growing from the Experiences of Everyday Life*. His point is simply that every personal encounter offers something worth learning. Any experience can be enlightening. When you realize that it is what *you* bring to experiences and opportunities that create meaning, foster

Continued on page 26

Continued from page 25

learning, and encourage understanding, you'll stop depending on others—especially others—to do all the teaching. You'll stop waiting to be pushed, forced, motivated, or coerced to learn; you'll start transforming your *own* life! People don't lack strength, they lack will.

The teacher we've always expected to lead, motivate, and energize us, is *us*! The teacher is us. Do you realize that that *is* the very goal of education: to instill the teacher in you!—to inspire the desire for learning in students. See, when your mind is set on fire, you *will* find ways to provide the fuel! So if you are going to be uninterested, uninformed, ignorant of what's going on in the world, you have no one to blame but yourselves. When I finally discovered that, the world became my classroom!

There are at least three hurdles (perhaps barriers)—probably many more than three—that prevent us from exercising this "and then some" philosophy—especially in our own lives: 1) our society, 2) other people, and 3) ourselves. Think about it, our society makes it so easy to become complacent and apathetic. Television and the VCR, alcohol and drugs, prepared meals and junk food, and with "the good life" portrayed to us at every turn, the message is "Relax, take it easy, calm down, become a 'couch potato.'" We are being bombarded daily with flashy, materialistic consumerism, and it is hard to resist.

And with the people around us adopting this lackadaisical philosophy of "the least possible effort," it is hard to break out from the pack. Other people actually become a barrier because if no one else cares, why should I? If no one else is doing anything, why should I? If everyone else has accepted the complacent, apathetic, "couch potato" lifestyle, why shouldn't I?

But beyond society and other people, the biggest hurdle is ourselves. What can you do to get yourself motivated? What can you do to stop putting everything off? See, that's where the "and then some" philosophy comes in. How badly do you *want* to be better?—better today than yesterday? More knowledgeable, more educated, more prepared. Think how great *you* would feel if you could end *every* day feeling you've made a contribution? You made some progress today!

It takes tremendous self-discipline. It's not easy. That's why more people don't do it. That's why I'm talking to *you* about it. But it's easy to talk about; *not* easy to do. So let me give you some inspiration. We're all success-oriented, that's why we're here. And the "and then some" philosophy is designed to either keep us, or to put us, in front! To become even more successful!

We have to destroy the mind set—the prison—that we lock ourselves in. All our previous behaviors—our habits and routines—bind us, hold us in, keep us secure. Some people have labeled these our "addictions." Our friends, too, want predictable, expected behavior—nothing new. Often, even our parents stereotype us as children and regard us the same year after year. It's enough to make you lose your motivation and *any* incentive to change. It is easy to be discouraged. What is the most normal response when teachers, friends, relationship partners, and parents hold us back or ignore or reject our efforts to shed our old skin and adopt a new philosophy? We sink back into our *old* selves—the prison (or womb) in which we feel so comfortable. Why try?

It's up to us and us alone! How badly do you want it? Do you think it's worth it? Worth the fight? Socrates said, "The unexamined life isn't worth living." We have to want to discover, to explore, to find out, to challenge our self and our life, to confront who we are and who we want to become. If not us, then who?

I like talking to *this* audience because all of you have been designated "peak performers"! It is for you, especially, that this philosophy of "and then some" is so appropriate. As a peak performer, you are one who:

—uses foresight.
—plans strategically.
—"stretches" to attain specific goals.
—has high self-confidence and self-worth.
—shows responsibility and takes control.
—learns from your mistakes and from the past.

—fully utilizes your time and capacities.
—knows that hard, creative work and perseverance will pay off.
—is an innovator.
—feels positive about your work and environment.
—believes in your own ability.
—acts decisively when opportunities present themselves.
—anticipates difficulties and opportunities.
—never rests on your laurels; you never stop learning.

Didn't know you were that good, did you? Just imagine what this list of credits would look like if "and then some" were already internalized, implanted, and in action?

All of us want the best out of life. We want to be healthy and happy and to have things that can enrich our experience. Yet, though we strive for these things, we can end up dissatisfied. We may have a "good" life. But if we do not tap into this "and then some" philosophy—to push, shove, and even kick us into doing that little bit more, we may never awaken to the joy of *real* living, the joy of knowing we've contributed, the joy of being truly informed, the joy of knowing we have *really* come to know ourselves—the joy of being transformed! At that point, we can say, "I know what joy is for I have done good work!" Remember, joy is not in things, it is in us. With *and then some*

Continued on page 28

Concluded fromon page 27

internalized—part of our everyday behavior—we will give more, we will get more, and we will want more from life! It will be a life *and then some!*

Questions

1. How does Weaver target his speech to a specific audience? How does he also make it a speech that appeals to an audience beyond those he is addressing first hand?

2. What specific suggestions does Weaver offer to help you improve your communication skills?

3. If you applied Weaver's "and then some" philosophy to your life, what would it call on you to do?

Keys to Interpersonal Communication

2

Learning Outcomes

After studying this chapter, you should be able to:

1 Explain the impact that nonproductive, destructive interactions have on business organizations.

2 Understand the benefits of being trained in communication skills.

3 Recognize the uses of interpersonal skills.

4 Identify and practice effective interpersonal skills.

INTRODUCTION

Up to this point, we've focused on two major points: (1) the need to become an effective communicator if you are to succeed in an informational society, (2) the necessity of assessing your own personality and understanding how it contributes to strengths and/or weaknesses as a communicator. Further, you learned that *change is possible;* negative habits that get in the way of career success can be exchanged for positive ones.

If you have accepted these two major concepts, you are now ready to switch from an introspective look at yourself to the actual process of becoming a more skilled interpersonal communicator. Earlier, we indicated that the two keys necessary to improving communication skills were *awareness* and *change.* Review the results of the communications quotient exercise you did in Chapter 1. Even though the exercise is not intended to produce a precise evaluation of your skills, it will give you a clear idea of your present strengths and weaknesses. Note your strengths, but focus on improving weaknesses.

To improve a particular communication skill, you need to learn the behaviors involved in the skill and how and when to use those skills. We will begin with interpersonal communication skills because most employers value those skills most highly.

AVOID DESTRUCTIVE, NONPRODUCTIVE INTERACTIONS

Some years ago, Dr. Eric Berne's best-selling *Games People Play* alerted the public and the business world to the need for improving employees' interpersonal skills. Berne theorized that, on the average, 55 percent to 85 percent of employees' time was wasted playing games, which he defined as destructive, nonproductive interactions between people, in which the real purpose of the interaction was not to achieve a productive goal but for one or both "players" to pursue some ulterior motive or satisfy some personality need. Berne identified over 90 games that people play. Many of these apply primarily to business organizations. Here are a few of them:

Why don't you . . . Yes, but . . .

- Played by people or groups who appear to want others to help them solve their problems.

- The initiator rejects all suggestions with reasons why the advice will not work, proving that, "No one can tell me what to do."

Kick me

- In this game the player does something to provoke a second player to criticize or otherwise make him or her feel inferior.
- They tend to attract opposite players who will take advantage of this weakness.
  "My report is late." (I'm a bad person.)
  "Again? You know I needed that report today." (Yes, you are a bad person, and here is your kick.)

Now I've got you

- This is a game in which a person tries to trap another in a mistake, lie, or other negative situation.
- If successful in trapping his victim, the player feels justified in taking some negative action: firing someone, not giving a raise, or writing a critical report.
  "Did you finish typing that letter I gave you this morning?"
  (Noticing it is still in the typewriter.)
  "Er . . . Yes, sir."
  "Oh? What's this then?"

Other business games

- *Blemish:* A supervisor finds major fault with a minor mistake.
- *Bear trap:* A supervisor coaxes an employee into doing a report, then overwhelms him or her with size and complexity of the job.[1]

Games not only interfere with honest, meaningful social relationships, but also get in the way of productivity and are obstacles to individuals and organizations reaching their goals.

After Berne's alarming report, more research followed. It quickly became apparent that skilled communicators wasted less time reaching their objectives and were more productive. When interpersonal communication skills improved, managers managed better and employees responded more enthusiastically. In other words, work became more productive, satisfying, and rewarding in direct relation to the improvement of interpersonal communication skills.

WHAT BEHAVIORS ARE INVOLVED?

Bruno Bettelheim, the noted psychologist and author, wrote that the person well trained in interpersonal communication should be able (1) to relate successfully to self and others, (2) to analyze personal and environmental experiences and make inferences from them for future behavior, (3) to understand self well enough to develop and maintain an individual sense of identity, and (4) to respond to life situations in accordance with his or her own interests, values, and beliefs without being insensitive to the values, interests, and beliefs of others.[2]

David Johnson, author of "Reaching Out: Interpersonal Effectiveness and Self-Actualization," expressed it slightly differently: The interpersonal skills that needed to be developed were:

1. Knowing and trusting one another.
2. Developing open and honest communication.
3. Accepting and supporting one another.
4. Resolving conflicts and relationship problems constructively.[3]

Two themes emerge from the research about interpersonal communication. An individual must have a positive self-image and be sincerely interested in another person or persons before he or she can communicate effectively to another. These basic principles of interpersonal communication apply to our social relationships as well as our business relationships, so there is a dual reason to work at them. However, our main concern in this text is *how* to improve interpersonal skills that will lead to career success. Here are some ways to do that:

1. Put interpersonal behaviors into practice: Be other-oriented. One central truth of all interpersonal transactions is that you must be genuinely concerned and interested in the person with whom you are communicating. You must be empathetic; that is, you must try to understand the other person's point of view or, to use the cliché, "put yourself in the other person's shoes." To do this requires discipline because our natural inclination is to impose our own viewpoint on someone else. This natural tendency leads to blocked communication, which is essentially wasting time. Open the channels to let ideas flow both ways. This open-minded approach leads to mutual respect and trust, which in turn leads to productivity.

2. Understand the objective of the communication. Knowing the true purpose of communication is vital to successful interpersonal exchanges. What is it you are trying to accomplish? Is it your purpose to pass on information or are you trying to motivate another person? Once the purpose is clarified, the methods of communication will follow logically. Your choice of tone, language, and approach will suit the situation. For example, the purpose of a job interview is clear. You want to be offered a job. To accomplish that objective, you need to do some very specific things. (See Chapter 12 on interviewing skills.)

3. Choose a proper setting for communication. This is an often overlooked yet crucial point about communication. Two people with the best intentions can have their communication spoiled by choosing the wrong time and place to interact. Don't expect to be well received if you stop a person in the street or in a hallway or crowded meeting to discuss issues of importance. Even an otherwise ideal office environment can be spoiled by telephones, radios, or other people as distractions.

Instead, be certain that both parties have ample time to devote to the issue being discussed. (This eliminates glancing at watches or wall clocks which is the death blow to communications.) Eliminate distractions. If the meeting is in your office, hold your telephone calls and ask not to be disturbed. Make your visitor feel comfortable and relaxed. Assure the visitor that he or she is important enough to receive your exclusive attention for a period of time. For example, "Mary, you and I have an hour to discuss this suggestion of yours before my next appointment. Let's see what we can do to make your ideas become company policy."

4. Clarify your thoughts before you speak. In our culture, many people seem uncomfortable with the silence that accompanies pauses in conversation. As a result, we too often rush to fill the void with words that are not carefully considered. The result can be a disaster. Think before you speak. Once your ideas are together, express them as best you can.

5. Seek the advice of others. One of the nicest compliments you can pay another person is to ask his or her opinion or advice about a subject. It tells the other person you value both the person and his or her ideas. Try it. Not only will you have made someone feel good, but you might learn something of value. Should this happen, be certain to give credit where it is due and let the person know you are appreciative of his or her contribution.

6. Think of tomorrow, not just today. Most of your interactions with people in business are ongoing; that is, you are likely to have continuing relationships with the same people over extended periods of time. Remember that and avoid the "Christmas party" scene where, after a few glasses of punch have loosened the tongue, employees have been known to tell their associates (or supervisors) just what they "really" think of them. The next day always arrives, and with it, feelings of remorse. Go easy on the emotions and try to cultivate relationships that will be satisfying and productive.

The last suggestions for interpersonal communication are to *listen well* and *be aware of the nonverbal means of communication,* two areas of communication that are so important that we have devoted entire chapters to them.

CAUSES OF INTERPERSONAL CONFLICTS

Nothing is as important to your happiness and success as being able to get along well with other people in both your private and business lives. Unfortunately, it is not always easy to do so. Human beings differ from one another in many ways; it is in these differences that the seeds of most conflicts are sown. The differences may be racial, ethnic, or religious, or they may be personal, political, or lifestyle. The possibilities for people to differ are endless. The problem is not so much that people differ, but the way that people think about those differences.

Instead of seeing individual differences as the source of a healthy diversity—something that adds interest to and enriches our lives and our society—too many people view those who differ as inferior or as threats to be feared. Sociologists explain that most human beings are naturally *ethnocentric* and, as such, consider their own way of life superior to all others. With education and maturity, people can learn to replace the extreme ethnocentrism that leads to conflict with a way of thinking called *cultural relativism.* This more enlightened approach encourages us to reach out and try to understand those who are different from us by learning to value these differences in their own contexts.

This is particularly important today as the global marketplace demands that we interact successfully with people from all over the world if we are to succeed.

Thus, the first step in resolving interpersonal conflicts is to determine what specific differences are causing conflicts. Whether you are an outsider or personally involved in the conflict, it is easier to handle conflict when the reasons for it are known. Once the causes of conflict are identified, a satisfactory resolution can be sought.

RESOLVING INTERPERSONAL CONFLICTS

All of us have experienced disagreements with others. Our first conflicts may have been with our parents or siblings. Later, we had disputes with our peers and teachers. It is reasonable to assume that the same patterns of conflict will continue in our careers. Indeed, studies point to unresolved conflicts in the workplace as major contributors to loss of productivity in the organization. That is why it is essential, as you prepare for your careers, that you learn to resolve conflicts in the most positive way.

Reactions to conflict take many forms. One reaction is *accommodation,* which means giving in to the other party. This may be appropriate if the issue is of little importance. Another possible reaction is *avoidance,* where the issue at question is not addressed. Avoidance is only a solution if nothing further depends on the resolution of the conflict. Another less-than-satisfactory tactic is *conciliation,* which attempts to smooth over the hostility but does little to resolve the actual problem.[4]

Despite their common use, none of the above strategies is ideal. You should strive to resolve conflicts according to a win-win approach, a progressive communications strategy based on the belief that both sides should gain something of value.[5] This approach requires skill at bargaining, compromise, and collaboration. Individuals who become skilled at resolving conflicts through win-win negotiations are on their way to becoming leaders in their communities and workplaces.

CONCLUSION

A final word on interpersonal communication: There is probably nothing as important to your happiness and success as being able to get along well with other people in your private and business lives. *Work at doing it well.* Remember, the two key factors necessary to improving communication skills are *awareness* and *change.* With this in mind, review the suggestions above and ask yourself whether you are presently doing these things well. If not, make a specific plan to change those behaviors. Then you can grow and improve as a communicator. When you change your behaviors, you will see immediate improvement in the quality of your interpersonal relationships and these benefits also will carry over into your business career.

NOTES

1. Eric Berne. *Games People Play: The Psychology of Human Relationships.* New York: Grove Press, 1964, pp. 84–85.

2. Bruno Bettleheim. *Surviving and Other Essays.* New York: Alfred A. Knopf, 1979, p. 342.

3. David W. Johnson. *Reaching Out: Interpersonal Effectiveness and Self-Actualization.* Englewood Cliffs, NJ: Prentice Hall, 1972, p. 3.

4. Gary Yuki. *Leadership in Organizations.* Englewood Cliffs, NJ: Prentice Hall, 1981, p. 263.

5. Andrew J. Dubrin. *Bouncing Back: How to Handle Setbacks in Your Work and Personal Life.* Englewood Cliffs, NJ: Prentice Hall, 1982, p. 15.

QUESTIONS FOR REVIEW AND DISCUSSION

Demonstrate that you have mastered the objectives of this chapter by answering the following questions.

1. On average, how much of employees' time is wasted in nonproductive, destructive interactions?

2. Can you describe some of the "games" people play?

3. How can both managers and employees eliminate this game-playing?

4. What are the benefits to the business organization of doing so?

5. What skills does Bettelheim believe that the person well-trained in interpersonal communications should have?

6. What two qualities must an

individual have before he or she can effectively communicate with another?

7. What natural tendency do we have to overcome to be "other-oriented?"

8. Why is the proper setting so crucial to communication?

9. What are the possible benefits of seeking the advice of others?

10. What are four possible reactions to conflict? Which is the most effective?

APPLICATION EXERCISES

1. Working with a partner, discuss how and where one of the following interpersonal communications should be handled. Write a brief script and perform it before the class.
   a. A supervisor must tell a subordinate to improve the quality of his or her work.
   b. A supervisor wishes to let an employee know that his or her work on a project is particularly well done.
   c. An employee wishes to tell a manager of a problem with a co-worker.
   d. An employee wishes to ask a boss for a raise.

2. Describe the environment in which you do most of your communicating. Is the environment helpful to communication and, if not, what can you do to change it?

3. Pick a controversial issue about which you feel strongly. Now, try to be other-oriented. Why do you think those who disagree with you feel the way they do?

4. Think about a recent significant conversation or discussion in your own life. Do you feel you truly understood both your objective and that of the other person? Was the conversation held in the best setting? Would you change anything about that communication now?

5. You can probably think of many examples, both personal and public, of the consequences of violating the rule of "think of tomorrow, not just today." Jot down a few public examples and be prepared to discuss them with the class.

6. One type of speech is the "impromptu" speech. The speaker has little or no time

to prepare and speaks spontaneously on a subject. To try this type of speech, every student should write one of the concepts or ideas discussed in this chapter on a piece of paper. These slips should be collected and pooled. Take turns drawing a piece of paper from the pool and giving a brief (one minute) impromptu speech on that subject. Not only will this help reinforce key concepts in the chapter, but it will help you to practice an important communication skill: the art of impromptu speaking!

FOR ADDITIONAL READING AND DISCUSSION

MANAGEMENT BY INSPIRATION
A Few Simple Reminders

by George F. Burns

George F. Burns, president of Consumer Products Division, SCM Corporation, delivered this speech at the Durkee Famous Foods Conference, in Lincolnshire, Illinois, on August 9, 1982. Burns's speech illustrates the connection between self-awareness and improving interpersonal skills, especially in the professional world.

Good morning. I'm very happy to be here with you today. First, my congratulations. Your efforts made it a great year for *Durkee Famous Foods.* As you know, this year was the best in our history. I'm pleased and proud of all of you. My sincere congratulations and deepest appreciation to Bill Miller, John Lowrie, Tom Stuckart, and each of you.

Now, I'll say no more about the past year or even our plans for the future. Others will provide particulars on them and on making next year even more successful!

Today I'd like to talk from a more personal perspective, on a topic that's vital to good business management, and to SCM.

As you may know I'll be retiring in December after 37 years with the company. Naturally, at this stage of a career, you look back and try, if possible, to put it in perspective. And reflecting on my experiences, I have some good sense of what makes people work and how they might be inspired to excel. We all have within us the power to succeed; the goal is to release it, in ourselves and in others.

The word *inspiration* comes from the Latin and means, to give life, to breath into, to put spirit into as God does to Adam in Genesis. Inspiration is a state of mind that's linked to productivity, in the sense that inspired artists are likely to produce better works of art. Imagine how Michelangelo felt as he contemplated painting the Sistine Chapel. There is a vital relationship between inspiration and production. In business, inspiration is often called *motivation*—a more recent term for the force that moves people to perform well, even under difficult conditions.

Published in *Vital Speeches of the Day,* October 15, 1982. Reprinted with permission

Continued on page 40

Continued from page 39

Just what is it that inspires a person to create or perform with excellence? There are external things like money, status, and power. For some, they are the spur to fame and fortune. But true inspiration is water from a deeper well. It comes from believing in yourself. It's a sense of self-worth and pride that you get from working hard and accomplishing things.

Remember the scene in the film *Chariots of Fire* where the runner asks himself "Where does the power come from to run the race to the end?" His answer: "The power comes from within." Of course, inspiration can also come from others. We are often inspired by heros, whether artists, athletes, or astronauts. These individuals can serve as role models and, on occasion, as teachers.

A man named Saul Yaffa hired me as a Smith-Corona salesman back in 1945. Saul was soft spoken and always a gentle man. At the outset he said to me: "George you can read all the books, and study your product till midnight. I can teach you the business and teach you how to work. But there's one thing I can't do— and that's make you want to work."

And Yaffa was a good teacher in the days before sophisticated sales training techniques were developed. Here's one of his favorite techniques. Every day, when you're finished, perhaps tired, and ready to quit, make one more call. Keep a record of these "extra" calls. And if the call is bad, make another one and keep going till you get a prospect. This way you not only go home on a high note, but you've structured your day with an upward momentum instead of just winding down. The ultimate call becomes something you psyche yourself up for. You leave feeling good about yourself and your work, ready to run again the next day.

This particular approach may or may not work for every individual. What makes a great salesman is something more natural: self-inspiration. It's a personal desire, a primary impulse to get going without anybody telling you. If you're self-inspired, you're halfway there. Anybody can be taught tactics, but the drive to win comes from within.

When I say self-inspiration is natural, I don't mean you're born with it. It's part of your nature because you put it there. How do you inspire yourself? Each person does it differently, but all of us have something in our makeup that triggers action. To find it, you must know yourself and be honest about your life's ambitions. Socrates challenged his students to know themselves and Plato suggested that an unexamined life wasn't worth living.

Inspiration, through self-awareness, is essential for success in any demanding endeavor, whether it's selling or skiing. Selling is a dynamic, challenging job. Unfortunately, it's among the less understood and unappreciated professions. The old image of the fast-talking, cigar-smoking huckster is due for an overhaul.

You can find dishonest individuals in any line of work including selling. I believe the salesman has become an important national figure. America could not have become the rich and productive nation it is without people selling its products. No matter what you produce, nothing happens until a sale is made. That is our moment of truth.

You have to be smart to sell well. Selling involves technical knowledge and interpersonal skills. Even in an age of automation, the sales force remains the backbone of a business organization. If your frontline troops fail to move products, the battle's over, the company's dead.

Now it appears that I'm preaching to the converted, but at times there's an exhilaration in rediscovering the truth behind clichés we hear. There's a lot of talk about the emerging era of leisure, and new industries have sprung up offering recreational goods and services. Some say hard work, as we know it, will become passé in a computerized society. Describing a "postindustrial" society where most people will work at home through computers, Alvin Toffler says: "We are moving toward a future economy in which very large numbers will never hold full-time paid jobs." He claims that the distinction between work and leisure will disappear.

That might be true by the year 2082, but today leisure exists in the context of work, and without this framework, leisure can become decadence. The fact remains that work gives meaning to life. It provides a sense of mastery and achievement, thus, enhanced self-worth. Recreation complements vocation. Work hard, play hard. But work before play. Why? Well, here's how I see it. If you really put yourself in your work, exercise total concentration, effort, and energy, several things will happen. First, you'll learn faster and get better at what you're doing. Second, as you confront tough challenges, you'll draw more fully on your intellectual and personal resources and develop them. Third, you'll succeed and success brings rewards, personal as well as material. Both mastering a skill and making money from it are sources of inner gratification and self-esteem.

To excel in any vocation, you must push yourself even when it hurts. In selling, as you know, perseverance pays off. But even the strong get weary. We've all heard about capable managers who've failed because they lacked the stamina to work under pressure or rebound from a setback. When fatigue hits and you feel headed for a burnout, here's what you might do to put yourself together.

First, try your favorite physical activity—swimming, golfing, running—it will help you relax. Second, keep your sense of humor. Joking about a difficult situation often puts it in a workable perspective and sometimes reduces stress. Third, recognize that you're human, that you will make mistakes, but they can be fixed. Recognizing your limitations is helpful

Continued on page 42

Continued from page 41

because it exposes areas that need more effort on your part. But in the end, like that British runner, a manager's ability to stay on course comes only from tenacious self-discipline. The French scientist Louis Pasteur said: "Let me tell you the secret that led me to my goal. My strength lies solely in my tenacity."

In the current business climate, you must persevere to survive. I know that stimulating a sales force today is a demanding task. You must be able to inspire yourself as well as others and encourage those under you to carry on when they get weak.

It's a tall order—because they're buffeted by a negative environment all day. The economy, the dealers, the customers who keep saying: "No, never mind, not this time, check with me next month." Your sales reps can come back in bad shape. Down, disappointed, sometimes depressed, they look to you for support and guidance.

You must be understanding and yet make demands, insist on productivity in spite of the desolation in the marketplace. Sometimes, a manager must sound an optimistic note against a chorus of pessimists, which is a subtle but indispensable management skill. Most of all, you must inspire your people to inspire themselves.

The word *manage* derives from the Italian "mano" for hand, and management connotes a skillful handling of people. Textbooks contain many useful ideas, but they can't teach you to inspire those working for you. When you get down on a one-to-one basis, an individual's instinct beats academic precept every time. Your approach may vary from friendly persuasion to the iron hand in the velvet glove, to no gloves at all. The aim is to make them feel that their work is important and that achievement can bring fulfillment.

The ability to manage people under stressful situations requires a delicate balance of firmness and compassion. You must offer constructive criticism together with words of praise. A wise man once said: "Praise, of all things, is the most powerful excitement to commendable actions, and animates us all in our enterprise." More mature individuals are instinctively able to strike this balance. Others cultivate it, over time, through self-scrutiny and a genuine interest in people. And there are those who never develop it. They become frustrated and angry with the human side of managing.

Yet, cultivating this interpersonal side doesn't mean you stop demanding results. That's another skill which involves psychological savvy. In fact, the capacity for making demands and getting people to meet them is among the most underdeveloped managerial talents.

Why? Making demands might appear risky. You might imagine they'll provoke resistance from subordinates and result in embarrassment for not reaching them.

A manager might also rationalize by saying he's already done everything possible in establishing expectations. That's a strategy for self-defeat.

On the other hand, if you're convinced that you want better results and are willing to put in the time and energy, you can get them. First, you have to figure out your objectives. In establishing them, it's wise to sound out your subordinates on opportunities for improvement. Their responses will provide clues about their readiness. But remember, sounding them out doesn't mean giving up concrete performance expectations. The next important step is to communicate precisely what you expect. It's crucial to make it absolutely clear that you're not asking permission to set goals or seeking advice on whether they're attainable, but saying unequivocally that they must be achieved.

Now, I know from experience that when a manager tells subordinates that better results are in order, they might at first not take him seriously or even resort to testing him. They might imply that his expectations are unrealistic. Such testing is sometimes an expression of their anxiety about meeting demands and a way of seeking reassurance from the boss. This situation presents a real chance to show leadership and inspire people.

If you have confidence in yourself, you'll be able to accept the testing, help subordinates deal with any feelings of incompetence, all this—without lowering your expectations for productivity. If you can "hang tough" on demands while truly helping people meet them, you'll no doubt find that many anticipated difficulties failed to materialize.

Instead, your subordinates will respond to more rigorous demands, become more productive, and take pride working in a results-oriented environment that you've created by fully exercising managerial authority.

Pollster Daniel Yankelovich says most Americans still believe in working hard because of an inner need to perform. He suggests that management emphasize the "soft" factors of production, like job dedication, and implies that capital investment isn't the only way to high productivity.

This brings me back to my main idea: If you can inspire dedication, you have a better chance of increasing productivity. So far I've said that people are inspired by believing in themselves and emulating others. I observed that the role of a manager is to be understanding and supportive of his or her staff, especially during tough economic times. It's often difficult to show genuine concern for your staff, without overidentifying with them and compromising the authority necessary for leadership. You must judge when it's OK to go for a drink with your staff after work. You should be able to discuss someone's family problems if you sense it might improve their job performance.

Continued on page 44

Concluded from page 43

Cultivating these skills does not relieve you of the obligation to provide practical, mundane assistance to your sales staff. If someone is having trouble with any aspect of the job, you must meet him or her more than halfway. If people have a chance to talk about problems in a candid and nonthreatening context, solutions might be found.

You might think it's easier to fire somebody and comfort yourself saying: "I'm sorry you just don't have the stuff to be a sales rep." If you say that after making every effort within your power to help an individual, you're home free. But, if you didn't give that person all you can, you've done an injustice and failed to carry out your supervisory responsibility. Think twice before you dismiss somebody and ask: "Did I do enough?"

I feel that the "exit" interview reveals much about the quality of management. In a situation where someone is leaving by choice, only one question need be asked. "Would you come back to the company?" Or put another way, "Would you recommend that a family member or friend work here?" A company, like an individual, gets its reputation from its dealings with people. And if it does not do well by them, some will just quit. Others who can't will stay on, becoming uninspired, cynical, and unproductive employees. A recent book put forth the theory of a unique corporate "culture," but this notion was already known to Shepard who wrote in his *Laws of Economics:* "Behind each corporation must be the singular force, or motive, that sets it apart from any other corporate structure and gives it its particular identity."

People indicate their feelings about an organization by deed as well as word. If they feel positive about it, chances are they'll be more productive. So, you can see that management through inspiration can have an impact on the bottom line. Each of you will succeed to the extent that you inspire yourself and those around you.

In this business, you must at times make tough decisions that could result in hardship to someone on your staff. Being hardnosed about productivity and profits never justifies undignified behavior toward anyone. That's something I learned from Saul Yaffa who was a compassionate person and competent manager. In this tradition, I would like to leave feeling that people thought of me as someone in whom they could confide, as one who could criticize their work if need be, and as one who was open to suggestions. I'd also like to be seen as one who made decisions and implemented them firmly and fairly.

I guess every man likes to pass on something of value to those with whom he's shared an important part of his life. This isn't meant to be my secret for success, but a few simple reminders:

First—Define yourself by what you do, by how you treat others, and how they see you.

Second—Define your business goals clearly, so that others can see them as you do.

Third—Praise good work loudly and criticize shortcomings softly.

Fourth—Follow your instincts, those undefinable feelings that can warn you of dangerous ventures or help you bring out the best in people.

Finally—Put all you have into each working day and you'll find the deep fulfillment you desire.

This is my legacy offered humbly with high regard for your work and sincere appreciation for your friendship.

Thank you.

Questions

1. According to Burns, what is the relationship between inspiration and production?

2. How does *your* definition of management compare or contrast with that of Burns?

3. Do you agree with Burns that the most effective management style is one that balances firmness and compassion?

Active Listening

Learning Outcomes

After studying this chapter, you should be able to:

❶ Define the importance of listening in daily communication.

❷ Identify the personal benefits of improved listening skills.

❸ Identify the professional benefits of improved listening skills.

❹ Understand the causes of ineffective listening.

❺ Practice better listening.

INTRODUCTION

One communication skill that has recently received great attention in our culture is listening. The combination of scholarly research into listening and its importance in business has changed the way we think about the skill. No longer do we take listening for granted as a process that happens instinctively as long as we are able to hear. No longer do businesses concentrate only on training their employees to speak and write more effectively. Today, typical employee seminars include training sessions on how to become better listeners. The best example of this interesting blend of academic findings and corporate concerns took place at the Sperry Corp. (now UNISYS), a large multinational corporation with 87,000 employees in 33 countries. The story is a logical place to begin as you start thinking about your own listening skills. After all, if the management of a corporate giant with billions of dollars of annual sales considers listening important, there must be something to it.

THE SPERRY STORY

In the fall of 1979, Sperry launched an external advertising program and an internal training program based on the importance of effective listening. In the first three years, the listening message appeared on television and in magazines and newspapers with a combined circulation of more than 65.5 million in the United States and 10.5 million in Europe. The central message of the advertising campaign was that Sperry employees work at listening and responding and that Sperry had made listening a fundamental philosophy of doing business.

Sperry's chairman and chief executive, J. Paul Lyet, was so serious about the program that he delayed the start of the advertising campaign six months until the employee training seminars in listening skills were well underway. The seminars were designed with the assistance of Lyman K. Steil, chairman of the Speech Communications Division at the University of Minnesota and a consultant to more than 300 corporations and government agencies.

From the beginning, the senior management at Sperry stated that the commitment to listening would be long term and, indeed, it continues to this day. Their motivation was clear. Improved listening would ultimately result in higher efficiency, increased productivity, and an improved company image. The company diverted thousands of hours to classroom training on listening skills at each of its five divisions.

In addition, internal mailings of 55,000 specially prepared phono-graph recordings and accompanying pamphlets sent the message to employees throughout the world. To date, approximately *25,000* employees have been trained and the effort continues.

What significance does the Sperry story have for young men and women who are planning careers in business? The answer to that question is simple. If the people at Sperry "understand how important it is to listen," you should too. *Begin now to learn how to become a more effective listener.*

WHAT WE HAVE LEARNED ABOUT LISTENING

Many of the new ideas and attitudes about listening are a result of up-to-date research. Research has proven that previous listening theories and practice contained many contradictions and misconceptions. For instance, even though we spend a greater percentage of our waking hours listening (45 percent) than we do the other communication skills—writing, 9 percent; reading, 16 percent; and speaking, 30 per-cent—we devote the least time (8 percent) to classroom teaching of the skill (reading gets 52 percent of classroom time).[1] Do you remem-ber the last instruction you received in listening?

A very common misconception among most people is that they are skilled listeners. However, the exact opposite is true because most people are *poor* listeners, which often causes problems in their pro-fessional and personal lives. Poor listening results in wasted time, loss of productivity, failed personal relationships, accidents, and other negative outcomes. For example, the average person retains only 50 percent of a short message immediately after hearing it. After 48 hours, retention drops to 25 percent. These figures are far below what people rate as their own listening effectiveness.

There is good news, however. *Anyone can become a better listener.* That positive note is reinforced by Dr. Ralph G. Nichols who researched, published, and taught in the area of listening for 35 years and claimed: "Listening is a collection of identifiable skills. It can be improved through training and practice, just as reading, writing, and speaking."[2] This is what the seminars at Sperry are about and what the rest of Part 1 is concerned with: improving listening skills. The bene-fits to your professional and personal lives are worth it.

WHAT CAUSES INEFFECTIVE LISTENING?

Our society rewards those people who write and speak well; as a consequence, our educational system devotes countless hours of training to perfect these skills. Listening, however, is not usually taught in school. We do not customarily associate listening with success and almost no time is spent developing proficiency as listeners. The result is that few people develop strong listening skills.

Most people are egocentric: that is, they tend to be self-centered and want to put their own wishes and desires first. As humorist Fran Libowitz noted, "The opposite of talking isn't listening. The opposite of talking is waiting." Writing and speaking allow people to assert their own personalities in an active way that satisfies the needs of their ego. On the other hand, listening requires that we be other-oriented, that we temporarily place the needs and concerns of another person in front of our own. When our ego prevents us from doing this, it becomes an obstacle to effective listening.

Some Common Causes

A very common cause of poor listening is daydreaming. Our minds wander from the subject at hand and travel to other times and places which may have no connection with the present. The reason we indulge our favorite fantasies rather than listen is because we are able to comprehend spoken words at a rate of 500 words per minute. Since the average speaker talks at a rate of 125–250 words per minute, we are left with a great deal of free time in which to daydream. If we do not use this free time productively, our listening will suffer.

Distractions are the next major cause of poor listening. In order to listen effectively, you must concentrate your attention on the speaker and what is being said. Anything that breaks that concentration interferes with the listening process. Ringing telephones, interruptions, word processors, and other office noises are all examples of potential distractions. In other words, a distracting environment can impede listening.

Finally, there are some poor behavioral habits that create blocks to effective listening. Most of these come from our attitudes toward the speaker and the subject. If, for example, we don't like the speaker or the way he or she looks, we may tune out and miss valuable content. If we react with anger or any excessive emotion to what is said, we may miss the message. If we have preconceptions that the material may be too easy or too difficult, we may close our minds to important information.

Covering our ears is a physical act that can prevent hearing. In much the same way, we often "cover" our minds with psychological barriers that prevent listening.

The cost of poor listening in our society is great. White-collar workers spend 40 percent of their time listening. Top management spends even more. Besides the obvious damage to productivity caused by a lack of listening, the University of Minnesota contends that 60 percent of misunderstandings in business are caused by poor listening. Poor listening is clearly one of the greatest communication problems on the job.

Not all the costs of poor listening can be measured in economic terms. Poor listening also damages relationships between husbands and wives, parents and children, and friends. Each year approximately 50 percent as many couples get divorced as get married. One of the major contributing factors to the growing divorce rate is the failure of partners to communicate with and listen to each other. Therefore, we can say that the inability to listen effectively hurts us not only in our careers but also in our interpersonal relationships.

BENEFITS FROM IMPROVED LISTENING

It follows that improved listening skills should produce worthwhile results, and they do. Robert Montgomery, a professional speaker and communication skills believer, states matter-of-factly that if working people were taught to listen effectively, the efficiency of U.S. business could be doubled.[3] With better listening, misunderstandings and the resulting problems are minimized. Managers manage more effectively and their subordinates react more positively when they sense an atmosphere of mutual trust. Quality information flows more freely through open communication channels, allowing for better decision making by management and clearer understanding of policies and objectives by employees. In short, improved listening contributes to productivity, which leads to success.

Business success is not the only by-product of improved listening. An equally predictable benefit is that better listening will have a direct effect on the day-to-day relationships we have with others in our social lives. Think about a friend or acquaintance whom you enjoy being with the most. Consider the characteristics of that person's personality. Chances are that among the traits you find appealing will be the fact that the person listens to you when you talk.

Good listeners are popular people. Further than that, effective listening tends to create reciprocal behavior in the other person. That is, after a person has been attentive and listened to what you have to say, it is natural for you to do the same in return. That, of course, is effective communication. The potential positive effect of improved listening on marriages, parent-child relationships, and friendships is enormous. *Try it. It works.*

HOW TO BE A BETTER LISTENER

Psychological Changes

Becoming a better listener requires psychological as well as behavioral changes.

1. Everyone can improve. You must accept the fact that *everyone* can become a more skilled listener if he or she has the desire to do so. Improvement doesn't just happen; it happens to those who want it to happen and are willing to work hard to see that it does.

2. Adopt a new attitude. You must be willing to adopt a new attitude about the act of listening. Put aside the old idea that listening is just a *passive* act that occurs naturally if you are able to hear. Instead, think of listening as an *active* behavior that requires an expenditure of energy like writing or speaking. Consider listening as hard work because that is what it is.

3. Suppress your ego. You must understand that effective listening requires that you suppress your ego and become other-oriented. This is quite difficult as it seems natural to think of ourselves first. We know, however, that this is a block to listening and so we must, for a time, put the person we are listening to first and try to accept and understand that person as he or she is. Once you are able to make these three psychological adjustments, you are ready to tackle the behavioral changes necessary for effective listening.

Behavioral Changes

1. Eliminate duologues. A dialogue is defined as an open and frank interchange and discussion of ideas between people, while a monologue refers to the remarks of someone speaking alone. No doubt you are familiar with these terms. Are you, however, familiar with the term *duologue?* "Duologue" is the tongue-in-cheek term given to a most common obstacle to listening, two people talking at the same time. It is so common as to be epidemic; yet, the cure is painless. All you have to do is *stop talking,* and *listen* to the speaker's entire message without interrupting. Lyndon Johnson made this point quite well when he said, "If you're talking, you aren't learning."

2. Create a good listening environment. Another crucial factor in listening is the place or environment in which communication occurs. To the extent that it is possible, you should try to create a comfortable, relaxed atmosphere from which distractions have been removed. This may mean many things. Put the speaker at ease by having him or her sit down; don't stand over a speaker who is sitting; hold telephone calls and ask not to be interrupted; seek a quiet spot that is appropriate for communication. Even though space is often at a premium in active businesses, individuals can take extra steps to make their space suitable to interpersonal communication and listening.

3. Use free time wisely. Earlier you learned that listeners are able to understand words at a rate of 500 words per minute while the average speaker talks at a rate of 125–250 words per minute. If you learn how to use this resulting free time wisely, you can become a better listener. Instead of daydreaming or thinking of what you are going to say next, discipline yourself to summarize mentally what is being said, relate it to what you already know about the subject, question or evaluate the message, and be mindful of nonverbal clues that the speaker may be sending.

4. Show willingness. This nonverbal aspect of communication is one of a listener's major responsibilities. You must show the speaker that you are willing to listen. The way to do that is to appear attentive by assuming an interested posture (learning toward the speaker is a sign of interest) and a receptive facial expression. Another way to show a willingness to listen is to maintain eye contact during communication. In our culture, it is considered normal for people to look at each other 40 to 60 percent of the time during communication. More than the normal amount of eye contact indicates increased interest while less than normal eye contact indicates disinterest on the part of the listener. Strive for 80 to 90 percent eye contact when listening.

5. Provide feedback. Besides nonverbal feedback, the listener can and should provide oral feedback during pauses by the speaker. Restate the basic ideas to be sure you have understood correctly, and ask questions which help the speaker elaborate and clarify his/her ideas.

6. Be open-minded. Finally, we can become better listeners if we are optimistic, open-minded listeners who refrain from negativism and emotional reactions. Expect the best of people until proven otherwise. Be willing to accept the views of others and don't always try to change them to your own ways. It won't work, so save your energy. You may not like a speaker's personality, but that same person may know something of value to you. Be aware of your own biases and preconceptions, so that you are able to minimize emotional reactions except when they are appropriate. Doing these things is not the same thing as saying you must *agree* with every speaker's point-of-view. What is being said is that before you dismiss or disagree with another point-of-view, you must first listen to it fairly and with an open mind.

CONCLUSION

You are ready now to put into practice what you have learned about listening. You will have an opportunity to do so in the exercises and activities that follow. Out of necessity, these are simulated exercises whose purpose is to reinforce effective listening skills. Ultimately, it is up to you and your willingness to try out the new ideas in your everyday encounters with family, co-workers, friends, and teachers that will decide whether you will be a better listener. If you do, you will have acquired another communication skill that will contribute to your career success.

NOTES

1. Florence Wolff; Nadine C. Marsnik; William S. Jacey; and Ralph G. Nichols. *Perceptive Listening*. New York: Holt, Rinehart and Winston, 1983, p. 27.
2. Ibid., p. 27
3. Robert L. Montgomery. *Listening Made Easy*. New York: Amacom, 1981, p. 12.

QUESTIONS FOR REVIEW AND DISCUSSION

Demonstrate that you have mastered the objectives of this chapter by answering the following questions.

1. What was the goal of the Sperry Corporation's emphasis on listening skills in their advertising campaign?
2. What percentage of our waking time is spent listening?
3. How much of a message will we typically retain 48 hours after hearing it?
4. How does the rate of the average speaker compare with the rate of words we can comprehend in a minute?
5. What are a few of the causes of ineffective listening?
6. How can our reaction to the way a speaker looks affect our ability to listen to his or her message?
7. What is the cost of poor listening to business?
8. What nonverbal cues indicate that you are willing to listen?
9. How can oral feedback improve one's ability to listen to a speaker?
10. Why is an open-minded attitude necessary to better listening?

APPLICATION EXERCISES

1. Separate the class into groups of three. Participants in each group should designate themselves as A, B, or C. In each group, one person should act as referee and the other two as participants in a discussion of one topic. One will be the speaker and the other the listener. Before beginning the exercise, choose three topics. For the most interesting and energetic discussions, choose current political or social controversies that everyone in the group has some knowledge of. Here are the rules for the exercise:

    a. The discussion is to be unstructured. Before speaking, however, each participant must first summarize, in his or her own words and without notes, what has been said previously.

b. The speaker and the referee are free to interrupt if they feel that the summary is inaccurate.

c. Participant A begins as speaker, choosing a topic from the list.

d. Participant B will be the listener and Participant C the referee.

e. Discuss the first topic for three minutes.

f. After three minutes, switch roles. Participant B becomes the speaker, C the listener, and A the referee. B chooses a new topic and the discussion proceeds for three more minutes.

g. After three or four rounds of discussion, members of the group should share feelings and reactions to the exercise by responding to the following questions:

  (1) *Which role was the most difficult?*

  (2) *Did you find you were not getting across what you wanted to say?*

  (3) *Did you have difficulty listening to others during the exercise?*

2. The entire class can perform a modified version of the above exercise. Choose a controversial topic and open up the discussion. The only rule is that all participants must acknowledge specifically what was said by the speaker before them.

3. Write a paragraph replying to these questions: How do you know when someone is not listening to you? How does it make you feel?

4. Describe someone in your life who is a good listener.

5. Pick a class in which you are a student and assess yourself as a listener, using the criteria suggested in this chapter.

6. Look around that same class next time you are there, and decide who seems like a good listener. Why?

7. Working with a partner, improvise scripts for the following situations. Perform in front of the class or in small groups and discuss both the oral and nonverbal feedback that is observed:

a. A customer service representative listening

to a customer complain
about a faulty product.

b. One spouse telling the
other that he or she must
help out more with
household chores.

c. A young adult listening to
a parent's advice on how
to budget money.

d. A worker listening to a
co-worker's constructive
suggestions about how to
improve the quality of a
joint project.

CHAPTER

4

Nonverbal Communication

Learning Outcomes

After studying this chapter, you should be able to:

❶ Understand the relationship between verbal and
nonverbal communication.

❷ Identify the benefits of improved nonverbal
communication.

❸ Understand how the nature of a communication affects
the use of nonverbal signals.

❹ Interpret nonverbal communication.

❺ Manage your own nonverbal communication effectively.

INTRODUCTION

There is a humorous story about President Franklin Delano Roosevelt deciding one evening to liven up a tiresome White House receiving line. As each guest came up and said, "Good evening, Mr. President, how are you, sir?" Roosevelt responded warmly with a pleasant smile and a firm handshake, "Fine, thank you, I just murdered my mother-in-law." Not one person going through the receiving line reacted to his comment. It's doubtful people even heard it. What is clear from this anecdote is that President Roosevelt was ahead of his time in his instinctive understanding of the power of nonverbal communication or body language. He knew his guests would pay more attention to his handshake, facial expression, and the tone of his voice than to the words he actually said. Today, through research in *kinesics,* the study of bodily movements and other nonverbal means of communication, we are more acutely aware of this important aspect of communication and how it contributes to success in business.

VERBAL VERSUS NONVERBAL COMMUNICATION

From your earliest years, parents and teachers have stressed the importance of learning a spoken language. Large amounts of time and energy are spent mastering language. When we work at using language properly, we choose our words consciously and carefully. Also, we place a high social value on using words well, and we often reward people who are skilled in the use of language with positions of power or prestige. In comparison, we devote relatively little time to learning about nonverbal communication. As a result, this part of our overall communication system often operates without direction. If, however, we pay attention to the findings of Albert Mehrabian, who conducted tests to determine how much body, voice, and words contributed to the total impact of a person's attitudes, we may have our priorities backward. Take this opportunity to take your own guess by penciling in the percentages you think apply. How much impact do these three areas have on communication?

Mehrabian's research indicated these results: body and other nonverbal cues contribute 55 percent of total communication; voice contributes 38 percent; and words (verbal) contribute 7 percent.[1] Are you surprised? If so, then you need to learn more about nonverbal communication.

Total Impact Theory:

Body and other nonverbal	_____ %
Voice	_____ %
Words (verbal)	_____ %
	100%

What Is Nonverbal Communication?

While verbal communication refers to the words that we use, nonverbal communication is more broadly based. It includes tone of voice, facial expression, eye contact, body posture, gestures, body movement, physical appearance including dress, and use of space. Because we have been trained for years to use language, we can manipulate and disguise our verbal messages with ease. This is not true for the nonverbal channels. Our bodies are predisposed to convey only the true meaning of our expressions. This can cause problems when there is a conflict between verbal and nonverbal messages. When this happens, the listener will rely on the nonverbal message, confirming the old truism that actions speak louder than words. Knowing this, you can see that there are two major benefits to be gained through knowledge of nonverbal communication. First, as receivers of communication *(listeners),* we can look for evidence that will help us understand more fully the message of the speaker. Second, as communicators *(speakers),* we can take steps to be sure that our nonverbal behavior is supportive of the words we choose to say.

LISTEN WITH YOUR EYES AS WELL AS YOUR EARS

In Chapter 3, you learned that an essential part of listening is to be mindful of nonverbal clues. To be a more alert communicator, you must *see* the message as well as hear it. Seeing nonverbal messages is one thing; interpreting them is quite another and requires some knowledge of generally accepted nonverbal principles. A word of caution at the outset: nonverbal signs often may be interpreted in more than one way and this makes the task of "reading" them more difficult. For example, if a person attempts to get very close to another person, it may be a sign of warm feelings of friendship or, in another context, it might mean provocation or aggression. For this reason, you must be alert to both verbal and nonverbal messages and notice whether they are consistent with one another or whether there is a conflict. Also, one nonverbal sign by itself may be meaningless. Taken together with two or three other nonverbal messages, the message may suddenly become very clear. Following are some common nonverbal signals and what they might mean.

READING NONVERBAL SIGNS

It is known that facial expressions and bodily movements provide clues to attitudes and feelings that are normally concealed. The eyes and mouth can indicate surprise, disgust, or frustration. Even if people try to hide these feelings, small, fleeting changes provide insights into the true feelings of the individual. Open-mindedness is reflected by open hands and an unbuttoned coat while defensiveness is indicated by arms crossed over the chest, crossed legs, and aggressive gestures. If a person is suspicious, he or she may glance sideways, rub the nose or eyes, button a coat and move away from another individual. People of higher status indulge in more relaxed and expansive postures; for example, a manager might lean back in a chair with feet on a desk when talking with a subordinate. The subordinate, on the other hand, signals his secondary status by sitting upright and appearing attentive.

Wringing of hands, rubbing the back of the neck, or running hands through the hair are seen as signs of frustration, while biting fingernails and chewing pens or pencils indicate insecurity. Nervousness is shown openly by clearing your throat, smoking, covering your mouth with your hand as you speak, jingling pocket money, tugging at your ear, fidgeting in your chair, and not looking at the other person. In contrast, the confident person will often sit up straight and place his or her hands behind the back; a man will place his hands in his coat pockets with the thumbs out. Thinking something over or evaluating a matter is often indicated by stroking your chin, tilting your head, hand-to-face gestures, peering over your glasses, taking your glasses off or cleaning them, and putting your hand to the bridge of the nose.

THE USE OF SPACE

Paying attention to nonverbal signals also means noting the space between participants in a communication transaction. Research has revealed that the space between participants in communication depends on the *nature* of the communication. Our personal space reaches out to one and one-half feet from us and is reserved only for those with whom we have an intimate relationship. Friendly, casual relationships take place between one and one-half and four feet. The rest of our communications, impersonal and secondary relationships, occur outside of four feet.

People in the United States are particularly sensitive to the use of space and feel uncomfortable in situations where informal space restrictions are violated. You can see proof of this in a crowded elevator. The people in the elevator will be uncomfortable because their private space has been entered by strangers with whom they are forced to stand in close proximity for the duration of the ride. People show their discomfort by staring at the floor or at the floor indicator in strained, embarrassed silence. Handshakes and other forms of touching dissolve interpersonal space and may signal a willingness to explore a more personal relationship. There is still much that we have to learn about this aspect of human communication.

The message is clear. As you begin to further develop your communication skills, you need to see the message as well as hear it. Remember the caution that one nonverbal signal may be ambiguous, easy to misinterpret. Look for a number of signs which together may provide additional insight into the speaker. Finally, be cautious of those who would manipulate others through the use of nonverbal communication.

CONTROLLING YOUR NONVERBAL MESSAGES

Next, it is necessary to learn how to use your knowledge of nonverbal communication as an asset that will help in business and social relationships. The word *asset* is used deliberately for, to be sure, the person insensitive or unaware of nonverbal communication can certainly create a *liability* that will work against success. You can offend or antagonize others and create a negative image of yourself just as easily without words as you can with words. Political candidates who use television to get their message to voters know full well the power of nonverbal communication. They concern themselves as much with their appearance as with the words they will say for there is a long list of candidates from Richard Nixon to Bill Clinton whose cause has either been harmed or helped by the way they appear to television audiences.

To be truly effective as a communicator, you must not only be skilled verbally and nonverbally, but you must make both messages *consistent* with each other. Remember that when inconsistency occurs, the listener will rely on the nonverbal message, and the transmission of this kind of missed or contradictory message will give an overall negative feeling to the communication. With this key point in mind, here are some suggestions on how to make your own nonverbal communication work for you.

MANAGING YOUR NONVERBAL SIGNALS

Eye Contact

Dorothy Sarnoff, a communications consultant whose clients have included presidents and business leaders, stresses the importance of eye contact: "Speaking without eye contact is like talking with a bag over your head."[2] You need to know that your eyes convey messages of approval, love, interest, sincerity, credibility, enthusiasm, and excitement as well as all of the negative emotions. Be aware that eye contact projects confidence and trust; conversely, the lack of eye contact suggests a negative self-image, feelings of inferiority, and even a neurotic personality. Work at maintaining eye contact 80 to 90 percent of the time during a communication without staring.

Americans are not comfortable when others stare at them; if you wish to test the truth of this statement, begin staring at a stranger as he or she approaches you on a sidewalk. Within seconds, the stranger will feel uncomfortable and suspect that something is wrong. You don't have to stare to use your eyes effectively. Look directly at a person, but move your eyes so that they do not linger too long on the same point of focus. Later, in the chapter on delivering speeches, you will learn how important it is to sweep your eyes across your audience to be effective. The importance of eye contact also applies to one-on-one interpersonal exchanges.

Facial Expressions

During a few of your next classes, look around at the faces of your teachers and your classmates. What messages do their facial expressions signal? If your classes are typical, you will see expressions of interest and enthusiasm as well as boredom and weariness. Which of the people seem more alive, more appealing? Can you tell, without hearing a word that is spoken, who is really involved and who is more likely to be benefiting from the class? What messages are you sending by the expression on your face?

Cultivate a habit now that will help you in your business career. Let your face come alive and tell the world that you enjoy what you are doing. Smile and show acceptance and interest when appropriate. Enthusiasm is contagious but people need to know you have it before they can catch it.

Posture and Gestures

Some people seem to have more "presence" than others. When they walk into a room, they make an immediate impact. Often, the explanation for this quality lies in the physical appearance or manner of dress of an individual. However, part of that same impact is explained by body posture and gestures, the way a person sits or stands, and the hand movements that accompany the spoken message. The key word here is *energy*. You need to feel that you are spending energy by maintaining a fairly erect posture, leaning forward, and using natural hand gestures that add to or complement the words you are speaking. Above all, avoid a slumping, sagging body posture and hand motions that distract the attention of the listener from your message.

More Hints

1. Try to maintain a reasonable distance of four to six feet during your business exchanges and realize that most people feel uncomfortable when their personal space is invaded.

2. Speak at a reasonable pace, so that your listener will have no difficulty understanding you. Vary the tone of your voice to avoid a tiresome monotone.

3. Your clothing and overall personal appearance should be suited to the occasion. Studies have indicated that when dress and appearance are inconsistent with position—for example, a banker who wears casual clothing to the office—people are less trustful and unwilling to place confidence in that person.

NONVERBAL COMMUNICATION IN A MULTICULTURAL WORLD

In a typical university or college, you will meet people from all over the world in your classes. After you graduate, you will enter a business world that is becomingly increasingly geared toward the global marketplace. The interpretation of nonverbal cues differs from culture to culture. An awareness of this will increase your chances of successful communication in both social and business exchanges. The following are illustrations of cultures that interpret certain gestures differently than Americans:

> In China, putting your hands in your mouth (even biting your nails!) is considered disgusting. In addition, the Chinese do not use their hands when speaking and are distracted by speakers who do. In contrast, Americans might find this a sign of nervousness but would not be disgusted.
>
> In Germany, it is impolite to wave or beckon to get someone's attention. Instead you should raise your hand. In the United States, we wave and beckon without thinking twice about it.
>
> In Malaysia, a handshake usually lasts for 10 to 12 seconds and is often done with both hands. Consider how different that is from the brisk, one-handed American greeting.
>
> In the Arab world, the left hand is considered unclean. When visiting these countries, you should avoid touching others with this hand and avoid both gesturing and eating with it as well. Also, the "thumbs-up" gesture is considered offensive.
>
> A circled thumb and forefinger means "OK" to Americans and "money" to the Japanese, but in other cultures as diverse as Brazil and Norway it is considered insulting.
>
> In Sri Lanka, a nod of the head means no while shaking your head from side to side means yes—the opposite of the American interpretation.[3]

CONCLUSION

These few examples show that whether you are communicating with someone from your own culture or another culture, you should take the time to learn some of the differences in nonverbal cues. If you will be traveling to another country for business or pleasure, take the time to learn how to properly communicate in that country. One thing is certain: If you are to be successful in the 21st century, you will have to interact comfortably with peoples from many different countries and cultures.

NOTES

1. Albert Mehrabian. *Nonverbal Communication.* Chicago: Aldine-Atherton, 1972, p. 182.

2. Dorothy Sarnoff. *Make the Most of Your Best.* New York: Holt, Rinehart and Winston, 1983, p. 39.

3. Terri Morrison; Wayne A. Conaway; and George A. Borden. *Kiss, Bow, or Shake Hands.* Holbrook: Bob Adams, Inc., 1994.

QUESTIONS FOR REVIEW AND DISCUSSION

Demonstrate that you have mastered the objectives of this chapter by answering the following questions.

1. What are kinesics?

2. How much do body, voice, and words contribute to the total impact we make on other people?

3. What does the phrase "nonverbal communication" refer to?

4. When there is a conflict between the verbal and the nonverbal message, on which will the listener rely?

5. What are two major benefits of learning about nonverbal communication?

6. How can the eyes suggest emotion?

7. How does one signal nervousness?

8. How does one signal confidence?

9. In what ways does the use of space in a communication transaction depend on the nature of the communication?

10. Describe an American gesture that could be misinterpreted by someone from another culture.

APPLICATION EXERCISES

1. Identify and describe one of your favorite public speakers. What nonverbal cues does this speaker use that makes him or her so charismatic?

2. Pick one of your least favorite public speakers. Is this person using any of the nonverbal signals we have identified as negative?

3. Discuss some of the benefits and possible problems of learning more about nonverbal behavior.

4. Choose two students in the class and have them demonstrate the three different distances at which the various types of communications take place. Identify your own comfort level with the use of space in impersonal communications.

5. Videotape yourself delivering a speech and watch it with the sound turned off. Assess your posture, hand gestures, eye contact, and other nonverbal behaviors.

6. Working with a partner(s), improvise a brief script and act out the following situations. Practice in small groups and then present your action to the class. Students should interpret and critique each other's nonverbal behavior.

   a. The first three minutes of a job interview, during which the candidate enters the room, sits down, and introduces him or herself.

   b. A manager who is introducing three employees to the new president of the company.

   c. Two best friends, one of whom is asking the other for advice on a difficult family situation.

   d. A manager who is trying both to offer sympathy and to maintain a professional demeanor with an employee asking for advice with personal problems.

FOR ADDITIONAL READING AND DISCUSSION

OPPORTUNITIES FOR HISPANIC WOMEN
It's Up to Us

by Janice Payan

Janice Payan, vice president of U.S. West Communications, delivered this speech at the Adelante Mujer (Onward Women) Conference in Denver, Colorado, in May 1990. Payan suggests that members of a minority in U.S. society will encounter barriers to success, but if they recognize their shared experiences and work together, they can overcome these obstacles.

Thank you. I felt as if you were introducing someone else because my mind was racing back 10 years, when I was sitting out there in the audience at the Adelante Mujer conference. Anonymous. *Comfortable.* Trying hard to relate to our "successful" speaker, but mostly feeling like Janice Payan, working mother, *glad for a chance to sit down.*

I'll let you in on a little secret. I *still am* Janice Payan, working mother. The only difference is that I have a longer job title, and that I've made a few discoveries these past 10 years which I'm eager to share with you.

The first is that keynote speakers at conferences like this are *not* some sort of alien creatures. Nor were they born under a lucky star. They are ordinary *Hispanic women* who have stumbled onto an extraordinary discovery.

And that is: *Society lied to us.* We *do* have something up here! We *can* have not only a happy family but also a fulfilling career. We *can* succeed in school and work and community life, because the key is not supernatural powers, it is *perseverance.* Also known as *hard work!*

And God knows Hispanic women can do hard work!!! We've been working hard for centuries, from sun-up 'til daughter-down!

One of the biggest secrets around is that successful Anglos were not born under lucky stars, either. The chairman of my company, Jack MacAllister, grew up in a small town in eastern Iowa. His dad was a teacher; his mom was a mom. Jack worked after school, sorting potatoes in the basement of a grocery store. Of course I realize, he could have been

Published in *Vital Speeches of the Day,* September 1, 1990. Reprinted with permission.

Continued on page 70

Continued from page 69

hoeing them, like our migrant workers.

Nevertheless, Jack came from humble beginnings. And so did virtually every other corporate officer I work with. The major advantage they had was living in a culture that allowed them to *believe* they would get ahead. So more of them did.

It's time for Hispanic women to believe we can get ahead, because we can. And because *we must.* Our families and workplaces and communities and nation need us to reach our full potential. There are jobs to be done, children to be raised, opportunities to be seized. We must look at those opportunities, choose the ones we will respond to, and do something about them.

We must do so, for others. And we must do so, for ourselves. *Yes,* there are barriers. You're up against racism, sexism, and too much month at the end of the money. But so was any role model you choose.

Look at Patricia Diaz-Denis. Patricia was one of 9 or 10 children in a Mexican-American family that had low means, but high hopes. Her parents said Patricia should go to college. But they had no money. So, little by little, Patricia scraped up the money to send herself.

Her boyfriend was going to be a lawyer. And he told Patricia, "You should be a lawyer, too, because *nobody can argue like you do!*" Well, Patricia didn't even know what a lawyer was, but she became one—so successful that she eventually was appointed to the Federal Communications Commission in Washington, D.C.

Or look at Toni Panteha, a Puerto Rican who grew up in a shack with dirt floors, no father, and often no food. But through looking and listening, she realized the power of *community*—the fact that people with very little, when working together, can create much.

Dr. Panteha has created several successful institutions in Puerto Rico, and to me, *she* is an institution. I can see the wisdom in her eyes, hear it in her voice, wisdom far beyond herself, like Mother Teresa.

Or look at Ada Kirby, a Cuban girl whose parents put her on a boat for Miami. Mom and Dad were to follow on the next boat, but they never arrived. So, Ada grew up in an orphanage in Pueblo, and set some goals, and today is an executive director at U.S. WEST's research laboratories.

Each of these women was Hispanic, physically deprived, but mentally awakened to the possibilities of building a better world, both for others and for themselves.

Virtually every Hispanic woman in America started with a similar slate. Let's do a quick survey. If you were born into a home whose economic status was something *less than rich* . . . please raise your hand.

It's a good thing I didn't ask the *rich* to raise their hands. I wouldn't have known if anyone was listening.

All right. So you were not born rich. As Patricia, Toni, and Ada have shown us, it doesn't matter. It's the choices we make from there on, that make the difference.

If you're thinking, "that's easy for *you* to say, Payan," then I'm thinking: "little do you know . . ."

If you think I got where I am because I'm smarter than you, or have more energy than you, you're wrong.

If I'm so smart, why can't I parallel park?

If I'm so energetic, why do I still need eight hours of sleep a night? And I mean *need*. If I hadn't had my eight hours last night, you wouldn't even want to hear what I'd be saying this morning!

I am more like you and you are more like me than you would guess.

I'm a third-generation Mexican-American, born into a lower-middle-class family right here in Denver. My parents married young; she was pregnant. My father worked only about half the time during my growing-up years. He was short on education, skills, and confidence. There were drug and alcohol problems in the family. My parents finally sent my older brother to a Catholic high school, in hopes that would help him. They sent me to the same school, to *watch* him. That was OK.

In public school, I never could choose between the "greasers" and the "soshes." I wanted desperately to feel that I "belonged." *But I did not like feeling that I had to deny my past to have a future.*

Anybody here ever feel that way?

Anyway, the more troubles my brother had, the more I vowed to avoid them. So, in a way, he was my inspiration. As Victor Frankl says, there is meaning in every life.

By the way, that brother later died after returning from Vietnam.

I was raised with typical Hispanic female expectations. In other words: If you want to *do* well in life, you'd better . . . can anybody finish that sentence?

Right!

Marry well.

I liked the idea of loving and marrying someone, but I felt like he should be more than a "meal ticket." And I felt like *I* should be more than a leech. I didn't want to feel so dependent.

So, I set my goals on having a marriage, a family, *and* a career. I didn't talk too much about those goals, so nobody told me they bordered on insanity for a Hispanic woman in the 1960s.

At one point, I even planned to become a doctor. But Mom and Dad said, "Wait a minute. That takes something like 12 years of college."

I had no idea how I was going to pay for 4 years of college, let alone 12. But what scared me more than the cost was the time: In 12 years I'd be an *old woman*.

Time certainly changes your perspective on that.

My advice to you is, if you want to be a doctor, go for it! It doesn't take 12 years, anyway.

Continued on page 72

Continued from page 71

If your dreams include a career that requires college, go for it!

You may be several years older when you finish, but by that time you'd be several years older if you *don't* finish college, too.

For all my suffering in high school, I finished near the top of my graduating class. I dreamed of attending the University of Colorado, at Boulder. You want to know what my counselor said? You already know. That I should go to a business college for secretaries, at most.

But I went to the University of Colorado, anyway. I arranged my own financial aid: a small grant, a low paying job, and a *big* loan.

I just thank God that this was the era when jeans and sweatshirts were getting popular. That was all I had!

I'm going to spare you any description of my class work, except to say that it was difficult—and worth every painful minute. What I want to share with you is three of my strongest memories—and strongest learning experiences—which have nothing to do with books.

One concerns a philosophy professor who, I was sure, was a genius. What I liked best about this man was not the answers he had, but the questions. He asked questions about the Bible, about classical literature, about our place in the universe. He would even jot questions in the margins of our papers. And I give him a lot of credit for helping me examine my own life.

I'm telling you about him because I think each of us encounter people who make us think—sometimes painfully. And I feel very strongly that we should listen to their questions and suffer through that thinking. We may decide everything in our lives is just like we want it. But we may also decide to change something.

My second big "non-book" experience was in UMAS, the United Mexican American Students. Lost in what seemed like a rich Anglo campus, UMAS was an island of familiarity: people who looked like me, talked like me, and *felt* like me.

We shared our fears and hopes and hurts—and did something about them. We worked hard to deal with racism on campus, persuading the university to offer Chicano studies classes. But the more racism we experienced, the angrier we became.

Some members made bombs. Two of those members died. And I remember asking myself: "Am I willing to go up in smoke over my anger? Or is there another way to make a difference?"

We talked a lot about this, and concluded that two wrongs don't make a right. Most of us agreed that working *within* the system was the thing to do. We also agreed not to deny our Hispanic heritage: not to become "coconuts"—brown on the outside and white on the inside—but to look for every opportunity to bring *our* culture to a table of many cultures.

That outlook has helped me a great

deal as a manager, because it opened me to listening to all points of view. And when a group is open to all points of view, it usually chooses the right course.

The third experience I wanted to share from my college days was the time they came nearest to ending prematurely. During my freshman year, I received a call that my mother had been seriously injured in a traffic accident. Both of her legs were broken. So was her pelvis.

My younger brother and sister were still at home. My father was unemployed at the time, and I was off at college. So, who do you think was elected to take on the housework? Raise your hand if you think it was my father.

No???

Does anybody think it was *me?*

I am truly amazed at your guessing ability.

Or is there something in our Hispanic culture that says the women do the housework?

Of course there is.

So, I drove home from Boulder every weekend; shopped, cleaned, cooked, froze meals for the next week, did the laundry, you know the list. And the truth is, it did not occur to me until some time later that my father could have done some of that. I had a problem, but I was part of the problem.

I *did* resist when my parents suggested I should quit school. It seemed better to try doing everything than to give up my dream. And it was the better choice. But it was also very difficult.

Which reminds me of another experience. Would it be too much like a soap opera if I told you about a personal crisis? Anybody want to hear a story about myself that I've never before told in public?

While still in college, I married my high school sweetheart. We were both completing our college degrees. My husband's family could not figure out why I was pursuing college instead of kids, but I was. However, it seemed like my schoolwork always came last.

One Saturday night, I had come home from helping my Mom, dragged into our tiny married-student apartment, cooked a big dinner for my husband, and as I stood there washing the dishes, I felt a teardrop trickle down my face.

Followed by a flood.

Followed by sobbing.

Heaving.

If you ranked crying on a scale of 1 to 10, this was an 11.

My husband came rushing in with that that "puzzled-husband" look. He asked what was wrong.

Well, it took me awhile to figure it out, to be able to put it into words. When I did, they were 12 words:

"I just realized I'll be doing dishes the rest of my life."

Now, if I thought you'd believe me, I'd tell you my husband finished the dishes. He did not. But we both did some thinking

Continued on page 74

Continued from page 73

and talking about roles and expectations and, over the years, have learned to share the domestic responsibilities. We realized that we were both carrying a lot of old, cultural "baggage" through life. *And so are you.*

I'm not going to tell you what to do about it. But I am going to urge you to realize it, think about it, and even to cry over the dishes, if you need to. You may be glad you did. As for me, *What have I learned from all this?*

I've learned, as I suggested earlier, that Hispanic women have bought into a lot of myths through the years. Or at least *I* did. And I want to tell you now, especially you younger women, the "five things I wish I had known" when I was 20, 25, even 30. In fact, some of these things I'm *still* learning—at 37.

Now for that list of "five things I wish I had known."

First, I wish I had known that I, like most Hispanic women, was underestimating my capabilities.

When I first went to work for Mountain Bell, which has since become U.S. WEST Communications, I thought the "ultimate" job I could aspire to would be district manager. So, I signed up for the courses I knew would help me achieve and handle that kind of responsibility. I watched various district managers, forming my own ideas of who was most effective—and why. I accepted whatever responsibilities and opportunities were thrown my way,

generally preparing myself to be district manager.

My dream came true.

But then it almost became a nightmare. After only 18 months on the job, the president of the company called me and asked me to go interview with *his* boss, the president of our parent company. And the next thing I knew, I had been promoted to a job *above* that of district manager.

Suddenly, I was stranded in unfamiliar territory. They gave me a big office at U.S. WEST headquarters in Englewood, where I pulled all the furniture into one corner. In fact, I sort of made a little "fort." From this direction, I could hide behind the computer. From that direction, the plants. From over here, the file cabinet. Safe at last.

Until, a friend from downtown came to visit me. She walked in, looked around, and demanded to know: "What is going on here? Why was your door closed? Why are you all scrunched up in the corner?"

I had all kinds of excuses.

But she said: "You know what I think? I think you're afraid you don't deserve this office!"

As she spoke, she started dragging the plants away from my desk. For a moment, I was angry. Then afraid. Then we started laughing, and I helped her stretch my furnishings—and my confidence.

And it occurred to me that had I pictured, from the beginning, that I could become an executive director, I would have been better prepared. I would have pictured myself in that big office. I would have spent more time learning executive public speaking. I would have done a lot of things. And I began to do them with my new, expanded vision of becoming an officer, which subsequently happened.

I just wish that I had known, in those early years, how I was underestimating my capabilities.

I suspect that *you* are, too.

And I wonder: *What are you going to do about it?*

Second, I wish I had known that power is not something others give you.

It is something that comes from *within yourself,* and which you can then share with others.

In 1984, a group of minority women at U.S. WEST got together and did some arithmetic to confirm what we already knew. Minority women were woefully underrepresented in the ranks of middle and upper management. We had a better chance of winning the lottery!

So, we gathered our courage and took our case to the top. Fortunately, we found a sympathetic ear. The top man told us to take our case to *all* the officers.

We did. But we were scared. And it showed. We sort of "begged" for time on their calendars. We apologized for interrupting their work. Asked for a little more recognition of our plight. And the first few interviews went terribly.

Then we realized we deserve to be on their calendars as much as anyone else does. We realized that underutilizing a

group of employees is not an interruption of the officers' work—it *is* the officers' work. We realized that we should not be asking for help—we should be *telling* how *we could help.*

So we did.

And it worked. The company implemented a special program to help minority women achieve their full potential. Since then, several of us have moved into middle and upper management, and more are on the way.

I just wish we had realized in the beginning where power really comes from. It comes from within yourself . . . and which you can then share with others.

I suspect you need to be reminded of that, too.

And I wonder: *What are you going to do about it?*

Third, I wish I had known that when I feel envious of others, I'm really just showing my lack of confidence in myself.

A few years ago, I worked closely with one of my co-workers in an employee organization. She is Hispanic. Confident. Outgoing. She's so likable I could hardly stand her!

But as we worked together, I finally realized: She has those attributes; I have others. And I had to ask myself, Do I want to spend the time it would take to develop her attributes or enjoy what we can accomplish by teaming up our different skills? I realized that is the better way.

I suspect that you may encounter

Continued on page 76

Concluded from page 75

envy from time to time.

And I wonder: *What are you going to do about it?*

Fourth, I wish I had realized that true suc-cess is never something you earn single-handedly.

We hear people talk about "networking" and "community" and "team-building." What they mean is an extension of my previous idea: We can be a lot more effective working in a group than working alone.

This was brought home to me when I was president of our Hispanic employees' organization at U.S. WEST Communications. I wanted my administration to be the best. So, I tried to do everything myself, to be sure it was done right. I wrote the newsletter, planned the fundraiser, scheduled the meetings, booked the speakers, everything.

For our big annual meeting, I got the chairman of the company to speak. By then, the other officers of the group were feeling left out. Come to think of it, they *were* left out.

Anyway, we were haggling over who got to introduce our big speaker. I was determined it should be me, since I so "obviously" had done all the work.

As it turned out, I missed the big meeting altogether. My older brother died. And I did a lot of painful thinking. For one thing, I was glad my team was there to keep things going while I dealt with my family crisis. But more important, I thought about life and death and what people would be saying if *I* had died.

Would I prefer they remember that "good ol' Janice sure did a terrific job of arranging every last detail of the meeting?" Or that "we really enjoyed working with her?"

"Together, we did a lot."

All of us need to ask ourselves that question from time to time.

And I wonder: *What are you going to do about it?*

Hispanic women in America have been victims of racism, sexism, and poverty for a long, long time. I know, because I was one of them. I also know that when you stop being a victim is largely up to you. I don't mean you should run out of here, quit your job, divorce your husband, farm out your kids or run for president of the United States. But I *do* mean that "whatever" you can dream, you can become.

A couple of years ago, I came across a poem by an Augsburg College student, Devoney K. Looser, which I want to share with you now.

> I wish someone had taught me long ago
> How to touch mountains
> Instead of watching them from breathtakingly safe distances.
> I wish someone had told me sooner
> That cliffs were neither so sharp nor so distant nor so solid as they seemed.
> I wish someone had told me years ago
> That only through touching mountains can we reach peaks called beginnings, endings or

exhilarating points of no return.
I wish I had learned earlier that ten fingers and
the world shout more brightly from the tops of
mountains
While life below only sighs with echoing cries.
I wish I had realized before today
That I can touch mountains
But now that I know, my fingers will never
cease the climb.
Please, my sisters, never, ever,
cease the climb!
Adelante Mujer

Questions

1. Why does Payan begin her speech by claiming a background similar to that of members of the audience?

2. What are some of the "myths" she says Hispanic women have "bought into"?

3. When Payan uses business catchwords such as "networking," what exactly is she urging Hispanic women to do?

CHAPTER 5

Leadership and Communication Skills

Learning Outcomes

After studying this chapter, you should be able to:

❶ Explain the growing interest in the subject of leadership as an academic discipline.

❷ Write a definition of leadership.

❸ List at least six general personality traits that are associated with successful leadership.

❹ Discuss the behaviors associated with the six general personality traits.

❺ Write a paragraph outlining an individual plan to strengthen your own leadership ability.

CHAPTER

Leadership and Communication Skills

5

Learning Outcomes

After studying this chapter, you should be able to:

❶ Explain the growing interest in the subject of leadership as an academic discipline.

❷ Write a definition of leadership.

❸ List at least six general personality traits that are associated with successful leadership.

❹ Discuss the behaviors associated with the six general personality traits.

❺ Write a paragraph outlining an individual plan to strengthen your own leadership ability.

INTRODUCTION: A NEW INTEREST IN LEADERSHIP STUDIES

Each summer the University of Richmond in Virginia hosts an academic conference on leadership studies. The conference is held at the Jepson School of Leadership and is attended by representatives of many U.S. and international universities. They gather to share ways to teach leadership skills effectively to their students. They return to their own campuses to create new courses and, in some cases, new programs or majors in leadership studies. The reason for all this activity is that interest in leadership studies as an academic discipline is growing rapidly as educators and students realize the enormous potential benefit that a widespread improvement of leadership skills can have for society, for organizations, and for individuals. If leadership courses or activities are available on your campus, it would be a wise investment in your future for you to become involved. In this chapter, you can start by learning about the relationship of communications and leadership skills.

LEADERSHIP DEFINED

The heightened interest in leadership skills is part of a growing societal awareness of the need for improved leadership in our political and business institutions. Apparently many people agree with a statement by Ken Hines, president of the American Hotel and Motel Association, that "leadership may be the fastest dwindling natural resource in our country."[1]

The renewed interest in leadership is a healthy sign. There are many different ideas and definitions of *leadership.* Grace Hopper, the first female admiral in the United States Navy, has this view: "You manage things, but you lead people." Richard Cooley, an American banker, states, "Leadership is an action, not a word." [2] There are many other definitions as well, but a consensus definition might include the idea that leadership is the ability to inspire or motivate others to work to their potential for the purpose of achieving shared objectives or a common vision. Typically, an extended definition will make the distinction between how management and leadership differ from one another and how leadership and communication skills relate to one another.

THE POTENTIAL FOR LEADERSHIP

As you consider these definitions of leadership, it is natural for you to make a self-assessment; that is, to ask what your own potential for leadership may be. Some of you may already have experienced success in leadership positions; others may not have had an opportunity. Evidence from research seems to indicate that personality differences make some people more "natural" leaders than others. Certainly everyone can benefit from understanding theories of leadership if only to become better followers themselves.

At this point, it is helpful to recall what you learned about personality traits and the possibility of changing those traits (see Chapter 1). You learned that your personality is largely the result of biological and cultural factors. You also read that the adult socialization process allows us to change overt behaviors and to acquire specific skills. In other words, change is possible, but first you must become aware of the parts of your personality you wish to change. The key to interpersonal skills needed by the modern leader are listening, questioning, and getting along with others. These skills can be developed or improved at any age once you become aware of the need to work on them.

Further research indicates other general personality traits that contribute to successful leadership. Andrew J. DuBrin identified those traits and the behaviors associated with them (see Figure 5–1).[3]

Personality Trait	Behavior
Self-confidence	Self-assured—cool under pressure
Honesty, integrity, stability	Generates trust in others
Dominance	Imposes will on others, domineering
Extroversion	Outgoing
Assertiveness	Willing to speak up and be heard
Emotional stability	Controls emotions appropriately
Enthusiasm	Openly energetic and enjoys work
Sense of humor	Comedic, laughs easily
Warmth	Sincere, reaches out to others
High tolerance for frustration	Copes with difficulty
Self-awareness and self-objectivity	Aware of strong points and weaknesses

Figure 5–1
Personality Traits that Contribute to Successful Leadership

Source: Andrew J. Dubrin, *How to Handle Setbacks in Your Work and Personal Life.* Englewood Cliffs, NJ: Prentice Hall, 1982, p. 31.

Review each of these personality traits by asking yourself, Is this a strength or weakness of mine? Be candid; there is no reason not to be. If you are uncertain about a particular trait, ask a friend how he or she would rate you. When you are finished, you will have a clear idea of the personality traits or communications skills you need to work on to improve.

FIVE STEPS TO BECOMING A BETTER LEADER

In addition to doing your own self-assessment of your leadership potential, there are five other specific things you can do to become a better leader:

1. Go to your library and pick up some of the more recent books on leadership. Read for the purpose of increasing your broad knowledge of leadership.
2. Sign up for a leadership class, seminar, or workshop.
3. Join a student organization and try to get involved in a position of leadership. This is often easier than you think.
4. Run for office in your student government or work actively for one of the candidates for office.
5. Observe how effective leaders conduct themselves. This can be done on your campus, in your communities, or by keeping abreast of our national leaders from the president to members of Congress to leaders of finance and industry. Imitation or "modeling" is a legitimate way to learn.

CONCLUSION

If you take some of the suggestions discussed here and go beyond this chapter to develop a real interest in the study of leadership, the benefits in the future will almost certainly be worth the extra effort. As Admiral Stark notes in his speech at the end of this chapter, regardless of the difference in our professions, the importance of learning leadership skills is something we all have in common.

NOTES

1. Ken Hines. "Luncheon speech" delivered at Johnson and Wales University, May 15, 1995.
2. Executive Speechwriter Newsletter. Vol. 10, no. 5, 1995.
3. Andrew J. Dubrin. *How to Handle Setbacks in Your Work and Personal Life.* Englewood Cliffs, NJ: Prentice Hall, 1982, p. 31.

QUESTIONS FOR REVIEW AND DISCUSSION

1. To what can we attribute the renewed interest in leadership skills?

2. Write a consensus definition of leadership.

3. How can you benefit from understanding theories of leadership, even if you do not intend to assume leadership roles yourself?

4. What is the connection between general personality traits and successful leadership skills?

5. How does the trait of dominance manifest itself in behavior?

6. What behavior can result from the trait of assertiveness?

7. What behavior can result from the traits of self-awareness and self-objectivity?

8. How can you assess your own leadership skills?

9. What leadership possibilities exist for a student?

10. From whom can you learn leadership skills?

APPLICATION EXERCISES

1. Write a self-assessment and then ask a friend or family member to write one for you. Compare and contrast the two.

2. In class, prepare a written assessment of the leadership skills of a well-known leader. Then compare your notes with those of other students to see if you agree in your assessment.

3. List all of the different "groups" to which you belong. These can include family, community, political, social, and so on. Ask yourself, Are you a "follower" or a "leader" in these groups? Does your role change from group to group? Why or why not?

4. Working in small groups, choose one of the tasks below and appoint a leader to guide the group through the task solving. When you are through, assess each other's success as leaders and followers.

   a. Organize a student group or union (choose a common interest or goal).

   b. Decide how to address a current problem on campus.

   c. Form a study group and study plan for a forthcoming test or project.

FOR ADDITIONAL READING AND DISCUSSION

LEADERSHIP

*by Rear Admiral J. R. Stark, president of the Naval War College
in Newport, Rhode Island*

Admiral Stark delivered this speech as part of the Leadership Colloquium sponsored by the John Hazen White School of Arts and Sciences at Johnson and Wales University, Providence, on March 14, 1996. You will find it a succinct and effective statement on leadership.

Good morning. I want to thank all of you for inviting me to be with you today. It's been a real treat to tour the campus and see all the things that go on here. Of course, I've known for a long time about the culinary and hospitality schools here at Johnson and Wales—they're pretty famous. But I hadn't realized until today that there is so much else going on.

Today, I want to talk about a subject that each one of you needs to be familiar with as you prepare for your careers. That subject is leadership. And even though your professions and mine may be very different, the importance of knowing how to exercise good leadership is something all of us have in common.

Several years ago, I had the chance to speak at a seminar at the American Enterprise Institute, a think tank in Washington. It was in the opening days of Operation Desert Shield, shortly after the Iraqi invasion of Kuwait. Since I had recently come back from commanding a guided missile cruiser that had been deployed in the Persian Gulf, the AEI scholars were interested in some first-hand observations on the area.

So, I talked for a bit about the challenges of operating in a very inhospitable region—the heat that feels like you've just been shoved in a pizza oven, the humidity that always seemed to hover around 95 percent, and the dust storms that aren't anything like the movies—they're more like a Rhode Island fog, except they consist of a talcum-powder like grit that gets into everything.

And at the end, almost as an afterthought, I remarked that one of the most inspiring aspects of my experience in the Gulf was the performance of our sailors. In my crew, we had people from every religion—Catholics, Protestants, Evangelicals, Jews, Muslims, even a Buddhist. We had every race and ethnic group—white, black, Hispanic, Native

Continued on page 86

Continued from page 85

American, Arab, Filipino, Chinese, Vietnamese, and Samoan. We had sailors from farms and factory towns, from suburbs and urban slums. And they came by and large from modest, sometimes tough, backgrounds—working class, some poor, many from broken homes.

All of us know the statistics. America's schools are failing. SAT scores have been steadily declining for the last 30 years. Students graduate from high school with only a rudimentary knowledge of reading. They can't handle the math necessary to balance a checkbook. Half the students in Texas don't know that the nearest foreign country is Mexico. Violence is a way of life.

As a parent, I share those concerns. And yet . . . that wasn't my experience aboard ship. My crew, diverse as they were, lived together 40 or 50 to a room, stacked in bunks three high, under conditions so arduous that, had we been a federal prison, it would have been considered cruel and unusual punishment. They worked long hours, under constant stress and often in danger, in heat that would blister your hand if you touched metal—and the whole ship was metal. And they performed *wonderfully.* Here were kids that six months ago couldn't get their dad to give them the keys to the family car, and now they were operating multimillion dollar equipment in a combat zone.

How do we do that? How does the Navy take these young people, train them, motivate them, and make them part of a smoothly functioning team, so that the whole is greater than the sum of its parts?

Well, there are lots of answers. Part of it is that we have high expectations for them. We set high standards, and we make sure they meet them. Part of it is because we give them good examples, older petty officers to supervise them and help them along. And part of it's because we give them the training and tools to succeed.

But I think the key—the real answer—is that we provide them a type of leadership that brings out their true potential. I'm not talking about me, because what I observed on my ship was typical of most ships. And I think it's pretty representative of all the military services. One of the great success stories of today's armed forces is that we have created a culture that is built on effective leadership at every level.

So what is leadership? We talk about it a lot, and I suppose we recognize it when we see it. But do we really understand it?

For many people, the concept of military leadership conjures up a picture of a drill sergeant shouting orders at a bunch of frightened recruits. But anybody who's been in the service will tell you that no operational unit functions like that. And yelling orders at people isn't leadership—any idiot can do that.

Recently, I've seen lots of books and theories that seem to equate leadership with management. But that doesn't have much appeal for me either. Management seems much too sterile—a science being applied to what is really an art. Don't get me wrong. Management is extremely important. It helps you set up an efficient organization, make proper decisions, and analyze how you're doing. But it's not the same as leadership. I rather like the old saying that "you can manage things, but you have to lead people."

So I'll ask my question again . . . what is leadership, anyway? Many years ago, when I was a young officer starting out, an old chief petty officer told me that "leadership is getting people to do things they normally wouldn't like doing . . . and having them *want* to do it." And while I know that definition may not be applicable to every situation, I think it captures the essence of what leadership is all about.

Just recently, I found a second definition that appeals to me. I was reading General Colin Powell's autobiography, *My American Journey,* and I came across a quote: "Leadership is the *art* of accomplishing more than the science of management says is possible." I like that. It really gives a sense of the fact that leadership is about motivating people to accomplish great things, more than they ever believed was possible.

One of the things I've concluded over the years is that leadership is hard work and, consequently, leaders are seldom born—they're made. I'm sure each of you has seen a few individuals that seem to have a natural talent for inspiring others. They're articulate, they're charismatic, they inspire confidence. They make you *want* to follow them. But most of the time, people like you and me have to work very hard to develop the ability and experience to be a good leader.

I think one of the best ways to learn how to lead is by watching effective leaders go about their jobs. And we learn it by watching *bad* leaders at work, too. And believe me, you'll see both. But the interesting thing is that, good or bad, you can learn a lot from either one.

If you're fortunate enough to have a good leader as a boss—somebody who really motivates people to do their best—you need to sit down and analyze why he or she is so effective: how he or she plans, how he or she treats others, how he or she communicates . . . and then you copy it. It's that simple. And you do the same thing for people you hate to work for, except in reverse. If you have a boss who is ineffective and fails to get the most out of his or her people, figure out what the boss is doing wrong. It's a great lesson in what *not* to do.

But think about what I just said. To be a truly effective leader, you have to first learn how to follow. It's part of being a professional. You have to see the business from the bottom to really understand it, to know the details, to avoid the little errors that mark the amateur. It means you get a chance to see more

Continued on page 88

Continued from page 87

experienced people at work, and to learn from them. And it means you get an appreciation for the little guy, the folks who do the heavy lifting for you, the ones who have to come in early and stay late. And hopefully, when you move up, you'll remember what it was like to be in their shoes.

So, what does it take to be a good leader? Well, I hardly consider myself an expert, but I want to give you seven lessons I've absorbed over the years. They're certainly not exhaustive, but I think they give a sense of what I'm talking about.

First, *know yourself,* and don't be afraid to *be* yourself. There are lots of different leadership styles. Every single one of them can be effective under the right circumstances. But trying to copy someone else's personality, as opposed to his or her leadership techniques, won't work. Figure out what's best for you, what makes you comfortable and gets the job done, and then use it.

Second, you have to *know your job.* Whether you get that knowledge from school, from working your way up through an organization, or a combination of the two, you can't be successful if you don't know enough to make the right decisions, because that's what people count on you for. That means understanding the details of your business, whether it's setting up for a missile shoot at sea, brokering a merger on Wall Street,

or running a restaurant. I'm not saying that you have to know every little fact. But you have to know enough to have credibility with your workers. Even more important, you have to be able to know when things aren't going right, so you can step in and fix them. If you're good, you'll see a problem before anyone else knows it's there.

Third, *know your people.* Part of that means being able to size people up—being a good judge of character—knowing who you can count on, who does sloppy work, and who will be less than honest with you. But it also means getting to know people as individuals. I'm talking about more than just knowing their names. It means understanding their backgrounds, what their special problems and interests are, and what motivates them. Another fine line you have to walk is being friendly, without being *too* friendly. People who work for you aren't really looking for you to be their friend. They've got lots of friends, and so should you. Sure, everybody wants a boss who's nice, and understanding, and easy to be around. But even more, they want somebody they can *respect,* someone who treats them fairly and can be trusted to look out for them.

Fourth, *listen to your people.* You'll find that most of them know when there are problems in the workplace, because they have to live with them every day. And they probably have some pretty good ideas about how to fix things and make the organization more efficient. Remember, everyone likes to be proud of their job, to be a part of a successful team. You need to involve them as much as possible in identifying areas for improvement and deciding how to implement the changes. That doesn't mean you always have to take their ideas. Some will work and some won't. But whichever way you go, they'll appreciate being consulted.

Fifth, *set high standards,* make sure everybody understands them, and then hold people accountable. A leader has to have a passion for excellence and never be satisfied with just good enough. I know just how easy it is to walk by something that's a little bit wrong—whether it's a piece of trash in the corner, or a product that's not quite right, or somebody goofing off. But never forget, once you do that, you've just set a new standard—a *lower* one. And pretty soon, you won't even notice the dirt in the corner, or the end products that are no longer good enough. In your business as in mine, it's *results* that count. Good intentions that never get anywhere aren't worth much, not even as an excuse. And always remember the old saying: praise in public, criticize in private. When things go well and people meet those high expectations, never miss a chance to pat them on the back in front of their friends and family.

Sixth, leadership is based on *loyalty.* A leader has every right to expect loyalty from those who work for him. That means getting to work on time, doing your job to

the best of your ability, and—this is important—telling your boss when you think he or she is going in the wrong direction. I know that can be hard to do. And with some bosses, it can be downright dangerous. But the ability to hear about problems is especially important for the boss himself. People who kill the messenger who brings them bad news are guaranteeing that, when something does go wrong—and it always does—they'll be the absolute last to know. But leaders sometimes forget that loyalty goes *both* ways. A leader owes a debt of loyalty to his subordinates—a debt that he pays by treating them fairly, by protecting them from unreasonable demands from on high, and by helping them get promoted.

Seventh, you need to *make integrity the cornerstone* of your personal and professional behavior. Today, we hear a lot about situational ethics—that everything's relative. People talk about business ethics, or military ethics, or medical ethics. But as far as I'm concerned, they're all part and parcel of the same thing. We *all* know what's right and what's wrong. We all know when we're rationalizing a course of action that shaves the truth or cuts across the lines of ethics, and there's nothing relative about it. I'm not talking about little white lies. If my wife buys a new dress that I don't particularly like and asks for my opinion, I'll probably say it looks fine, but not as nice

Continued on page 90

89

Concluded from page 89

as her blue one—after all, I've been married nearly 30 years. I'm talking about doing what's right, even when it hurts or even when it's embarassing. In my profession, where our lives depend on people doing the right thing, honesty and trust are the glue that holds us together. I don't see how it could be any different for you.

Those are the seven points I want to get across about leadership. They're certainly not conclusive. But before I stop and open the floor to your questions, I want to talk about two final topics that I think are important for each of you as you prepare to start your careers.

First, think about what you would want from your workers if you were running a business. Obviously, you're not going to be starting out as president of the corporation, but if you can put yourself in your boss's place for just a few minutes, then you'll have a better idea what he wants from *you*. Sure, the boss is looking for loyalty, dependability, initiative, energy, and hard work. But remember, bosses are very busy people who are trying to juggle a half-dozen things all the time. So, they appreciate people who can operate without a lot of detailed supervision. If you have a problem, don't just dump it in your boss's lap and expect him or her to give you the answer. Learn how to tell your boss about a problem in a constructive way. Tell the boss what the problem is, what the various alternatives are, and how *you* intend to solve the problem.

Then, if there's something you can't do by yourself, go ahead and ask the boss to give you the outside assistance you need.

In the process, you've just done three things. First, you've kept the boss informed, which will be appreciated. We've got a saying in the Navy that you never want to surprise your boss. And I think it's just as true for you as it is for me. Second, you've just shown your boss that you can be counted on to be part of the solution instead of part of the problem. And finally, your boss will appreciate the fact that you came to him or her for something that you couldn't fix yourself.

My second point applies to every single one of you. As you get ready to finish your education here at Johnson and Wales, never forget that learning is a lifelong pursuit. It *never* stops. I remember finishing high school, and the feeling of relief that I was all done. And then I felt the same thing again when I finished college, and then again with my PhD. But I was wrong. No matter what your profession, there's *always* going to be more to learn. There will *always* be new technologies, new techniques . . . and new competition. And if you ever stop learning, if you begin to stagnate, that competition will pass you by.

Learning is something you always *want* to do. It's something to look forward to as you grow in experience, and in ability, and in leadership. It becomes a familiar friend as you go through life.

And so as each of you get ready to start

out on your own personal journey into the 21st century, I wish you every success. You and your generation are the future of this country. We're counting on you. I know you won't let us down.

Thank you.

Questions

1. According to Stark, what is the essence of leadership?

2. What steps does he suggest you take to begin the process of becoming a leader?

3. Stark mentions the importance of considering learning to be a lifelong process. Is this currently a part of your own philosophy? To what extent do you think this philosophy is needed to be a leader?

Public Speaking for Business and Community

Preparing for the Speech

6

Learning Outcomes

After studying this chapter, you should be able to:

❶ Explain why public speaking is an important career skill.

❷ Use your own personal interests as well as audience analysis to choose a suitable topic for your speech.

❸ Conduct different types of research to gather information on your topic.

❹ Write a thesis statement that clearly states the primary purpose of your speech.

❺ Outline a speech so that you have a "blueprint" to follow as you begin writing a speech.

INTRODUCTION

Of all the communication skills that you need to master, perhaps none is more challenging and demanding than presenting a speech to a group of people. Unlike other skills, speech making requires you to stand alone on "center stage" before an audience whose entire attention is focused on you. To be effective takes much planning and practice, but the rewards to be gained are certainly worth the effort. There is no better way to favorably impress people with your knowledge, personality, and ability to communicate than by presenting an effective speech. The opposite is equally true. Which impression you make will depend on how hard you work to learn and put into practice the ideas in this book. One thing is *certain:* Once your career in business begins, you will have the opportunity to speak in front of a group much sooner than you may think.

PUBLIC SPEAKING AS A CAREER SKILL

Most of you will be required to give speeches or talks before groups as part of your job responsibilities. Many of you will begin very early in your careers. Most companies have established rituals that are followed faithfully year after year. One ritual is to have new employees give a short speech to fellow employees at a business meeting or social function. It is a convenient way for the established employees to become acquainted with and to form impressions of new arrivals. The newcomer is generally asked to present a brief biography and share first impressions of working with the organization. The ritual is a kind of *initiation.* How you perform it can either ease your acceptance into the new group or make it more difficult.

There are many other occasions when you will be asked to speak before groups. The types of situations you face will depend on your chosen occupation. Here are some other possibilities that may require speech making:

- To fill in for a superior.
- To a group of visitors touring your place of business.
- To the local chamber of commerce on behalf of your firm.
- To a group of colleagues explaining new office procedures or changes in employee benefit programs.

- To a college or high school class who requested a representative from your company.

- To church groups, school board meetings, city council meetings, and zoning commission meetings.

- To union meetings.

These are only a few of many possible occasions where you may be asked to talk publicly. There are many others, but all have this in common: The success of your efforts will be directly proportionate to the quality of your preparation.

Unlike the written word that can be studied and dissected, reread, and even redone, the speech is a one and only interaction. It is truly a "one-shot deal." It is delivered to the audience quickly, and is normally finished in a short period of time. As discussed in Chapter 3, the average rate of delivery for most speakers is 125–250 words per minute. If most people don't listen well, then much of the subject matter will be forgotten or even ignored. Only the most prepared and rehearsed speakers will engage, capture, and sustain an audience's interest. Therefore, you should approach speech preparation with a strategy that is both organized and efficient.

TOPIC SELECTION

It is true that in some formal speaking situations, you may be asked to speak on a specific subject. More often, however, you will have to begin your speech preparation by selecting a topic. This first step is crucial to the success of the entire speech process; everything that follows rests on how well you pick a subject. Here are suggestions to get you started on the right track:

Use intrapersonal communication to decide on a topic. Go through your "memory banks" and reflect on those topics that you find interesting. What are your likes and dislikes? What are your hobbies or avocational interests? What is your field of expertise? On what subjects do you normally speak well? Select subjects you find stimulating and then pick a topic you can "believe" in and "sell." Your audience will sense if you are not personally interested. *You can excite an audience only if you are genuinely involved in your subject matter.*

Complete an audience analysis to help you decide on a topic. Once you have reflected on your interests and strengths, you should do the same for your audience. Too many speakers make incorrect assumptions about their audiences and wonder why their speeches fail. A little homework or research on your audience will reveal important factors to consider as you develop your ideas. In many college speech classes, you will get to know your audience through speeches of introduction that students are required to give.

Audience Analysis

It is wise to do an informal demographic or statistical study of your audience. In the classroom and later in business, you will want to consider the following demographic factors:

Average age of group. A young audience will tend to be interested in different topics than an older audience. For example, if your class is composed mostly of 18-year-old freshmen, then an informative speech on the ways to adjust to dormitory life might be appreciated. However, that same speech would strike an audience composed of 30- or 40-year-old people attending a night school class as irrelevant.

Male-female distribution. It would be a mistake to think that certain topics are more interesting to males than females or vice versa. Instead, make sure that your approach to a topic does not appear to exclude either males or females in the audience. Avoid language that might be perceived as sexist and references that rely on stereotypes.

Educational level. The more educated your audience is, the more likely they are to know about topics you may choose. They will appreciate an effort to support your points with strong research, including expert testimony and recent data. They also will be more likely than an uneducated audience to detect flawed logic or inadequate research.

Economic class. Chances are, your audience includes a wide variety of income levels. Again, choose topics of interest and value to everybody. For example, we can all appreciate a speech on the importance of investing in our future—regardless of how much money we make. Keep in mind, you may have to explain unfamiliar terms.

Occupational types. People in a group may share common work interests or career goals. If everybody in the audience is in the hospitality field, they will be interested in a speech on how computers are revolutionizing that industry. If the audience is from a different field, then look for common concerns or interests in these fields instead of focusing on your own field.

Ethnic composition. Both college campuses and businesses are becoming increasingly diverse. This can create an enriching experience in which group members can educate each other about varying customs and experiences. Understanding that the members of your audience may come from different ethnic backgrounds also can help you to avoid inadvertently offending or confusing members of your audience who may not be familiar with some of your customs or experiences.

Political affiliations. Knowing that the audience has strong Republican or Democratic leanings can help you determine how to approach your subject. If, for example, you were giving a speech advocating drastic welfare reforms to a staunchly Republican audience, you could assume that most would agree with you and would react to your speech favorably. However, that same speech could perhaps be modified to anticipate and address the concerns of an audience that you knew felt differently about this issue.

A careful analysis of these and other factors will reveal what subjects are likely to be of interest to the group and which are not. Further, such a study will suggest the values and attitudes that members of the audience are likely to have. This combination of self-inventory and audience analysis will allow you to pick a topic that is suited to both you and the people who will be listening to your speech. Be certain the topic will fit the audience's expectations, the time constraints you have been given, and the occasion for the speech.

RESEARCHING YOUR TOPIC

Check the available resources. Once you have chosen a topic, you still need to be certain that sufficient information is readily available on the topic, so that you may develop the subject to its fullest extent. Naturally, if you have chosen a real-life personal experience to talk about, your need to obtain information elsewhere will be less important. With other subjects, you need to recall Cicero's warning to aspiring orators: "No man can be eloquent in a subject he does not understand." Understanding comes from information, and information comes from researching a topic. Find out if information is available before making a final choice of topic. The following are possible sources that can be used singly or combined:

Personal experience. As mentioned above, personal experience may be the entire basis of a speech. However, it also can serve as a source in a speech which relies on other types of information. A personal anecdote or testimony can add interest to a speech which otherwise relies on "hard" data such as statistics. You may speak of experiences from your past or you may create personal experience in the course of researching your speech; for example, a speech on AIDS might be greatly enhanced by a description of your visit to an AIDS resource center.

Reference areas. In the reference section of your library, you will find encyclopedias, almanacs, atlases, biographical resources such as *Who's Who in America,* the *Reader's Guide to Periodical Literature,* and books such as *Bartlett's Familiar Quotations,* all of which can provide valuable information and substance for your speech.

Card catalogs. You will need to research your topic in your library's information catalogs. Books and other publications are cataloged by author, title, and subject either on cards or on computer. Even if you do not know how to use a computer, you can easily learn to use the computerized card catalog. Most librarians are willing to help you, and the computers themselves have easy instructions to guide you along. A "keyword" search during which you type the key words describing your subject into the computer can save hours of research time. Many libraries now have electronic databases. ProQuest and Infotrac are two popular periodical indexes which give you access to many databases and provide you with abstracts of articles and often the articles themselves.

Internet. If either your library's computers or your own computer have access to the Internet, it is also a source of up-to-the-minute information. To access the Internet, you need a computer, modem, and appropriate software. Well-known on-line services include America Online and Compuserve. Find out what is currently on-line by checking such sources as "What's On Line," a weekly column that runs in many newspapers. Public access computer networks give users limited access to the Internet's World Wide Web where you will find among other things, access to library networks, the *Federal Register,* and the *Congressional Record.*

Public agencies. Don't limit your investigation to the above sources. Community organizations such as Alcoholics Anonymous, the Samaritans, Planned Parenthood, the Right to Life Movement, and most municipal, state, and federal agencies are often excellent sources of material. They may have pamphlets or brochures with current information on your topic.

Interviews. An interview may also be a useful source to consider. Members of college and university faculties can be helpful if you are researching a topic in their field of expertise. Local businesspeople may provide you with their perspective on a subject. For example, if you are writing a speech about career opportunities in the hospitality field, an interview with the manager of a local hotel would add depth and interest to your research. If you are speaking on a controversial issue, an interview with a person directly affected by this topic can create an unusually moving speech. For example, a speech on "gays in the military" might include an interview with someone who currently serves in the military and who can provide a personal account of how current policy affects him or her. Always remember that an interview should be conducted properly. You should prepare a list of questions ahead of time, verify all information with the interviewee, and write a thank-you note after the interview. As a courtesy, you should provide the person interviewed with a copy of the speech, so that he or she may see how you used the information provided.

The point is that information can be found in many places. However, before you continue with your speech preparation, determine if *enough* information is available on your topic.

DETERMINING YOUR PURPOSE

Determine the purpose of your speech. When we listen to a speech, we frequently have only a vague notion of what the speaker wants us to do with the information. Sometimes we are not even sure what the speech is all about. We usually are not sure of the purpose of the speech when the speaker hasn't defined the topic clearly and hasn't made any attempt to include a central idea or thesis statement. You should include a thesis statement or central idea (sometimes called a controlling concept) in your speech to help the audience focus on your purpose. This also will remind you of your reason for speaking and it will help the audience listen and comprehend.

Write your purpose in a thesis statement (a single, declarative sentence is easiest) before you begin writing the speech. For example, you might wish to inform a group about first aid procedures within a factory. You may put that into a thesis statement as follows: "When an emergency strikes, everybody should follow the first aid procedures I have listed from the *Red Cross Handbook*." The thesis statement should capture the essence of the concept or information that you are trying to communicate. Include that statement or a close variation in your introductory remarks.

There are other ways of revealing your purpose, but the beginning speaker should stick to a simple, clear formula. Always ask yourself, What am I trying to communicate to this audience? Am I trying to persuade, to inform, to entertain, or some combination of all three? When your purpose is clear in your mind, it will be clear to the audience. With your purpose clear and materials gathered together, you are now ready to structure your speech.

OUTLINING YOUR SPEECH

Once you have chosen your topic, completed your research, and clarified your purpose, you need to formulate a specific outline of your material. At this stage, you are much like a builder who has a general idea of a house he plans to build. The builder must draw up a specific blueprint before moving to the construction phase. Your blueprint is an outline that lists in order the specific steps you plan to take in your speech. See Figure 6–1 for a sample speech outline.

Figure 6–2 shows how your outline can serve as the format for an actual speech.

Figure 6–1

Sample Outline for
a Speech

Title of Speech: _____

Purpose of Speech: _____

Thesis: _____

Time of Speech: _____

Type of Audience: _____

I. Introduction
    A. Use one or a combination of suggested approaches.
    B. Preview the speech.
       1. Set the tone.
       2. Give your thesis or main idea. Make sure your focus is clear.
       3. Give your intentions for the topic and set the parameters of your speech.
       4. Arouse interest in yourself as a speaker.
       5. Arouse interest in your subject.

II. The Body or Discussion Area
    A. Support your thesis.
    B. Use the most appropriate pattern of organization.
    C. Elaborate on main points.
       1. Give major ideas larger treatment.
       2. Divide speech to accent those major ideas.
       3. Subordinate minor or lesser ideas.
       4. Develop ideas well enough for the comprehension level of your audience.
       5. Check your logic for these points:
          a. Unity and continuity
          b. Coherence
          c. Emphasis
       6. Never make a statement without considering the support you will give it. If an idea is not generally agreed upon knowledge, then consider elaborating and developing that idea more fully. (Again, the capability of your audience should help to determine the development of an idea.)
       7. Finally, when you check your discussion area, ask yourself if you fulfilled the expectations and intentions of your Introduction. Make sure you do what you told the audience you were going to do.

III. Conclusion
    A. Use one or more of the suggested approaches.
    B. Sum up, review, or refocus the main areas of the speech. Make sure the "essence" or "reason to be" is now entirely clear. By this time your thesis should be self-evident. A reminder of that position can help your audience to retain it.
    C. Make the last few words of your speech appropriate for your audience.
    D. Disengage yourself positively from your audience. Know exactly how you are going to conclude and *always be decisive*. In those last few moments the audience will make their final assessment about you. Once you have concluded, thank the audience for their attention, and then sit down.

Figure 6–2

The actual flow of the outline should look like this:

Your Name: Paul Smith

Title of Speech: "A MAN FOR ALL SEASONS"

Purpose of Speech: TO REINFORCE THE HIGH OPINION OF THE AUDIENCE FOR

POW ADMIRAL STOCKDALE

Thesis: ADMIRAL STOCKDALE'S COURAGE BOTH AS SOLDIER AND PRISONER OF

WAR IS A SOURCE OF INSPIRATION TO US ALL.

Time of Speech: 10 MINUTES

Type of Audience: MILITARY PERSONNEL AND THEIR FAMILIES

I. Introduction
   A. Refer to the audience and the occasion.
   B. Use "factors of attention": familiarity, reality, and proximity.
   C. Preview.

II. The body of the speech
   A. Reasons for praising Admiral Stockdale.
   B. Use the "chronological" sequential pattern.
   C. Discussion of Admiral Stockdale's entrance into the military to his role in
      Vietnam and his eventual detention in North Vietnam as a POW.
   D. Examples and illustrations of his unusual bravery and courage.
   E. Use testimonial by fellow POW.

III. Conclusion
   A. Refer to another illustration; refer to the audience; end with a climax.
   B. Use a quote from the president of the United States about Admiral Stockdale
      and all POWs and then disengage from the audience.
   C. Ask for applause from audience for Admiral Stockdale.

CONCLUSION

You will have many occasions as a student and later in your career to listen to and appreciate skilled public speakers. Many of those speakers will appear completely at ease, almost effortlessly keeping their audience's attention and interest. You may think the speaker was "born with this gift" or is a "natural." This is a mistake. With very few exceptions, the most successful public speakers are those who put the most time and effort into preparation. Learn from their success. Cultivate the habit of working hard at the preparation steps outlined in this chapter. Your success as a speaker will be your reward.

QUESTIONS FOR REVIEW AND DISCUSSION

1. What are three groups to whom you may give a speech during your career?

2. What is the average rate of delivery for most speakers?

3. What is the first step in speech preparation?

4. Why is it so important to be genuinely involved in the subject matter of your speech?

5. What are five demographic factors to consider when analyzing your audience?

6. How can an audience analysis contribute to the success of your speech?

7. In addition to the library, where else can you obtain information on a topic?

8. What is a thesis statement and why is it so important to the success of a speech?

9. Where does the thesis occur in the speech?

10. At what point in the speech preparation process should you begin outlining? In what way is the outline like a "blueprint"?

APPLICATION EXERCISES

1. Make two separate lists: one of your hobbies and interests and another of your special skills. Exchange lists with another student. Each student should select a subject of interest from the other's list and jot down five questions about it. Discuss the results with your partner. Sometimes when you are very familiar with a subject, you overlook the possibility that others may not know as much about it and may be interested in learning more. Do your partner's questions help you to see the subject in a new light? Could you write a speech that would answer those questions?

2. Pick a topic that you believe would be interesting to the following audiences whose demographics are described below. How would the demographics determine your approach to that topic?

a. A group of 18-year-old freshmen, half of whom are international students new to the country and the rest are American. All are business students.

b. A group of senior citizens on fixed incomes. All are women who have never worked outside of their homes.

c. An audience composed of recent college graduates, including business and liberal arts students. All are in the job market and the ratio of men to women is approximately 3:1.

d. A community volunteer group composed of middle-income people with strongly conservative political and religious beliefs. The age range is 35–60.

3. Perform an audience analysis of your class. Divide the class into groups and assign tasks to each: One group should determine the average age, another the ethnic backgrounds, and so forth. Your group should first discuss which questions to ask, then briefly interview each member of the class. Pool your findings and discuss the overall demographics of the class.

4. Based on the demographics you determined, make a list of topics to which you think the class would respond positively. Which topics would the class find less appealing?

5. Choose a topic and develop a list of possible sources to use. Visit your school library and find at least five sources—perhaps three magazine or journal articles and two books. Next, add two possible nonprint sources that would *not* be found in the library. These might include professors; experts in the field who are willing to be interviewed; federal, state, and local agencies, and so forth.

6. Using the topic above, write a possible thesis statement and be sure to include the speech's purpose. Then, develop a rough outline for this speech.

FOR ADDITIONAL READING AND DISCUSSION

THE QUALITIES OF SUCCESS
Leadership, Diversity, Community Service and Career Development

by Richard Lidstad

Richard Lidstad, vice president of Human Resources for 3M, delivered this speech before the Carlson School of Management, University of Minnesota, in Minneapolis, May 31, 1995. Lidstad links the concepts of leadership, diversity, community service, and career development. All are essential elements to success in the modern business world.

Good evening. It's a real pleasure for me to be with you tonight to take part in these festivities honoring students who have completed the requirements for the Emerging Leadership Program. I want to applaud all of you who have accomplished this feat.

I was asked to talk to you today because I have always felt a strong, personal link to the University of Minnesota. My bachelor of science in business degree was from the University, more years ago than I'd like to remember. My relationship with the University has been strengthened over the last few years, partly because I have been a part of the Executive Mentoring Program for MBA students. I'll talk a little more about that later.

Before I begin my remarks, I want to issue two caveats. First, unlike many people today, I have spent my entire business career at one company, 3M. So anything I say is colored by my experiences there.

Second, you need to know that I don't consider myself an intellectual. I don't know everything.

That's not all bad, however, since President Dwight Eisenhower once said: "An intellectual is a man who takes more words than necessary to tell more than he knows." With that in mind, I'll try to keep these remarks short.

I'm going to spend the next few minutes talking about the criteria that are emphasized in the Emerging Leadership Program: leadership; diversity, community service, and career development. I think these qualities are right on, since they are all important qualities for anyone who wants to succeed in modern business.

Let's talk about leadership first. This is

Published in *Vital Speeches of the Day,* July 1, 1995.
Reprinted with permission

Continued on page 108

Continued from page 107

the single most important criterion for those of you who aspire to a management position . . . and it's almost as important for those of you who don't. That's because a lot of teaming is going on now in corporate America. And these teams are not hierarchical. Leadership is passed around, so the ability to get the most out of people is a critical skill for everyone.

The traditional method of management—command and control—is dead. (Well, perhaps still kicking and screaming in a few quarters.) Now we are looking for managers who can act as teachers, as coaches, as cheerleaders. Businesses need people who are visionary and who know how to reward those who work for them.

I hope you'll excuse a sports analogy here. The old hierarchical corporation looked and acted like a football team. In football, there is narrow specialization of function. Each man plays only one position, and they all look to the quarterback or the coach for the next play. And when the play is executed, each person has a carefully defined job to execute.

The new way to look at business is more likely a hockey team. There is rapid, continuous action . . . and everyone must pass, shoot, and play defense, even though each player may have a primary role. Teamwork is the most critical element in hockey, since individuals play multiple and often interchangeable roles. Success depends on how well those roles

are blended. It's also true that when the puck drops, nobody knows for sure what's going to happen. Yet, a skilled and well-coached team gets amazing synergy from these interactions.

The change from traditional top-down management to this new leadership model is difficult to learn for many of us from the old school. It's tough for us to grasp this new style, which instead of stressing command, stresses interpersonal skills such as listening, questioning, and getting along with others. This change is good, however, and very necessary.

Not too long ago, we went through an issues prioritization exercise in Human Resources at 3M. Guess what? The number one issue globally is the identification, assessment, and development of leaders. And as you know, leaders can come from any background.

That leads me right to the next criterion: diversity. Learning to work with others who may be different from yourself is a critical part of being a good leader. Recently, I read that the old model saw America as a melting pot, with all the various races, religions, and cultures merging into each other until they represented a whole. Ideally, it visualized an "homogenized" America, sort of like Velveeta Cheese.

The new model is more like a salad bowl. The dressing binds the ingredients together, but they remain separate while enhancing and enriching each other. Each individual keeps his or her own identity and unique attributes, while working together toward a common goal.

If you accept this concept of diversity, that means you respect people with different backgrounds and different points of view. It doesn't mean you just tolerate people who aren't like yourself, it means you embrace them and their cultures. You see how their viewpoint can be valuable to the team.

In the end, respect is what diversity is all about. When we first started talking about diversity at 3M about 20 years ago, I realized that my first lesson in diversity actually occurred right after I started work at 3M more than 15 years earlier.

You're much too young to remember but, in the 50s and 60s, business attire, which some still say is an oxymoron, was in the very distant future. Men—and I stress men—wore white shirts, navy blue suits, narrow ties, and a hat. We had short haircuts, and we were clean shaven.

So I was very surprised, during my orientation in the laboratory where I worked, to see a guy who was wearing a sport shirt and Hush Puppies and sporting a scraggly beard. That man turned out to be one of our top inventors. He had 13 patents. People had so much respect for what he had accomplished that they had learned to ignore the way he dressed. He could wear anything he wanted to wear, and he still got respect because of his contributions.

And that's the way it should be. One should get credit for what one does, not be judged by the way one looks or speaks or thinks.

You can take that little story of mine and transfer it to the whole issue of diversity. Remember, you don't just have to look at obvious differences like race, age, or gender. Look at the family traditions people celebrate, look at the differences in culture that make up the various individual backgrounds.

One way to learn more about diversity is to work with some of the key charitable organizations here in the Twin Cities. You'll find a lot of diversity at the Red Cross, United Way, Salvation Army, and Goodwill. And you'll learn that it is because of their broad outlook—their diversity—that these organizations succeed.

Obviously, that brings me to the third criterion for your program: community service. My own experience tells me that nothing I have done in my career has been more valuable to me than my experience as a volunteer. I love the work I do for the United Way, for example.

It's extra work and it takes time I don't have, but it is extremely rewarding. It helps me understand where 3M fits into the community at large, and it frequently takes me out of my comfort zone, so I learn new things.

Earlier I mentioned that I mentor four MBA students at the Carlson School of Business. I thoroughly enjoy my relationship with these students. I get as much, if not more, from them as they get from me.

Continued on page 110

Continued from page 109

Sometimes I can bring what I learn from them back to 3M and apply a fresh perspective to my work. And when you've reached my mature age (in the human resources field, we call it chronologically gifted), bringing a fresh, new perspective to the job isn't easy. The relation-ship I have with these students helps to make this possible.

If I have any regrets about my community service, it's that I didn't really get active in it until about five years ago. Once you leave school, you'll be busy building your careers and perhaps your families as well, but you need to take time to give something back to your community, too.

And you're sure to find that community service helps you develop skills that will make you more valuable on the job. I'm talking about skills like leadership and finding a balance in your lives. Of course, there is another obvious advantage to community service. It enhances your network of friends and business associates. But the real payoff of volunteerism is very personal; you feel good about your contributions.

The last criterion I'm going to discuss is career development. And the first thing I'm going to tell you is that when you plan your career and set your personal goals, I want you to be very selfish. This is one area that definitely needs to be "me colored."

The first thing you have to ask yourself is "What do I really like to do?" Involve your emotions in this decision, and don't feel guilty if you find out you don't want to be CEO of a company. Of course, if you want to be a trapeze artist or a rock star, you probably shouldn't be attending the Carlson School of Business. But let's assume you want to go into business. The question is, Which spot is the right one for you?

Whatever makes you happy is where you should concentrate your efforts, because that is what you will be the best at. You have to please yourself before you can please anyone else.

Only when you follow your own instincts will you be happily successful. Intellectually, you may think you should strive to be CEO. But if that isn't what makes you happy, you'll probably fail to achieve your goal.

British journalist Katharine Whitehorn said, "The best career advice given to the young is, 'Find out what you like doing best and get someone to pay you for doing it.'" I can only echo those remarks.

When I came to 3M in 1958, I came because I was offered a good job, not a career. I was there several years before I gave much thought to what I wanted to do with the rest of my life. As a matter of fact, I didn't even have my college degree when I joined 3M, although I worked to remedy that rather quickly thanks to the evening and summer sessions offered at the University of Minnesota.

I've been pretty successful at 3M because I followed my instincts about what was fun and interesting to do. For example, I once turned down a quality manager's position to become a technical instructor. I did it, because I love to teach . . . and I'm pretty good at it, too.

So, the management position waited a few years, but guess what? I wound up managing a technical education center, plus a lot more.

There are too many students today who, in trying to crack the puzzle of career success, do all the right things like going to the right school, studying the right things, and getting the right grades. To some extent, every student in this room is doing that.

I want you to promise yourself that, after tonight, you'll spend a little more time being selfish. Because if there isn't some "me" in the equation, you won't be successful.

The other thing you have to do to succeed in meeting your career goals is to be prepared for a lifetime of learning. Good organizations have to continue to grow to meet new challenges. Some of you may think that your education is finished once you get your degree (or degrees), and that's wrong—even if your degree is from a good school like the University of Minnesota.

Over the last decade, lifelong learning has received renewed emphasis at 3M and, from what I've heard from my HR colleagues in other companies, that's true almost everywhere. We encourage all 3Mers—our top executives, scientists, marketers, manufacturing employees, and clerical people—to continuously improve their capabilities every year.

After all, how can a corporation like 3M get better every year unless its people do? 3M is its people, and that's true of every other company as well.

This learning can involve formal training or participation in teams or task forces or new assignments. Companies today cannot be competitive in the global marketplace unless all their people renew their old skills and develop new ones.

You need to be willing to leave your comfort zone. As Alvin Toffler said, "The illiterate of the future are not those who cannot read or write, but those who cannot learn, unlearn and relearn." That's a real challenge, but it's one you will face again and again in your careers. Learning is what will keep your mind young, even when you are as old as I am!

I've shared my thoughts with you on leadership, diversity, community service, and career planning, and I hope you found them helpful. I hope some of what I've said may make your travels down your career path a little easier.

I'd like to congratulate the University of Minnesota and the Carlson School for sponsoring this program, because it is so contemporary and forward looking.

And, once again, I want to congratulate tonight's honored guests. And I want to wish all the students here the kind of career I've had, one that is happy,

Continued on page 112

111

Concluded from page 111

personally fulfilling, and satisfying in every way.

Thank you again for inviting me. And thank you for listening.

Questions

1. What was the traditional management style that Lidstad says is now "dead"? How does he describe the new management style? What skills does he feel are needed for this new style?

2. What are the personal and professional benefits of community service according to Lidstad?

3. How does he define "lifelong learning"?

Writing the Speech and Using Visual Aids

Learning Outcomes

After studying this chapter, you should be able to:

1 Organize a speech into three distinct parts: introduction, body, and conclusion.

2 Write effective introductions.

3 Develop the body of the speech in four different patterns: topical, sequential, casual, and problem-solution.

4 Write effective conclusions.

5 Incorporate visual aids into the speech in ways that strengthen your presentation.

INTRODUCTION

Most speeches are written out first, often in essay form. Knowing this, you can make up your mind to follow the basic Aristotelian rule that all good writing contains a beginning, a middle, and an end. Learn to write each of these three parts separately and in the correct proportion to one another and your speeches will be better received by your audience.

Organization is the key to a successful speech. If your speech is not organized, it will be difficult to understand and follow. Listeners will be confused if you jump around haphazardly. You can make your speech coherent by separating it into three parts: introduction, body, and conclusion. Remember that your listeners have no way of sitting down and studying your speech like a book or a letter.

There is no second chance for the listeners. Clear organization helps you develop ideas, so that each one is a stepping-stone to the next. If you destroy the organization of your speech, you destroy its clarity. If the speech is not clear, meaningful interaction with the audience will not take place.

INTRODUCTION TO THE SPEECH: 10–15 PERCENT

Though the introduction of a speech should represent only 10 to 15 percent of the entire speech, many consider it to be the most important part. During your introduction, you create that vital first impression and predispose your audience to feel positively or negatively toward the rest of what you have to say.

The first words you deliver are crucial. Several things ought to happen at the outset of your speech: You should be setting a tone, making an impression, arousing interest in yourself as speaker, attracting interest in the topic, developing the boundaries of the topic (some call this signposting the speech) for the audience, and giving the audience your intentions for the speech. If the audience is not with you at the beginning, they will not be with you at the end. *Work at effective introductions.*

Approaches to Making an Effective Introduction

The following approaches are recommended for your introductions. Consider combining some of them when appropriate.

1. Refer to the audience. "It is a pleasure to be addressing such an important organization as the Big Brothers of America. You as Big

Brothers bring love, care, and inspiration and guidance to many boys without a male role model. I am honored to speak to you today."

2. Refer to the occasion. "The Fourth of July is a historic and important celebration in the history of our nation. It is a time when we are reminded of the roots of our independence, our freedom, and the spirit of our American character. It is a time when we praise all who have gone before us and sacrificed themselves for the glory of our democratic Republic."

3. Refer to the subject. "My speech today is about that old romantic ritual, the high school prom. My hope is to persuade you that the high school prom should be done away with and replaced by an occasion that is safer, much less expensive, more democratic, and far less traumatic."

4. Refer to a quote. "As the German philosopher and poet, Friedrich Nietzcshe, once stated: 'He who has a *why* to live for can bear almost any *how*.' It is my pleasure to applaud your inspiration and thank you for showing the world the truth of Nietzcshe's remark. As former POWs [prisoners of war], you have shown us that life is worth living, no matter how hard the circumstances may be."

5. Using a startling statement. "Have yourself a good long look, because you are looking at a crazy man. A man who has lost his marbles. A man who needs a straightjacket. Because according the standards of American society, I'm crazy!"

6. Use a rhetorical question. "Have you ever felt fear? Have you ever panicked? Have you ever felt like flipping out? Have you ever lost control because of anxiety? If you answered yes, you may have a phobia."

7. Use humor. "Tonight, at your graduation ceremonies, you have asked me to share my wisdom with you. Though that part of my speech will only take a few seconds, I believe I can still inspire you. I reflect on the inspiration my coach gave me when I was pitching in a close baseball game. He said: 'Son, it may seem like a bad spot to be in, but receive hope from this—that even a blind squirrel finds some nuts.' "

Whatever approach or combination of approaches you decide to use, be certain that your introduction connects logically and smoothly to the body of your speech.

THE BODY OF THE SPEECH: 70–80 PERCENT

The body or the discussion section of your speech should be 70 to 80 percent of the whole. The basic problem with many speakers is that they think too much like writers and not enough like speechmakers. Your audience cannot study, reread, or dwell on any one point for an extended period of time. Unlike written information, oral communication flows like a river and cannot be stopped in any one place. There is an old speech saying that states: "Tell them what you are going to tell them, tell them, and then tell them what you told them." If there is any type of communication that needs a little "redundancy," it is speech communication. You must help your audience to retain, and repetition is certainly called for in your speeches.

The organizational set up that you follow should be selected with the audience in mind. Only a few organizational patterns are recommended for the beginning speaker. The following patterns are recommended: topical, sequential, causal, and problem-solution.

The Topical Pattern

As the name implies, the topical pattern is a speech arrangement that is divided according to well-known topics or categories that you can easily classify. For example, you may want to speak on the top three U.S. automobile manufacturers. You could easily arrange this as follows:

    I. Ford Motor Company
       A. History and Development
       B. Present Day Activity
       C. Future Innovations

    II. General Motors Company
       A. History and Development
       B. Present Day Activity
       C. Future Innovations

    III. Chrysler Motor Company
       A. History and Development
       B. Present Day Activity
       C. Future Innovations

The thing to remember about the topical pattern is that it can be used to classify almost any speech. Simply break down your subject according to types, kinds, categories, reasons, groups, traits, parts, advantages, disadvantages, and so on, and you are using the topical pattern.

The Sequential Pattern:

This type of arrangement is based on space and time. Many sources call this "spatial" arrangement and "chronological" arrangement. The spatial approach could be used in a discussion of the geography of the coastal New England states. You could arrange your speech by moving in sequence from the state of Maine to the state of Connecticut (north to south). An example of the north-south sequence is the following:

I. State of Maine
   A. Physical characteristics
   B. Economic characteristics
   C. Demographic characteristics

II. State of New Hampshire
   A. Physical characteristics
   B. Economic characteristics
   C. Demographic characteristics

III. State of Vermont
   A. Physical characteristics
   B. Economic characteristics
   C. Demographic characteristics

IV. State of Massachusetts
   A. Physical characteristics
   B. Economic characteristics
   C. Demographic characteristics

V. State of Rhode Island
   A. Physical characteristics
   B. Economic characteristics
   C. Demographic characteristics

VI. State of Connecticut
   A. Physical characteristics
   B. Economic characteristics
   C. Demographic characteristics

In the sequential pattern, physical space or geographic proximity is used to show relationship and to produce unity. The "chronological" approach is simply the use of *time* in a systematic way. If you are giving a speech on how to fill out your income tax forms, you can talk about what needs to be done first, and then progress to the next point. Or if you were giving a speech on the Persian Gulf War, you could begin with the invasion of Kuwait and end with the surrender of Iraq.

The chronological approach is an excellent one for how-to speeches or historic speeches.

The Causal Pattern

The causal arrangement shows a relationship between certain factors and what follows them, that is, an arrangement that shows causes and effects. You could show how watching television produces antisocial behavior in children and adolescents. You could cite increases in violent crime and threatening behavior after "gang" movies were shown on major networks in large cities. An example of an outline for this type of speech would look like this:

I. Cause: Violent TV programming
   A. Violence in "action" cartoons
   B. Violence in adult-oriented action dramas
   C. Violence in "gang" movies
II. Effect: Increasingly violent behavior in children
   A. Increased aggression in children of kindergarten age
   B. Increased number of disturbances in elementary schools
   C. Increased number of gun-related incidents in high schools

The Problem-Solution Pattern

This is an effective arrangement when you are proposing a change or suggesting an alternative to a present-day problem. If you were to give a speech on drug addiction and make suggestions for solutions to the problem, this type of pattern is ideal. You could set up the speech easily by showing the seriousness of the problem and then conclude your speech by making recommendations for the solution:

I. Health-related problems of drug addiction
   A. Physical deterioration
   B. Mental deterioration
II. Work-related problems of drug addiction
   A. Loss of productivity
   B. Possible loss of job
III. Family-related problems of drug addiction
   A. Withdrawal from family structure
   B. Emotional hardships for spouses and children
IV. Solution: increased social awareness and support
   A. Educating the public about drug addiction and its dangers

B. Government-assisted programs
C. Compassionate policies in the workplace
D. Counseling for both individual and family members

COMMUNICATION IS THE GOAL

Whatever pattern you decide to use, always remember that your goal is communication. Many speakers lose their audiences because they never make organizational selections based on the capability of their listeners. Always subscribe to the principles of unity, coherence, and emphasis. Make sure every part of the speech fits together well with the others. Don't confuse the audience by jumping around, bringing in extraneous information, or failing to elaborate on your statements.

Your plan should give you a singleness of purpose: one that shows your speech is *unified*. Also allow your audience to see the continuity, the consistency, and direction of your speech. *Coherence* means the logical ordering of the thoughts you utter. Your plan should not be a random selection of material and supporting information. Again, you need to have unity and continuity in the production of your thesis. The last point to remember is to use *emphasis* in your organization. You should give prominence to some ideas and subordination to others. You can achieve emphasis by using:

1. *Proportion*—the length of time you devote to an idea.
2. *Repetition*—the number of times you repeat your ideas in the same way or in a slightly different way.
3. *Position*—the location of your ideas in the speech.

The last type of emphasis, position, is largely a psychological matter. You have to decide where the best position is for an idea in your speech. Generally, your strongest and most attention-getting material—logical, well-thought-out supports, shocking statistics, unusual facts or anecdotes—should be at the beginning and at the end of a speech. By placing them at the beginning, you catch the audience's attention quickly. By placing them at the end, you leave the audience with a strong impression of your handling of the topic. Weaker material—points that are still relevant but perhaps of less *immediate* interest—should be sandwiched between these stronger points to complete the speech.

CONCLUSION OF THE SPEECH: 10–15 PERCENT

Many untrained speakers don't know how to disengage themselves from the audience. They either hem and haw, ramble on and on without knowing where to stop, or stop too abruptly as if they had to jam on the brakes at a light that suddenly turned red. In so doing, they spoil the last opportunity they have to make a desired impact on the audience. They are ignoring that old truism of communication theory: "That which is said first is usually the attracting or arousing thing; that which is said last is usually the thing that is most remembered, most retained." Your conclusion should be remembered as the climax of the speech. It is the last thing the audience will hear. A good conclusion should do the following:

1. Let the audience know you are ending (use concluding words such as *so, thus, finally, to conclude, to sum up, my final remarks, let me finish by restating my thesis, therefore,* and so forth).
2. Restate what you want listeners to understand about your topic.
3. Leave a final impression.
4. Disengage yourself from the audience in a meaningful way.

Like any good business letter or any good musical piece, your conclusion should be looked upon as a closure or a finale. Make your last few words important. Don't forget to signal your conclusion to the audience by using the appropriate words.

Many of the ways you can introduce a speech can also be used for concluding a speech. You have to decide what the best way is for your purpose.

Select the most appropriate approach below. Decide on your purpose and use the following effective method. You may want to combine approaches.

Approaches to Concluding a Speech

1. Refer to the audience. "So, tonight, as I leave this meeting, I will receive strength from the knowledge that all of you here will not abandon the cause. You are the type of people who have ideals and pursue them, and I am encouraged in my efforts because you stick to the fight when you're hardest hit." This approach could be used when addressing a group of community volunteers or a student group whose efforts you hope to encourage.

2. Refer to the occasion. "Finally, as we reflect on this Veterans Day, let us recall the many men and women who have served this country well. Let us remember their sacrifices, so that today, we can truly call ourselves free Americans." This type of conclusion would obviously be used to highlight the ceremonial nature of your speech.

3. Refer to the subject. "My speech this afternoon has focused on the need for dialogue between management and labor. All management personnel should institute the four main steps of the dialogue process in their respective departments. Copies of my speech will be distributed via E-mail to help you in this crucial process." This type of conclusion reminds the audience of the informative purpose of the speech and leaves them with a clear sense of what they are expected to have learned.

4. Refer to a quote. "As I conclude tonight, I recall the words of the great New England poet, Robert Frost: 'The woods are lovely, dark and deep, but I have promises to keep, and miles to go before I sleep, and miles to go before I sleep.'" The use of a quote such as this would provide an effective conclusion for a speech that revealed personal goals and dreams.

5. Refer to a story or illustration. "Let me end by sharing with you a brief story about a businessman who had a dream, and turned that dream into a multimillion dollar enterprise which today is Microsoft." A story such as this would effectively conclude an persuasive speech addressed to a corporate, community, or collegiate audience.

6. Refer to a rhetorical question. "So, is it not better for us to be in full discussion with management than to close down negotiations and go on strike?" The rhetorical question forces the audience to engage themselves in your topic, mentally answering the question by pondering the information you have given them. It, too, is an effective ending for a persuasive speech.

7. Issue an appeal or challenge the audience to action. "Since the next few months are critical to our company, I ask all of you to hold the line on your budgets. If we can do that, we may be able to forgo the expected layoffs, and get all of our employees back to work." This conclusion not only reinforces the main purpose, but also points out future implications to the audience.

8. Summarize your main points. "Each person is asked to follow the steps I have outlined for the computer's use. To highlight the main points again, I recommend the following . . ." This is an effective conclusion for a speech that has detailed information which may be difficult for the audience to process. The repetition of main points eliminates the possibility of confusion, leaving the audience with a clear summary of the information.

LANGUAGE AND EFFECTIVE SPEECHES

In addition to following a three-part organizational pattern, you must pay close attention to the words and phrases that you choose to deliver when writing a speech. Each of us would like to coin lasting terms such as the "Iron Curtain" (Winston Churchill) or to write memorable phrases such as, "Ask not what your country can do for you, but what you can do for your country" (John F. Kennedy). Indeed, that is what you should strive for, to write and deliver the best speech possible. Your chances of doing that will be much greater if you follow these suggestions:

1. The level of complexity of your language choice should depend on your audience. However, a fundamental rule to follow about word choice is to avoid the artificial, lengthier, and unfamiliar words and choose the simpler words that tell it as it is.

2. Be brief. Avoid wordiness. Find out how much time you have for your speech and stay within that time limit. Remember the overly long speeches you have had to sit through. Don't do the same thing to your audience.

3. Choose words and phrases that sound effective when you hear them. Rehearse aloud and change words or phrases that you have trouble pronouncing or that don't have the right sound to them.

4. Avoid jargon. Jargon is technical language that pertains almost exclusively to some special field of interest such as medicine, the law, or computers. If your audience consists of all doctors or lawyers, then medical or legal terminology might be acceptable. If not, do not use technical terms unless you provide an accompanying explanatory definition to help understanding.

5. Avoid clichés. Clichés are words or phrases that have been used too often and have lost their original freshness and appeal. Look for fresh ways of saying things that are clearly original.

These basic rules serve you well as guidelines to the part language choice plays in your speeches.

USING VISUAL AIDS

As you plan your speech, you may also decide that visual aids would be a helpful supplement. You have heard the expression, "A picture is worth a thousand words"—but consider the following advice:

> A picture is worth a thousand words . . . if it supports rather than distracts from the message, if it accurately conveys the message, if it can be seen by everyone in the audience, and if it is easily interpreted by the audience. A picture is worth a thousand words when the correct visual technique is used and it is well designed.[1]

Any visual aid must meet three criteria: visibility, clarity, and simplicity. To meet these criteria, the number of words used on charts should be few, visual aids should be colorful, and graphs or charts should be simple and unified.[2]

Also, be sure that your graphics are suited to the place where you are speaking. Don't assume there will be chalk and chalkboards, projectors, or electrical outlets at your disposal. Check ahead of time to be certain the place is suitable and whatever equipment is needed will be there.

Options in the Use of Visual Aids

Some of the many options to consider when planning the use of a visual aid in a presentation follow.

Use of volunteer from the audience. When giving an informative speech, you can use a volunteer to help demonstrate a procedure. For example, a speech about the techniques of karate might benefit from a brief demonstration using a willing volunteer. Always remember to ask your volunteer *before* the speech and to rehearse with them as well, if possible.

Use handouts. It might be helpful to hand out one or two sheets to each member of the audience. For example, during a persuasive speech asking for a ban on animal testing, you might hand out a list of companies that practice testing and those that do not. The audience can refer to the list as you speak. However, the audience can become distracted by handouts; this option works best if you distribute the handouts toward the end of speech. Do not make the mistake of handing them out before you wish the audience to look at them. Make sure you have enough for everyone in the audience and consider enlisting the aid of a volunteer to help you distribute them quickly and efficiently. Explain their purpose as you hand them out, so that your presentation is not interrupted.

Use a chalkboard. The advantage of using a chalkboard is that it is very convenient and requires no planning. It can lend an air of spontaneity to your presentation. The disadvantages are that it doesn't have the professional appearance of other visual aids and it cannot take advantage of color variation. If you do use the chalkboard, remember to angle your body so that you still partially face the audience and project your voice toward *them* not the chalkboard.

Use flip charts. This is an inexpensive option popular with students. You can use the flip chart to present graphs that you have drawn yourself. The flip chart allows you to focus the audience's attention on a few pieces of information at a time and unlike the chalkboard, the flip chart can use color to highlight information. Check to make sure you have access to an easel; the flip chart does not work well against a chalkboard or when the speaker attempts to hold it! The audience should be limited to no more than 30 to ensure visibility. If your sheets are not attached to one portfolio, place them neatly behind each other as you use them; a common mistake is to simply drop sheets to the floor as they are used.

Use an overhead projector. This is best for complex and detailed topics. Presenters often demonstrate a formula or concept on the overhead projector as they speak. It allows you to present to a slightly larger audience than the flip chart will. Consider using a pointer to direct the audience's attention to particular points. To ensure a smooth presentation, practice using the overhead before your speech. A disadvantage is that both you and the equipment may block the view of some members of the audience, so remember to stand to the side to avoid blocking the audience's view. Overheads are often hand drawn but computer-generated overheads have a more professional appearance and also allow you to use color.

Use a slide projector. Like the computer-generated overheads, slides lend an air of professionalism and preparation to a presentation. With a properly sized screen, you can present to a large audience. A disadvantage, however, is that the room must be darkened and you must be careful to keep the audience's attention from straying. Again, remember to practice—many presenters have been flustered by finding their slides were out of the correct order.

There are many other possibilities when considering the visual aid that best suits your purposes. When explaining to your audience how the space shuttle works, consider how helpful it would be to use a model of the space shuttle. When trying to persuade your audience of the benefit of generic brands over that of name brands, consider letting your audience see the two products face to face. This could mean comparing boxes, lists of ingredients, or even contents. If you have never used a visual aid in any presentation, consider using one when you perform your first informational speech. Visual aids are particularly helpful in this type of presentation.

CONCLUSION

Interacting effectively with your audience and engaging them in your speech requires an understanding of the different parts of a speech *and* the different strategies required of a speaker when delivering the introduction, body and conclusion. Most importantly, remember that visual aids should enhance your presentation not detract from it. Like the speech itself, you must *plan* the use of a visual aid and then *practice* in order to use it effectively.

NOTES

1. Lee Pitre and Larry Smeltzer. "Graphic Reinforcement for an Oral Presentation." *ABCA Bulletin.* December 1982.
2. Ibid.

QUESTIONS FOR REVIEW AND DISCUSSION

1. What percentage of the speech should the introduction be?

2. What are at least four goals an effective introduction should accomplish?

3. Describe at least four strategies for introductions.

4. What percentage of the speech should the body be?

5. List four possible organizational patterns. For what type of topics would each be appropriate?

6. What percentage of the speech should the conclusion be?

7. What should a good conclusion accomplish?

8. What are five possible strategies for concluding a speech?

9. What three criteria must any visual aid meet?

10. How can you make sure the graphics you wish to use are suited to the place where you will be speaking?

APPLICATION EXERCISES

1. Read the sample speech by General Colin Powell at the end of this chapter and critique its introduction. What strategy does it employ? Do you find it effective? Why or why not?

2. As a class, brainstorm and list several possible speech topics on the chalkboard. Next, decide which organizational pattern might best be used to develop a speech.

3. Watch a political speech and notice how the presenter uses the conclusion to leave a lasting impression. What strategies does he or she use?

4. Describe for the class an effective use of visual aids which you have recently observed (perhaps in another class). How did the presenter handle the aid? How did it contribute to your knowledge of the subject?

5. Assess your classroom as a site for using visual aids. Walk around the classroom and determine which visual aids could be used and which could not. Would the room require any special preparation?

FOR ADDITIONAL READING AND DISCUSSION

U.S. FOREIGN POLICY IN A CHANGING WORLD
Keeping Democracy Alive

by General Colin L. Powell

General Colin L. Powell, then Chairman of the Joint Chiefs of Staff delivered this speech to the Town Hall of California, Los Angeles, on March 23, 1990. Read his speech not only for the message, but for his use of the speech-writing strategies we have discussed.

Thank you for that most generous introduction, Jack [Dean Borsting]. Chairman Miscoll, President Medawar, members of the Town Hall of California, honored guests, ladies and gentlemen—I am pleased to be back in California. I came here frequently in my last job as Commander in Chief of the U.S. Army Forces Command—to Fort Ord to visit the 7th Infantry Division, to the Presidio of San Francisco to visit the U.S. 6th Army headquarters, and to Fort Irwin at Barstow to visit the fine young troops in training at our National Training Center.

I am especially pleased to have this opportunity to speak to such a prestigious group. For over half a century, Town Hall of California has provided a distinguished forum for the discussion of public issues. And your reach is more than local—*The Town Hall Journal* and your radio broadcast, "Town Hall on the Air," provide for wide dissemination of your discussions.

You provide a valuable service by informing the American public and increasing their knowledge of critical issues. In her letter of invitation to me, President Medawar wrote that the members of Town Hall of California "are firmly-convinced that knowledge of international and national issues in today's world is not merely a social or intellectual asset—it is vital."

Today, such knowledge is indeed vital. Today, the world is changing with such dizzying speed that it demands the earnest involvement of every citizen if we are to shape and mold this change to the benefit of our nation—and, ultimately, to the benefit of the world.

The change is electrifying. Democracy is on the move everywhere. Free

Published in *Vital Speeches of the Day*, May 1, 1990.
Reprinted with permission

Continued on page 128

Continued from page 127

economies, responsive to market pressures, are being studied by yesterday's most ardent Marxists. Freedom of speech occurs between East and West German policemen talking over the rubble of the Berlin Wall that is now a monument to the past rather than a barrier to the future. The votes for self-determination fill ballot boxes in East Germany, in Nicaragua, and, yes, even inside the Soviet Union.

These changes are a result of the power of ideas: the power of freedom, the power of democracy, the power of free economies, and the power of people in control of their own destinies. And ultimately the power of human dignity.

These changes are also a direct result of the steadfast commitment of America and her allies to the policies of collective security, peace through strength, and the rule of law. These policies created today's world in which freedom and democracy are now the dominant forces at work.

Almost half a century ago, George Kennan advocated a policy of containment. If we held firm, he said, the inherent weaknesses of communism would bring it down. We held firm. And the walls of communism are coming down.

Since 1945, the major threat to peace in the world has been the Soviet Union and its allies. Today, in what seems in the broad scope of history little more than the time required for a sound bite on CNN, the Soviet Union seems to have abandoned its aggressive foreign policy,

encouraged several of its allies to do the same, and is increasingly focusing on its own critical internal problems.

Those Soviet client states who remain unmoved, such as Cuba and North Korea, are pariah nations in the world community. They are economic basket cases, and their leaders wait in great anxiety for the sunlight to shine suddenly on them and expose all the underlying rot. Fidel Castro, a pathetic, irrelevant, aging starlet, still shows up for casting calls carrying faded, dog-eared 8×10 glossies, and accompanied by a crew of bodyguards that needs 10 tons of weapons to feel secure.

In the words of an old song, "What a difference a day makes!"

Only three and a half years ago I was a corps commander in Europe. My 72,000 young volunteers were positioned astride the Fulda Gap, one of the classic invasion routes into Germany from the east. We were poised to stop a Soviet invasion into West Germany. My corps had been there for almost 40 years with virtually that same mission. In fact, I began my career in that same corps as a second lieutenant 28 years earlier.

Across that border, opposite my corps, was the Soviet 8th Guards Army that I knew could engage my corps with just a few days warning. I also knew that behind the 8th Guards Army was another Soviet army—a tank army that could perhaps threaten my corps while I was engaged with the lead army. And there were other armies behind those two. It might take nuclear weapons to stop them all. For me and my soldiers, this wasn't a game. It was for real. Every time I visited my border units at Fulda, I could look over the wire and see the enemy. This was before perestroika, glasnost, and Gorbachev took hold.

But what a difference a day makes.

Two months ago in Vienna, I met with my counterparts in the East European armed forces and my counterpart in the Soviet armed forces, General Moiseyev. One message I got loud and clear: Soviet armies were rolling all right, but not west; they were rolling east, back into the Soviet Union. Within the past month, the Soviet armies in Hungary and Czechoslovakia continued their march home—125,000 more men to be gone by June of 1991. Soviet armies still in Poland and East Germany—430,000 troops—will also eventually start to go home.

These armies are withdrawing because they knew they couldn't win, and they learned they could not intimidate us any longer. They leave empty-handed. Soviet strategy has failed. It failed because of the systemic strength of the Free World: our values, our resilient economies, our powerful political processes, our rule of law, our belief in human rights, and our strong and well-supported armed forces together in even stronger alliances. Our systemic strength has beaten the Soviet juggernaut before it could be unleashed on Europe.

I can visualize a small travel item in the *Los Angeles Times* in about 1993. Some reporter will have been to Germany and will end the travelogue piece with a description of a visit to the town of Fulda:

> And in this historic German city, lying at the foot of the Vogelsberg Mountains—once on the border, now situated in the heart of the new, unified Germany—I was caught up in a sense of history as I visited the second oldest church in Western Europe, and as I noted a bronze marker on a hill just outside of town, near what's referred to as the Fulda Gap. The marker was inscribed as follows: "Dedicated to the American men and women whose 40-year watch at this spot gave Eastern Europe her freedom and changed the course of history."

Throughout Europe dramatic change is the order of the day. In the Soviet Union, dramatic change seems to be the order of the hour. So much so that we know the Soviet Union will never be the same. The real question, what will it be? Will it become a real democracy, or will it become something else we cannot yet see clearly or define?

Irrespective of which future course the Soviets follow, East Europeans will be moving swiftly ahead toward democratically-elected, noncommunist regimes.

As we try to analyze all of this incredible change, we have to be careful. As Clausewitz said, "Beware the vividness of transient events." Amidst these incredible changes, we have to identify the principal factors that affect our interests and sort

Continued on page 130

Continued from page 129

them out from the cascade of more glamorous but essentially transient events.

First, we must understand what is really happening to Soviet military capabilities. We know that right now their armed forces appear to be the instrument of a much more benign foreign policy. But we also know that while reductions and restructuring are in fact ongoing, the Soviets are not demobilizing or disarming. Mr. Gorbachev is making a virtue of necessity where he can. Yes, the Soviet army is going home. But it is not disbanding. When this is all over, the Red Army will still be modern and capable and several million strong. Still the major Eurasian military power. Others may wish to ignore that or say it doesn't matter. I am charged not to ignore it; and it does matter.

And as far as their nuclear capacity is concerned, the Soviets are not giving up any capabilities that will be allowed under a new strategic arms agreement. The Soviet nuclear arsenal that threatens our very homeland is still intact and it is being modernized to the state of the art.

Second, we have no way of knowing what is in store for the Soviet Union. I am confident that even the Soviets don't know. It will take some years for them to sort out the mess that they have created over the past 70 years and to try to become an economic as well as a military superpower—to try to become a responsible, participating member of the world democratic community.

Third, the world has not ceased being a place where America's interests are sometimes threatened. We are not approaching Utopia. I have been involved in several crises using military force in the six months I have been chairman. They have provided me with stark evidence of how dangerous the world remains and how on-guard we must remain.

These three factors remind us of the importance of the strength that brought the Free World this victory in the first place. One of the keys to that strength is our alliance structure.

We are an Atlantic nation, so I believe we need to stay in Europe—in a strong NATO. Our allies want our armed forces to stay in Europe. We are not an occupying power like the Soviets; they are being asked to leave, we are being politely asked to stay. So long as that invitation stands, I believe we must stay to ensure the peace. Let no Soviet leader ever look back and not see us on guard.

Notwithstanding the momentous, riveting events in Europe and the Atlantic Community, we must never forget we are also a Pacific nation—we are in Pacific alliances as well.

In East Asia and the Pacific, more so than in Europe, our alliances were never based totally on a response to the Soviets. We have interests in the Pacific and East Asia that would remain even if the Soviets disappeared completely from the region. Not that I believe they will disappear; their Pacific fleet alone dissuades me from that belief.

So we need to stay in East Asia and in the Pacific. Nature and politics can't tolerate a vacuum. Were we to depart from the region, it would create one of the largest political vacuums in history—a vacuum we cannot afford to have.

As we remain involved in East Asia and the Pacific, we will adjust to the realities of a changing world. Strong regional security relationships will be crucial to our involvement, so let me briefly review our principal Pacific relationships.

Korea

The security relationship we have with the Republic of Korea has kept the peace on the Korean peninsula for 37 years. The teeth in that relationship are the U.S. and Korean forces standing shoulder to shoulder on the ground in Korea. So far North Korea has felt none of the tremors that have rocked dictatorships in Eastern Europe and elsewhere. South Korea meanwhile has become an economically prosperous democracy.

I believe we can adjust our forward military presence in Korea to accommodate the realities of a mature and economically prosperous South Korea. But we should not leave South Korea entirely or even disengage in a major way. To do so would be unwise. We did it once before to our regret.

What would not be unwise and what we would dearly love to see would be for Mr. Gorbachev to apply more pressure on the North Koreans to open up their closed society and to share in a meaningful and productive dialogue with the South. And to submit immediately to the international inspection regime for nuclear facilities and the possible presence of weapons-grade nuclear material. However monolithic and reactionary the North Korean regime has been all these years, the historic winds of change will eventually reach Pyongyang.

Australia

Down under, the U.S.-Australia bilateral relationship is alive, well, and kicking. And it is an important relationship, particularly in the Southwest Pacific and in the Indian Ocean. I believe Australia will always be a solid member of the Free World's alliance structure—as those brave people were throughout World War II. Only now they participate in a rigorous peace rather than a bloody world war.

The Philippines

Turning to the Philippines, you are aware that our security relationship there is undergoing some understandable tensions as we approach negotiations on the future of the U.S. military presence. Our principal objective in the Philippines is not the U.S. facilities, not the dollars involved, and not the contribution of those facilities to regional stability— though each of these things is important. Our principal objective is to support the Philippines as a democracy, a democracy firmly embedded in the Free World's

Continued on page 132

Continued from page 131

great system of nations.

We would like to keep our facilities in the Philippines. Our presence there contributes to stability in Southeast Asia and in the Southwestern Pacific and Indian Oceans. Other regional friends know this. That is why Singapore, for example, has offered publicly to help us stay in the area should we have to depart the Philippines.

These are decisions we cannot make alone. The Filipino people will tell us their decision and we will abide by that decision. But our fondest hope is that, irrespective of the outcome of the base negotiations, the Philippines remains a friend and an active participant in the regional alliance structure.

Japan

Our relations with Japan, one of our most important allies, are incredibly complex and multidimensional. The economic and security dimensions affect our interests most powerfully today. The interplay of these two dimensions frequently gives us cause for concern.

Let me give you a presidential statement of concern over our relationship with Japan:

"In common with other western powers," said the president of the United States, "our relations with Japan have been brought into serious jeopardy. . . . It is hoped, although not with entire confidence, that these difficulties may be peacefully overcome."

The president who spoke these words was not George Bush but Abraham Lincoln in 1863.

Lincoln's words fit perfectly our modern image of the economic problems a majority of Americans believes exist between our country and Japan. And the modern sound of the last of Lincoln's words—that we may lack complete confidence that we can solve our problems—fits our present situation too perfectly indeed.

And that perception of a lack of confidence in our ability to keep U.S.-Japan economic relations on an even keel, affects the other dimensions of our relationship with Japan, whether we want it to or not. Let me concentrate for a moment on why it's important we understand this interplay between the economic and security dimensions of our relations with Japan:

First, as a military man, I must tell you that Japan is absolutely critical to our ability to keep the peace in the Pacific. Keeping the peace in the Pacific without Japan would be a burden very few Americans would want to bear—and rightfully so.

Second, again as a military man, I will tell you that in terms of sharing the defense burden of keeping the peace in the Pacific, no finer ally than Japan exists today.

Japan has the third largest defense budget in the world, second only to the Soviet Union's and our own. That budget has been increasing at an average rate of 5 to 6 percent per year for the past 10 years. The Japanese pay 40 percent of the costs of keeping U.S. forces in Japan—2.5 billion dollars last year—a higher percentage than any of our other allies. The magnitude of Japanese burden-sharing is enormous—and the Japanese have indicated they are willing to do even more.

The Japanese are responsible for the air and land defense of Japan and for the security of sea lines of communications out to 1,000 nautical miles. They have embarked on an ambitious modernization program to expand their naval and air forces to meet these clearly defensive responsibilities.

In short, the U.S.-Japan security relationship is in good shape. In fact, as Secretary Cheney said in Tokyo last month, it "has never been better."

Our economic relations, on the other hand, need a great deal of work. Unfortunately, much of the trade squabble between the United States and Japan is a kabuki play, full of smoke and mirrors and a great deal of dancing in the dark. We need to clear the air of the smoke, remove the mirrors from the room, and deal with the real issues that divide us. The early March meeting in Palm Springs between President Bush and Prime Minister Kaifu, and the meeting between the president and former Prime Minister Takeshita in Washington two weeks ago, have energized the process of getting at the issues.

The United States and Japan are so economically intertwined that neither of us will be successful in the years ahead without the other. The people of both our great nations must come to understand this interdependence.

Just as the United States without California would be a much reduced country, America without her Japanese ally would find it difficult to continue being the leader the Free World depends on to keep alive the powerful global movement toward peace and prosperity.

We could do it without Japan. We could still be a superpower, but we would need to increase dramatically the cost to the American people and the investment they would have to make. And there is simply no necessity for us to expend so much of our national treasure in that manner if we can keep collective security alive and well. And in the Pacific, the key to that collective security is the U.S.-Japan relationship in all of its many dimensions.

We cannot permit any single dimension of our relations with Japan to compromise our friendship and our need for one another. We must solve our economic differences. It's as simple—and, as difficult—as that.

China

I would be remiss if in my quick sweep over the Pacific and East Asia I omitted the nation that holds almost a fourth of the world's population. Our national feelings about China have waxed and waned over the years between love and hate,

Continued on page 134

Continued from page 133

between understanding and incomprehension. There is perhaps no better example of the desire for freedom than that vivid image of the young man standing alone near Tiananmen Square against a column of tanks. We want to see such a desire for freedom fulfilled; yet we understand that it may require time and patience.

I believe we can best assist the people of China to join the ranks of free peoples everywhere by the pressure of our example, and by our willingness to stay involved in the Pacific and Asia. I believe our current policies toward China, including military-to-military relations, reflect the right balance of this pressure, concern, commitment, and understanding.

One of the fascinating aspects of today's world, and especially of the Pacific region, is that we have so many friends without any formal treaty mechanisms.

In the Pacific, we have friends like Thailand, Indonesia, Malaysia, the South Pacific island nations, Papua New Guinea, and a host of others. There's a reason for this. That reason has many dimensions, among them our values, our economic system, and our altruism. Also, there is the dimension of power—in our case, of superpower.

We are a superpower. At the moment, in many respects, we are the only superpower in each of the critical aspects of power. The Soviet Union retains only the aspect of military power.

Superpower status imposes responsibilities on us. Our outlook must be global and it must encompass the strong alliances that are critical to the future peace of the world. America must invigorate these alliances. America must lead the world into the 21st century if it is to be a century of peace.

If we are to stay a superpower, we must keep intact all the aspects of power—political, economic, technological and, yes, military. We can take advantage of the incredible change in the world and the commensurate reduction in the threat to our interests. We can reduce the size of our military forces and prudently adjust our forward presence around the globe. We can cut our defense budget over time. President Bush, Secretary Cheney, I, the Joint Chiefs of Staff—we must do it carefully over time. But there is a bottom line; there is a base force which this country needs beneath which we dare not go.

Such a base force must provide for our forward presence in the Atlantic Community. It must provide for our forward presence in the Pacific and East Asia, and in the Persian Gulf region when necessary. Moreover, it must provide a pool of contingency forces in the United States. And it must provide the needed mobilization and reinforcement capabilities to support our forward presence around the world, and to back up our contingency forces. We must have a navy second to none. And we must ensure that our strategic nuclear forces are strong enough to deter any nuclear threat to us.

We must find the balance between our superpower base force requirements and what the American people are willing to pay for. That is what the budget debate in Washington is all about. Secretary Cheney and I are determined to make sure that paying a peace dividend does not leave America weak and unable to lead.

Will Rogers spoke in 1932 on the anniversary of California's statehood. "Eighty-two years ago today," Rogers said, "California entered the Union—on a bet. The bet was that the country would eventually be called California and not America."

But we are America. We are America because our Union is greater than its individual states.

Today, we hear similar bets about the future world. We hear bets on a future world dominated by Japan. We hear bets on a future world dominated by a united Europe. And we hear bets on an American domination as well.

Well, I'll take those bets. Because I believe that as long as America leads the Free World, there will be no dominating state or region. The peace of the future will be a peace of all the democracies and of all the free peoples in the world. In fact, I believe that is the only way to make it a true peace—a peace that is enduring, that brings equal opportunities for economic prosperity to all, and that at the same time establishes safeguards for the liberty of all free people.

And the proper safeguards are the same safeguards that have secured the Free World's liberties for over four decades: our strong values, our resilient democracies, our vibrant market economies, our strong alliances, and, yes, our proud and ready armed forces.

All of these things constitute our great systemic strength. That strength sustains the Free World, just as in America it sustains our great Union—of which California is such an important part.

And that strength will continue to add people to the Free World's ranks. From Prague to Managua and from Budapest to Brasilia, few dark corners remain, and it's only a matter of time until these few bastions of dark tyranny are consigned to the ashheap of history.

Now the task is keeping democracy alive, not fighting and containing communism. Now the task is helping the dozens of democracies that are just being born. Now the task is teaching the basics of government of the people, by the people, and for the people—to the people. Now the task, in the words of the playwright-turned-president Vaclav Havel, is to continue "approaching democracy"—to do so with hundreds of thousands of new recruits.

No one is better fitted for these tasks than America and her allies. If we stay strong and lead, the world will follow. Of

Continued on page 136

Concluded from page 135

that, I am sure.

Thank you very much.

Questions

1. What is the purpose of Powell's speech?

2. What strategies to attract the audience and set a context for his speech can you detect in the introduction?

3. How does he use transitions to knit this speech together?

PART

3

Presentation
and Practice

Delivering the Speech

Learning Outcomes

After studying this chapter, you should be able to:

❶ Know the most effective ways to cope with anxiety.

❷ Rehearse a speech in at least three different ways.

❸ Explain the difference between the four basic types of speech delivery: extemporaneous, impromptu, manuscript, and memorized.

❹ Explain and know how to use the four channels available for speech delivery: verbal, visual, pictorial, and aural.

❺ Understand and know how to use the speech evaluation form to evaluate other student speeches.

INTRODUCTION

It is time to take the next step as you move closer to your goal of becoming an effective public speaker. The last three chapters focused on speech preparation, writing the speech, the use of visual aids, and the ways that language choices can improve your speech. Now you must learn how to take the speech that you have written privately and communicate it publicly to an audience. This is the most challenging step of all but, as with most worthwhile challenges, the rewards are the greatest.

Faculty who teach public speaking at colleges and universities around the world may disagree on many points about how best to teach public speaking. This is to be expected. However, there is almost unanimous agreement on one point. The more opportunities that individuals have to speak in front of groups, the greater the likelihood that their skill level will improve. Knowing this, you can help yourself by taking advantage of every opportunity you have to speak to groups. But first you must overcome the fears and anxieties that most people go through when they think about public speaking.

OVERCOMING SPEECH ANXIETY

There is an old expression—"there are only two things in life that are certain, death and taxes." Well, it wouldn't be too far-fetched to add a third item; it is almost certain that you will experience some degree of anxiety when you think of yourself standing alone in front of an audience.

Just the idea of having to stand up and speak before an audience can cause many different types of responses within you. Some of these are psychological; others are physiological. Someone suffering from an extreme attack of stage fright might sum up the physiological responses in the following way:

> What's wrong with me? I'm losing control. My heart is racing, my head is pounding, my face is on fire, my hands are cold and shaking, my knees are twitching, I can't stop sweating, my stomach is in a knot, my muscles are stiffening up on me, and I can't breathe. Please help me!

It is highly unlikely that your symptoms of speech anxiety will be so extreme, but you *can* expect some reactions with lesser degrees of intensity, depending on a variety of other variables. Recognize these symptoms for what they are: the result of stress buildup and self-induced fear. Remember that these feelings are natural. By practicing in front of your classmates, you can become desensitized to the problem. *You can learn how to cope and manage your fear of public speaking.*

What happens when an anxiety attack strikes you? In his best-selling book, *The Relaxation Response,* Dr. Herbert Benson, associate professor of medicine at Harvard Medical School and director of the Division of Behavioral Medicine at Boston's Beth Israel Hospital, tells us that people "react in a predictable way to acute and chronic stressful situations, which triggers an inborn response that has been part of our physiologic makeup for perhaps millions of years. This has been popularly labeled the 'fight-or-flight' response."[1] This response is a natural, instinctual reaction due to the buildup of stress and fear over a speaking assignment. Extra adrenalin is released at the same time that increases in your blood pressure, heart rate, rate of breathing, and blood flow to the muscles and metabolism take place. You are now ready to stand for a "fight" or prepared to run and take "flight." Obviously, your speaking assignment hardly warrants a fight or flight, but it is hard to tell your body not to respond that way. No wonder you feel uneasy about your speech requirements.

What can be done to control your nervous responses? Being prepared is the best remedy for speech anxiety. Dale Carnegie, the famous speech teacher, taught his students that preparation is the key. He believed that "only the prepared speaker deserves to be confident."[2] James Harvey Robinson states in his book, *The Mind in the Making,* "It is fear that holds us back. And fear is begotten of ignorance and uncertainty."[3] Fear is overcome by thorough preparation. By complete planning beforehand, you will have something to say and you will be prepared. The Boy Scouts' motto, "Be prepared," is on target for the speech maker.

Practice

Rehearsing the speech in front of caring and constructive critics will reduce your apprehension. A good listener can reinforce your good points and help you smooth the rough edges. Perhaps you can enlist the help of a roommate, friends, or a family member. Talk the speech through with someone else. The practice will increase your confidence and make you more familiar with the content. We will talk about practicing in more depth later.

Always recall that a certain amount of nervous energy is a good thing and that you are in good company. Many public figures have experienced stage fright but managed to use it productively. Communications expert Dorothy Sarnoff observes of the fight-or-flight syndrome that though the one type of nervousness will make you want to flee, the other type is "racehorse" energy and can be used to help your performance. Political figures have not been immune from stage fright either. Sir Winston Churchill and Presidents Reagan, Carter, Ford, Nixon, Johnson, Kennedy, Eisenhower, and Truman all showed signs of nervousness in their speeches. Even the famous orator Cicero said: "I turn pale at the outset of a speech and quake in every limb and in all my soul." However, none of these men let their apprehensions stop them from succeeding. They were *determined* to perform for their audiences.

Use Your Energy

Try to channel your extra nervous energy into the delivery of your speech. Use your energy enthusiastically and remember that you are stronger than your anxieties. It is reassuring to note that most of the things that you worry about never materialize. If you behave confidently, you just may begin to *feel* confident. The American psychologist, William James, put it well:

> Action seems to follow feeling, but really action and feeling go together; and by regulating the action, which is under the mere direct control of the will, we can indirectly regulate the feeling, which is not.
>
> Thus the sovereign voluntary path to cheerfulness, if our spontaneous cheerfulness be lost, is to sit up cheerfully and to act and speak as if cheerfulness were already there. If such conduct does not make you feel cheerful, nothing else on that occasion can.
>
> So, to feel brave, act as if we were brave, use all of our will to that end, and a courage-fit will very likely replace the fit of fear.[4]

Remember also that you probably feel worse than you look. Very few speakers actually look nervous and more than likely your audience is rooting for you. Most audiences are not hostile and generally respond in a friendly way toward speakers.

Your fellow students will have their turns speaking to the class, so they are likely to be compassionate because they will soon be in your shoes.

Be Positive

Next, take the advice given by Dr. Normal Vincent Peale in his best-selling book, *The Power of Positive Thinking.*[5] *Think positively.* Positive thinking and confident behavior will improve your speech performance. Today's Olympic athletes are counseled by sports psychologists to visualize themselves performing exactly as they would hope to perform; that is, they are told to meditate and see themselves being successful. You can do the same thing. See and hear yourself standing before an audience delivering the best speech of which you are capable. Talk to yourself, tell yourself you can do the job. It works. As you come to learn more about yourself as a human being, you learn that there is a direct relationship between your self-image and what you are able to do. In many ways, all of us are the products of our own minds.

Be Active

Finally, we know that physical exercise is an effective way to reduce the extra adrenalin which contributes to stress and anxiety attacks. Exercise acts as a release for nervous energy, helps "clear the head," and reestablishes your equilibrium. Students who exercise regularly usually deal better with stress than those who don't. Ideally, some kind of physical exercise shortly before you give a speech will lower the effects of anxiety. Any type of aerobic exercise will do (walking, jogging, swimming, biking) as long as it gets your heart and lungs working hard.

Table 8–1 gives you seven tips that will help you become a better speaker.

REHEARSING THE SPEECH

After you have written out the speech in its entirety, you need to reread it. At the same time as you are committing much of what you have written to memory, you are practicing or rehearsing. Don't worry about memorizing the speech word for word; just get down the essence of what you have written in the order that you wish to deliver it.

Rehearsal may be done in a number of different ways:

- Speak it aloud while alone in an office or automobile.
- Deliver the speech to a friend or family member who will not be too critical nor too complimentary.
- Use any machines you have (tape recorder or videotaping unit) and play it back alone and in the company of a few critics. If you can't find anyone to practice in front of, at least use a mirror and check your facial expression and posture to

Table 8–1
Overcome your speaking fears

Seven Tips to Become a Better Speaker

1. *Know your stuff.* If you know your material, then you're doing your audience a favor by speaking to them. You're saving them time and effort (and maybe even money). Don't forget that they need you. What you have to say is more valuable for them to hear than for you to say. Make a list of what you already know and what you need to learn. Then go outside of the topic area to see whether there's something especially interesting or a little different that you can bring to your speech.

2. *Tell the audience what you're going to talk about, talk about it, then tell them what you talked about.* This simple outline has been used successfully by thousands of speakers. Keep your presentation short. If you have a maximum of 10 minutes, try to use only 5.

3. *Use your memory and don't read your speech.* Get help from notes or index cards if you need it and read *only* small segments that are direct quotes or are difficult to remember. If you know your material, your presentation will be easier on the audience.

4. *Admit your stage fright.* Find a simple or humorous way to admit that you're uncomfortable or afraid to speak in public. Sometimes a small joke will do the trick. Drink a glass of water (without any ice) just as you begin to speak. Say something like: "I had the ice taken out of this water so you wouldn't hear it rattle as my hand shook." You might even shake the glass a little, but not enough to spill water. Or, deliberately shake a glass of water with ice to make it rattle, saying, "It's a good thing I'm not nervous this morning."

5. *Speak conversationally* and refer to the here-and-now, not just to the topic of your speech. Make a comment about the weather, a noise from the back of the room, the city you're in, the color of the carpet—anything to reduce the formality of your speech. Your tension and the audience's will be considerably lowered if you make a natural everyday observation.

6. *Breathe deeply and slow down.* Take deep breaths as you speak and stop yourself from speeding up. Directly ask your audience a question if you find yourself going too fast.

7. *Practice, practice, practice.* Practice your speech in front of friends, in front of the mirror, to your children and pets, to a tape recorder or video camera. Push yourself to give presentations (short ones at first) and work your way up to speeches before large audiences.

Source: Miskell, Vincent and Jane R. Miskell, *Overcoming Anxiety at Work,* Burr Ridge, IL: Richard D. Irwin, 1993, p. 83. Used with permission.

see if your speech is "together." Once everything is together, you are ready to deliver the speech. Remember, the greater the preparation, the lesser the speech anxiety.

FOUR TYPES OF DELIVERY

All speeches and the situations in which they are given are different. Before proceeding to discuss specific kinds of speeches, we need to study the four methods of delivery for speech makers.

Extemporaneous Speech

The extemporaneous speech is one that is planned and rehearsed, uses a brief speaking outline or notes, and yet possesses an air of spontaneity. It is the type of delivery that your teacher will require most of you to use in your classroom speaking assignments. It gives you freedom to make adjustments as you deliver your speech and at the same time you have your speaking outline or "road map" before you so you know what must be covered. The extemporaneous method can be used in all types of business settings. A major advantage is the flexibility it allows. You are not locked into a script, you are freer to look at your audience, you are able to make audience adaptations quickly, and you have the "safety" of your notes before you. If you are going to speak to groups in your career, the extemporaneous approach is highly recommended.

Impromptu Speech

Unlike the extemporaneous speech, the impromptu speech is not prepared. It is given "off the top of your head." The impromptu speech requires thinking on your feet and speaking well enough to make your audience take notice. This type of speech is given all the time. You may be asked to say a few words in a meeting without any preparation or forewarning. You could deliver this type of speech at a PTA gathering or at a town budget meeting. The impromptu speaker must quickly assess the situation and come across as reasonable and knowledgeable. Although you have very little time for preparation, you should try to use the few moments that you have to structure your thoughts for a fluid delivery. The impromptu speech is a difficult method of delivery and should not be your standard approach to speeches. Even Mark Twain said it took him "at least three weeks to prepare a good impromptu speech!" If you must speak impromptu, you should use those things that have been addressed before your speech to maintain continuity between your topic and the others. Try to relate to the people who have spoken before you and remember that you cannot speak well for long without preparation. Get to the point and offer the floor to another. If you are the first to speak or if you are wondering how to focus your speech quickly, address the "journalistic questions"— who? what? when? where? why? and how? If these points are clear, more than likely your audience will be able to comprehend your message. There is a tendency in impromptu speaking to be vague because of the lack of preparation and the short time to speak. A good impromptu speaker can be a valuable asset in an organization. However, it is not recommended that you depend on your ability to "ad lib" to deliver. Preparation is always preferred.

Manuscript Speech

This method of delivery is just as the name implies. You use a manuscript or written text and read the speech to your audience. This is the type of speech that many top executives deliver because they have speech writers prepare their talks. The writer will usually type in large print that is spread out across the page (five to nine words per line), and spaced out with three to four lines between each sentence. The manuscript speech is also used where a speaker's information will be recorded verbatim, such as Congressional proceedings or courtroom situations. The manuscript speech can be used effectively in highly emotional settings, such as funerals. The eulogy speech can be a very emotional experience and having the script with you is a good idea. Senator Edward M. Kennedy used a manuscript when delivering the eulogy of his brother Senator Robert F. Kennedy at St. Patrick's Cathedral. The president and many national and state officials will use a manuscript when they address the press. Sometimes they give the press corps copies before they deliver it publicly, so the press can prepare their reports, questions, and analyses. This method has been used in most of the recent presidential inaugural addresses.

Any businessperson can use this approach to speaking and even hire a speech writer if the firm's budget allows. However, there is a tendency to "read" the speech and not really "deliver" it. It is easy to avoid eye contact with the audience. If someone else has written the speech for you, it may sound artificial and may not be written in your "style." You also may be unfamiliar with the content, which could hinder your credibility if questions arise. Further, if you are locked into a script, there is little room for audience adaptation. Still, for the beginning speaker in a class such as yours, using the manuscript method for your first few efforts may help you overcome some of the initial problems of stage fright. Your instructor can help you decide which method to select for the first few assignments.

Memorized Speech

Many beginning speakers believe if they memorize their speeches, they will have no problems. There is nothing further from the truth. Usually you are setting yourself up to forget the speech. If you lose your train of thought, you may panic and not be able to continue. Unless you are a practiced speaker, such as an actor or actress, or perhaps a tour guide or someone who gives the same talk repeatedly to groups, the memorized speech is not recommended. The business speaker would do better to concentrate on the extemporaneous or manuscript method of delivery. If you have a choice, use the extemporaneous speech. It gives you the most freedom to speak.

Figure 8–1 is a typical critique sheet used in college classrooms to evaluate a speech *after* it has been given. Look at it before you give a speech so that you are reminded of the things you need to do. Ask yourself these questions as you review:

1. Introduction: Is an effective strategy used to "hook" the audience's interest? Is there a clear thesis? A clear sense of how the presentation will proceed?

2. Purpose: Do you clearly indicate why you are giving this speech and what you expect the audience to get out of it?

3. Choice of words: Is your level of language appropriate to the occasion—formal, informal, or somewhere in between depending on the circumstances? Is it appropriate to the audience's level of education? Not loaded with jargon?

4. Is your posture upright and confident? Are your hands used to express points in a way natural to you and not distracting for the audience?

5. Do you make eye contact with the audience—clearly focusing on all parts of the room at various points in presentation? Do you smile at your audience—especially when beginning or ending?

6. Can you be heard by everyone in the room? Is the rate neither too slow nor too fast? Do you vary pitch, tone, etc.?

7. Do you seem sincerely interested in imparting your message to the audience? This can be demonstrated in level of energy, enthusiasm, and amount of preparation the presentation demonstrates.

Figure 8–1
Speech evaluation

Speaker _____ Subject of talk _____

Date _____ Evaluated by _____

	Poor 1	Very Weak 1	Weak 3	Fair 4	Adequate 5	Good 6	Very Good 7	Excellent 8	Superior 9
1. Introduction									
2. Clarity of purpose									
3. Choice of words									
4. Bodily action-gesture-posture									
5. Eye contact and facial expression									
6. Vocal expression									
7. Desire to be understood									
8. Poise and self-control									
9. Adapting material to audience									
10. Organization of material									
11. Conclusion									

8. Does the presentation run smoothly with no unplanned breaks or pauses?

9. Is your topic chosen with the audience in mind? Do you use material interesting and of benefit to *them?*

10. Is the presentation logically and clearly structured? Do you use transitions to show the audience the relationships between ideas?

11. Do you leave the audience with a satisfying sense of closure—a clear sense of what you have been talking about and what you are asking them to do or to think about?

CONCLUSION

Remember that your reactions from stage fright only *seem* to be acute. You are not losing control but responding naturally to stress. Speech anxiety may be the biggest obstacle to speaking effectiveness, but you can overcome it through understanding and applying some of the techniques described in this chapter, through your instructor's insights, and through gradual exposure.

NOTES

1. Herbert Benson. *The Relaxation Response.* New York: Morrow, 1975, p. 5.

2. Dale Carnegie. *Public Speaking.* New York: Association Press, 1962.

3. James Harvey Robinson. *The Mind in the Making.* New York: Harper and Brothers, 1950, p. 100.

4. William James. *The Works of William James.* Cambridge, MA: Harvard University Press, Harvard Up, 1983, p. 34.

5. Norman Vincent Peale. *The Power of Positive Thinking.* New York: Fawcett Crest, 1956.

QUESTIONS FOR REVIEW AND DISCUSSION

1. What is the "fight-or-flight" response and how does it affect your feelings of speech anxiety?

2. What is the single best suggestion for nervous speech makers?

3. What are four other ways to overcome speech anxiety?

4. Describe how positive thinking can affect your speech performance.

5. What are three ways to rehearse a speech?

6. Define extemporaneous speaking. What are the advantages of this type of speech?

7. In what situations might you make an impromptu speech?

8. In what situations is the manuscript speech

required? What are the disadvantages of this type of speaking?

9. Why is the memorized speech only recommended in certain situations? What is the difference between it

and the extemporaneous speech?

10. What are the four channels available for speech delivery?

APPLICATION EXERCISES

1. Write a paragraph describing what scares you about public speaking. What is it you think might happen? After you have finished writing, let one person collect these paragraphs and read several out loud. Do the people in the class share similar fears? Discuss ways to alleviate them.

2. Think of the last time you had to speak in front of a group. Review the suggestions in this chapter on overcoming speech anxiety and rehearsing the speech. How many of these steps did you use at that time?

3. With your classmates, compose a list of topics suitable for impromptu speaking. Each student should choose one and spend five minutes preparing an impromptu speech.

Deliver the speeches in front of the class.

4. Choose five or six "winners" from the impromptu speeches. Send these students out of the room. As a class, develop one question to ask of these students. The question could be a typical interview question such as, "Can you describe both your greatest personal strength and your greatest weakness?" Have them reenter one by one and, in front of the class, answer the question. When all have answered, discuss what you have learned about impromptu speaking.

5. Discuss effective examples of each of the four types of delivery. At what occasions have you observed them?

FOR ADDITIONAL READING AND DISCUSSION

PUBLIC SPEAKING AND OTHER CORONARY THREATS
The Value of Self-Improvement

by Max D. Isaacson

Max D. Issacson, vice president, administration of Macmillan Oil delivered this speech to Speechcraft Students at Des Moines City Hall, Des Moines, Iowa, February 1, 1980. Like you, his audience was learning the art of public speaking. His words and those of the well-known figures he quotes should alleviate some of your nervousness and remind you of the value of public speaking.

In my job and at other functions, I'm quite often called on to speak and my wife says that I get up so often that I'm living proof of the old adage that hot air always rises. But I have something a little more substantial than hot air to talk about today.

I'm glad you are here because that tells me you've had the dedication and the interest in this important Speechcraft course. I can tell you from personal experience that the ability to express oneself well in public is certainly valuable in my business and in every walk of life that I know of.

In addition to my interest in public speaking, I'm happy to be here for another reason. Since I'm on the staff of an oil company, I'm happy to be invited anywhere where there is a cordial reception . . . that's a pleasant accomplishment.

Speaking of accomplishments, your chairman asked me to speak on "Accomplishments Through Speechcraft." A more appropriate title might be *"Public Speaking and Other Coronary Threats!"* because in public speaking, many are called but few want to get up. You know and I know that it can be scary indeed to get up to address a group. But listen to these statements.

Daniel Webster said:

If all my possessions were taken from me with one exception, I would choose to keep the power of speech, for by it I would soon regain all the rest (of my possessions).

Sigmund Freud observed:

Words call forth emotions and are universally the means by which we influence our fellow creatures . . . by words, one of us can give to

Published in *Vital Speeches of the Day.* Reprinted with permission

Continued on page 152

Concluded from page 151

another the greatest happiness or bring about utter despair.

The eminent Dale Carnegie said:

Every activity of our lives is communication of a sort, but it is through speech that man asserts his distinctiveness . . . that he best expresses his own individuality, his essence.

Someone else has observed, and I certainly agree, that "self-confidence has always been the first secret of success." Of the known phobias—and there is a long list of them—the fear of public speaking consistently ranks at the top in public surveys. It's even more feared than death. But why should intelligent people fear public speaking?

Most of us have at least average intelligence and when we look around us—at co-workers, bosses, politicians—we know that our level of knowledge is as great or greater than theirs, but the thing that so often separates us is our inability to feel confident when expressing ourselves . . . we fear to speak up.

It's true that we make ourselves vulnerable when we speak up . . . vulnerable to criticism. It's usually easier and more comfortable to stay out of the spotlight and to languish in the comfort of the nonspeaker's role, to avoid the risk of feeling inferior.

But I've always been fond of quoting Eleanor Roosevelt on the subject of self-confidence. She said: "No one can make you feel inferior without your consent."

Think about that for a moment. "No one can make you feel inferior without your consent." Isn't that a remarkable statement?

And here are some remarkable figures to prove that man is his own worst enemy. *More persons kill themselves each year than murder others.* There are 25,000 suicides annually in the United States and 18,000 homicides. Suicide is the severest form of self-hatred. But a milder form of self-hatred is the inferiority complex many of us secretly harbor.

One of my kids recently told me a riddle. He said, "Dad, do you know what the largest room in the world is?" I replied that I did not. He answered, *"The room for improvement!"* That's why I believe in Speechcraft, because it's a valuable means for improvement. It offers what most of us need to become better public speakers.

Isn't it incredible that there is so little emphasis throughout our educational and business training on this needed skill of oral communication? I've found that in high school, college, military service, graduate school, and business, any emphasis on oral communication *has been conspicuous by its absence.* And yet, you and I communicate orally more than in any other way when dealing with people.

Some time ago, I attended a conference whose main speaker was a nationally known management expert. He said that we are not in the oil business, the insurance business, the government service business, the manufacturing business . . .

rather *we are in the people business!* It behooves us to do whatever we can to improve our communications among people in all walks of life in order to improve human relations.

Where will you go from here? What will you do with the valuable experience you've gained at these Speechcraft sessions? Unfortunately, most persons stop their training after the formal Speechcraft course has ended. They apparently are satisfied with their progress or don't want to make the effort to continue. But can you imagine a pianist stopping after 10 lessons and saying, "I've arrived—and I'm now accomplished!"? Public speaking takes ongoing practice, so I would encourage you to stick with it through regular Toastmaster training.

I'm convinced you'll do better on the job, in your community organizations, and in your house of worship. One of my biggest thrills was that of becoming a certified lay speaker in the United Methodist Church—just one of the many ways that experience in public speaking can be applied for personal fulfillment and self-realization.

Let me close with a thought that I've shared with graduating high school seniors and other groups concerning the value of self-improvement. It goes like this:

God said, "Build a better world,"
And I said, "How?"
The world is such a cold, dark place and so complicated now
And I so young and useless, there's nothing I can do,
But God in all his wisdom said, "Just build a better you."

Questions

1. How and why does Isaacson use the words of famous figures to emphasize the value of public speaking?

2. How do *you* interpret the words of Eleanor Roosevelt: "No one can make you feel inferior without your consent"?

3. Do you agree with Isaacson that although our society places great value on communication skills, we rarely experience training in oral communication in either education or business?

Four
Speeches for
Special
Occasions

Learning Outcomes

After studying this chapter, you should be able to:

❶ Deliver a speech of introduction.

❷ Deliver a speech of presentation.

❸ Deliver a speech of acceptance.

❹ Deliver a speech of announcement.

INTRODUCTION

We live in a society in which ceremony and ritual have become a daily part of our behavioral patterns. These occasions often require individuals to deliver speeches appropriate to the ceremony or ritual. These special occasion speeches differ from each other. However, they share something in common in that each situation has certain *expectations* that the speaker must meet. If you learn what is expected, establish a formulaic approach to fulfill the expectations, and apply the principles of public speaking you have already acquired, you will be prepared for any occasion. This last point needs to be stressed because often you will not be given much time to prepare your remarks.

Certain general principles apply to all special occasion speeches. You need to be consistent with the appropriate tone or mood the situation calls for, you should be brief (one to three minutes) without rushing, and you should remember that your role is subordinate to the ceremony's primary purpose, whatever it may be.

INTRODUCING A SPEAKER

When you are called on to introduce another speaker, the expectations for this kind of speech are clear. You are expected to provide information about the speaker and his or her topic and, in so doing, establish a friendly and warm atmosphere in which the speaker and audience can relate to each other. To do this, follow this formula. Ideally, you will use only the briefest of notes.

- Welcome audience and refer to the purpose of the occasion.

- Provide the name and background of the speaker. Be sure to pronounce the speaker's name correctly. It helps to do your homework researching the speaker's position, education, experience, and accomplishments. Be selective and include only significant data. (If you have advance notice and no other way of obtaining information, you may ask the speaker to send you a short, biographical sketch.) Do not overdo the buildup.

- Explain why the subject of the talk is meaningful to the audience and what they stand to gain from listening.

- Conclude by repeating the name of the speaker and the topic.

Model Introduction Speech

Good morning, ladies and gentlemen of the faculty. Welcome back to our annual faculty orientation day at Hastings College. I hope you are all rested and eager to go back to work teaching our students who will be returning to campus this Wednesday.

To start the new academic year off on the right track, we have invited Dr. Martha Munroe to speak to you this morning. Dr. Munroe comes to us with a distinguished academic and professional background. She received a bachelor's degree in communications from Northwestern University and a PhD from Stanford University. For the past eight years, she has been a communications consultant to businesses and government agencies. She has also found time to author four books, one of which, *Take Time to Talk,* is presently on the list of the top 10 best-selling, nonfiction books.

Dr. Munroe's topic, "Communication Channels in Classrooms," could not be more suitable. It is our hope that her remarks will act as a catalyst so that we can greet our students on Wednesday with fresh and enthusiastic approaches.

Ladies and gentlemen, I present to you Dr. Martha Munroe speaking on "Communication Channels in Classrooms."

Use the outline below as needed to write your own speech of introduction. Both the suggestions and the model speech above should serve as guidelines.

EXERCISE

1

Follow your instructor's directions for using this outline.

Outline of Speech

Name: _____

Title of speech: _____

Purpose of speech: _____

Thesis: _____

Type of audience: _____

Time of speech: _____

I. Introduction

   A. _____

    1. _____

    2. _____

  B. _____

    1. _____

    2. _____

  C. _____

    1. _____

    2. _____

II. Body of Speech

  A. _____

    1. _____

    2. _____

  B. _____

    1. _____

    2. _____

  C. _____

    1. _____

    2. _____

  D. _____

    1. _____

    2. _____

III. Conclusion

  A. _____

    1. _____

    2. _____

B. _____

   1. _____

   2. _____

C. _____

   1. _____

   2. _____

D. _____

   1. _____

   2. _____

SPEECHES OF PRESENTATION

From our earliest years, we have participated in ceremonies where achievements are recognized by the presentation of awards. The award may vary from Little League trophies to scholarships for academic excellence, but the ritual remains the same. Similar ceremonies are held by corporations. Awards are presented to outstanding salespeople, managers, and those who make special contributions to their community. Many companies present gifts to retiring employees in gratitude for years of loyal service. Because these situations occur so frequently in our culture, the expectations for the speech of presentation have become commonly accepted.

Formula

- Explain the background, significance, and criteria for the award.
- Point out what the recipient(s) has done to merit the award.
- Ask the recipient to come up physically to the podium to accept the award.
- Present the award with your left hand so that your right hand is free for a congratulatory handshake.

Model Speech of Presentation

The Garnett Award is given each year to a student who best balances academic achievement with meaningful extracurricular involvement. The award consists of a $500 check and a plaque commemorating the achievement. This is the 20th year that the Garnett Award has been given since it was begun by a distinguished alumnus, Mr. Orville Garnett, founder and president of Garnett Industries.

This year's recipient is Harold Brown, who comes to us from New Orleans, Louisiana. As a junior majoring in marketing, Harold has maintained a 3.8 cumulative average since his freshman year. Also, he has lettered in varsity basketball and tennis, served on the yearbook staff as a copy editor, been president of the Marketing Club, and served as treasurer of the local DECA chapter. If that isn't enough, Harold is also a volunteer in the campus Outreach program which sponsors visits and work sessions to the Whitestone Center. Here, Harold and other volunteers work with handicapped children.

Would Harold Brown please come forward to receive the Garnett Award, which he so clearly deserves.

EXERCISE

2

Follow your instructor's directions for using this outline.

Outline of Speech

Name: _____

Title of speech: _____

Purpose of speech: _____

Thesis: _____

Type of audience: _____

Time of speech: _____

I. Introduction

    A. _____

        1. _____

        2. _____

B. _____

    1. _____

    2. _____

C. _____

    1. _____

    2. _____

II. Body of Speech

A. _____

    1. _____

    2. _____

B. _____

    1. _____

    2. _____

C. _____

    1. _____

    2. _____

D. _____

    1. _____

    2. _____

III. Conclusion

A. _____

    1. _____

    2. _____

B. _____

    1. _____

EXERCISE 2

(concluded)

2. _____

C. _____

   1. _____

   2. _____

D. _____

   1. _____

   2. _____

SPEECH OF ACCEPTANCE

If you are fortunate enough to receive an award, you had better be prepared to make an acceptance speech because you will often be asked to do just that. There is no graceful way to refuse and to do so would certainly spoil the moment. It is better to do what is expected of you in a sincere and appreciative way.

Formula

- Thank both those who are giving you an award and those responsible for creating the award.
- Express your appreciation to the people who were instrumental in helping you win the award.
- Close by repeating your thanks. This speech is usually brief.

Model Speech of Acceptance

I wish to thank the faculty members who selected me to be the recipient of the Garnett Award. Also, I am grateful to Mr. Garnett and his company for their generosity.

Winning the award is of course a thrill. I am aware that I owe a debt of gratitude to the teachers, coaches, and to my fellow students whom I have enjoyed learning from and being with during the past three years.

Again, thank you very much.

Follow your instructor's directions for using this outline.

Outline of Speech

Name: _____

Title of speech: _____

Purpose of speech: _____

Thesis: _____

Type of audience: _____

Time of speech: _____

I. Introduction

    A. _____

        1. _____

        2. _____

    B. _____

        1. _____

        2. _____

    C. _____

        1. _____

        2. _____

II. Body of Speech

    A. _____

        1. _____

        2. _____

    B. _____

        1. _____

        2. _____

EXERCISE 3

(concluded)

C. _____

    1. _____

    2. _____

D. _____

    1. _____

    2. _____

III. Conclusion

A. _____

    1. _____

    2. _____

B. _____

    1. _____

    2. _____

C. _____

    1. _____

    2. _____

D. _____

    1. _____

    2. _____

ANNOUNCEMENTS

Many times the announcement of an important event, company policy, or occurrence is relegated to an inexperienced speaker or placed at the end of a program when people are not likely to listen. It is unfortunate that announcements are treated as afterthoughts. If you have an important announcement to make, have it prepared, make copies of it to be distributed immediately afterward or that same day through interoffice mail, and do not make the announcement at the end of a program or meeting. You should make all important announcements at the beginning.

Keep the announcement brief and get to the point(s) quickly. The journalistic questions of the public relations practitioner should be your guiding principles when you deliver the message. They are *who? what? when? where? why?* and sometimes *how?* Your audience should not be left questioning what is happening or what they should be doing with your information.

Formula

- Get the attention of the audience and quickly preview the purpose of the announcement.

- Make the announcement, providing all necessary facts (dates, times, places, amounts, etc.).

- If possible, ask for and respond to any questions from the audience.

- Repeat details and close on a motivational note.

Model Speech of Announcement

Every year at this time, all the employees of the Brown Company have an opportunity to assist our fellow human beings by contributing to the United Way. For the past three years, we have had the highest percentage of people who contribute through payroll deductions of any firm in the city. We would like to continue this record.

Here is all you have to do. Return the contribution card that will be in the mail this week to Pat Bourne in the Payroll Office by November first. Indicate the amount you want deducted. It is that simple. Remember, besides helping others in the community, you will be entered in the annual Bermuda drawing, which provides an all-expenses-paid week for two on Bermuda.

Are there any questions?

Fine, get the United Way card back to Pat Bourne in Payroll by November first. Your donation is tax deductible and you are helping a worthwhile cause.

Thank you.

EXERCISE

4

Follow your instructor's directions for using this outline.

Outline of Speech

Name: _____

Title of speech: _____

Purpose of speech: _____

Thesis: _____

Type of audience: _____

Time of speech: _____

I. Introduction

    A. _____

        1. _____

        2. _____

    B. _____

        1. _____

        2. _____

    C. _____

        1. _____

        2. _____

II. Body of Speech

    A. _____

        1. _____

        2. _____

    B. _____

        1. _____

        2. _____

C. _____

   1. _____

   2. _____

D. _____

   1. _____

   2. _____

III. Conclusion

A. _____

   1. _____

   2. _____

B. _____

   1. _____

   2. _____

C. _____

   1. _____

   2. _____

D. _____

   1. _____

   2. _____

CONCLUSION

The formulaic nature of ceremonial speaking makes it similar to social manners. Although it may seem daunting at first, the very fact that it *is* formulaic makes it easy to grasp and to practice. Once you learn what is expected of you, you can enter situations that require this type of speaking with confidence.

QUESTIONS FOR REVIEW AND DISCUSSION

1. Why are ceremony and ritual important in our society?

2. What general principles apply to all special occasion speeches?

3. Do ceremonial speeches generally call for a great deal of preparation?

4. What are the four steps of a speech of introduction?

5. What are some examples of the type of occasion in which you might give a speech of presentation?

6. What four steps should a speech of presentation include?

7. What three steps will a speech of acceptance include?

8. If you are conducting a meeting, at what point in the meeting should important announcements be made?

9. What journalistic questions should be your guiding principles when delivering the message?

10. What are the four steps in the formula of a speech of announcement?

APPLICATION EXERCISES

1. Working with a partner in the class, devise a ceremonial occasion at which one of you will present an award and the other will accept. Write your speeches, practice together, and perform for the class.

2. Watch an award show either on television or in your community and critique both presenters and accepters.

3. From the many written announcements commonly posted on college campuses, select one and change it into a speech of announcement. Write it and then announce to the class.

4. Introduce one of your classmates as if he or she were about to speak to the class on a subject about which the classmate is knowledgeable.

FOR ADDITIONAL READING AND DISCUSSION

The following speeches provide both additional examples of the types of speeches discussed in this chapter and of other types of ceremonial speaking.

IN SEARCH OF PEACE
This Honor Belongs to All the Survivors

by Elie Wiesel

Elie Wiesel delivered this speech at the University of Oslo in Oslo, Norway, on December 10, 1986, when he accepted the Nobel Peace Prize. Wiesel, who survived the Nazi death camps, was honored for his constant efforts to ensure that the world never forgets—and never repeats—the horrors of the Holocaust. As with any great ceremonial speech, Wiesel makes this a moment of not only personal, but universal, relevance.

It is with a profound sense of humility that I accept the honor you have chosen to bestow upon me. I know: Your choice transcends me. This both frightens and pleases me.

It frightens me because I wonder: Do I have the right to represent the multitudes who have perished? Do I have the right to accept this great honor on their behalf? I do not. That would be presumptuous. No one may speak for the dead; no one may interpret their mutilated dreams and visions.

It pleases me because I may say that this honor belongs to all the survivors and their children, and through us, to the Jewish people with whose destiny I have always identified.

I remember: It happened yesterday or eternities ago. A young Jewish boy discovered the kingdom of night. I remember his bewilderment, I remember his anguish. It all happened so fast. The ghetto. The deportation. The sealed cattle car. The fiery altar upon which the history of our people and the future of mankind were meant to be sacrificed.

I remember: He asked his father: "Can this be true? This is the 20th century, not the Middle Ages. Who would allow such crimes to be committed? How could the world remain silent?"

And now the boy is turning to me: "Tell me," he asks. "What have you done with my future? What have you done with your life?"

And I tell him that I have tried. That I have tried to keep memory alive, that I have tried to fight those who would forget. Because if we forget, we are guilty, we are accomplices.

And then I explained to him how naive we were, that the world did know and remain silent. And that is why I swore never to be silent whenever and wherever human beings endure suffering and humiliation. We must always take sides. Neutrality helps the oppressor, never the victim. Silence encourages the tormentor, never the tormented.

Sometimes we must interfere. When human lives are endangered, when human dignity is in jeopardy, national borders and sensitivities become irrelevant. Wherever men or women are persecuted because of their race, religion or political views, that place must—at that moment—become the center of the universe.

Of course, since I am a Jew profoundly rooted in my people's memory and tradition, my first response is to Jewish fear, Jewish needs, Jewish crises. For I belong to a traumatized generation, one that experienced the abandonment and solitude of our people. It would be unnatural for me not to make Jewish priorities my own: Israel, Soviet Jewry, Jews in Arab lands.

But there are others as important to me. Apartheid is, in my view, as abhorrent as anti-Semitism. To me, Andrei Sakharov's isolation is as much of a disgrace as Iosif Begun's imprisonment. As is the denial of Solidarity and its leader Lech Walesa's right to dissent. And Nelson Mandela's interminable imprisonment.

There is so much injustice and suffering crying out for our attention: Victims of hunger, or racism and political persecution, writers and poets, prisoners in so many lands governed by the left and by the right. Human rights are being violated on every continent. More people are oppressed than free.

And then, too, there are the Palestinians to whose plight I am sensitive but whose methods I deplore. Violence and terrorism are not the answer. Something must be done about their suffering, and soon. I trust Israel, for I have faith in the Jewish people. Let Israel be given a chance, let hatred and danger be removed from her horizons, and there will be peace in and around the Holy Land.

Yes, I have faith. Faith in God and even in His creation. Without it no action would be possible. And action is the only remedy to indifference: the most insidious danger of all. Isn't this the meaning of Alfred Nobel's legacy? Wasn't his fear of war a shield against war?

There is much to be done, there is much that can be done. One person—a Raoul Wallenberg, an Albert Schweitzer, one person of integrity—can make a difference, a difference of life and death. As long as one dissident is in prison, our freedom will not be true. As long as one child is hungry, our lives will be filled with anguish and shame.

What all these victims need above all is to know that they are not alone; that we

Continued on page 172

Concluded from page 171

are not forgetting them, that when their voices are stifled we shall lend them ours, that while their freedom depends on ours, the quality of our freedom depends on theirs.

This is what I say to the young Jewish boy wondering what I have done with his years. It is in his name that I speak to you and that I express to you my deepest gratitude. No one is as capable of gratitude as one who has emerged from the kingdom of night.

We know that every moment is a moment of grace, every hour an offering; not to share them would mean to betray them. Our lives no longer belong to us alone; they belong to all those who need us desperately.

Thank you Chairman Aarvik. Thank you, members of the Nobel Committee. Thank you, people of Norway, for declaring on this singular occasion that our survival has meaning for mankind.

Questions

1. In whose name does Wiesel accept this award?

2. Why does he feel both the award and the occasion have such tremendous significance for the past, the present *and* the future?

THE LESSONS OF LIFE

by Marian Wright Edelman

Marian Wright Edelman delivered this commencement address at the Yale University Class Day exercises in New Haven, Connecticut, on May 27, 1990. Notice how Edelman uses her speech not only to mark the occasion but to inspire her audience as well.

It is a great honor to share this day of accomplishment, celebration, and transition with the graduates of 1990 and your families. I am pleased that more than 80 of you applied to and 40 of you are going to participate in Teach for America, which sends graduates to serve in teacher-shortage areas. I hope many more of you will wander off the beaten career path and help redefine what success is in the America of the 1990s.

When I was growing up, service was as essential a part of my upbringing as eating and sleeping and going to school. Caring black adults were buffers against the segregated prison of the outside world that told black children we weren't important. But we didn't believe it because our parents said it wasn't so. Our teachers said it wasn't so. And our preachers said it wasn't so. The childhood message I internalized was that as God's child, no man or woman could look down on me and I could look down on no man or woman.

We couldn't play in segregated public playgrounds or sit at drugstore lunch counters so my daddy, a Baptist minister, built a playground and canteen behind the church. Whenever he saw a need, he tried to respond. There were no black homes for the aged, so my parents began one across the street and our whole family helped out. I didn't like it a lot at the time, but that's how I learned it was my responsibility to take care of elderly family members and neighbors and that everyone was my neighbor.

I went everywhere with my parents, and members of the congregation and community were my watchful extended parents. They reported on me when I did wrong and applauded when I did well. Doing well meant being considerate toward others, achieving in school, and reading. The only time my daddy wouldn't give me a chore was when I was reading. So I read a lot!

Children were taught that nothing was too lowly to do and that the work of our

Source: The H. W. Wilson Company. Reprinted with permission.

Continued on page 174

Continued from page 173

heads and hands were both valuable. As a young child, I was sent with an older brother to help clean the bed and bed sores of a poor, sick woman and learned just how much even the smallest helping hands can mean to a lonely person in need.

Black adults in our families, churches, and community made children feel valued and important. They spent time with us and struggled to keep us busy. And while life was often hard and resources scarce, we always knew who we were and that the measure of our worth was inside our heads and hearts and not outside in material possessions or personal ambition. Like Walker Percy, my elders knew instinctively that you could get all A's and still flunk life.

I was taught that the world had a lot of problems; that Black people had an extra lot of problems, but that I should face up to and was obligated to struggle and change them; that extra intellectual and material gifts brought with them the privilege and responsibility of sharing with others less fortunate; and that service is the rent each of us pays for living, the very purpose of life and not something you do in your spare time or after you have reached your personal goals.

I'm grateful for these childhood legacies: a living faith reflected in daily service, the discipline of hard work and stick-to-itiveness, and a capacity to struggle in the face of adversity. Giving up was not part of my elders' lexicon: You got up every morning and did what you had to do and you got up every time you fell down and tried as many times as you had to until you got it done right. They had grit. They valued family life and family rituals, and tried to be and expose us to good role models. And role models were those who achieved in the outside world, like my namesake Marian Anderson, and those who lacked formal education or money but who taught us by the special grace of their lives Christ's and Gandhi's and Heschel's message that the kingdom of God is within. And every day I still try to be half as good as those ordinary people of grace who were kind and patient with children and who shared whatever they had with others.

I was 14 years old the night my daddy died. He had holes in his shoes but two children out of college, one in college, another in divinity school, and a vision he was able to convey to me dying in an ambulance that I, a young black girl, could be and do anything, that race and gender are shadows, and that character, self-discipline, determination, attitude, and service are the substance of life.

I want to convey that same vision to you today as you graduate into an ethically polluted nation where instant sex without responsibility, instant gratification without effort, instant solutions without sacrifice, getting rather than giving, and hoarding rather than sharing are the too-frequent signals of our mass media, popular culture, and political life.

The standard for success for too many Americans has become personal greed rather than common good. The standard for striving and achievement has become getting by rather than making an extra effort or service to others. Truth telling and moral example have become devalued commodities. Nowhere is the paralysis of public or private conscience more evident than in the neglect and abandonment of millions of children of all races and classes whose futures we adults hold in trust. Their futures will shape the ability of our nation to compete morally and economically as much as yours as children of privilege.

Yet:

Every 8 seconds of the school day, an American child drops out (500,000 a year).

Every 26 seconds of the day, an American child runs away from home (1.2 million a year).

Every 47 seconds, an American child is abused or neglected (675,000 a year).

Every 67 seconds, an American teenager has a baby (472,000 a year).

Every 7 minutes, an American child is arrested for a drug offense.

Every 30 minutes an American child is arrested for drunken driving.

Every 53 minutes an American child dies from poverty in the wealthiest nation on earth (9,855 a year).

The 1990s will be an era of struggle for the American conscience and future. The battles will not be as dramatic as Gettysburg or Vietnam, but they will shape our place in the 21st-century world. The bombs poised to blow up the American dream and shred America's social fabric emanate from no enemies without. They are ticking away within ourselves, our families, our neighborhoods, and cities, and in our loss of national purpose and direction.

We have lost our sense of what is important as a people. And too many young people—white, black, brown, rich, and poor—are growing up unable to handle life in hard places, without hope and without steady compasses to navigate the morally polluted seas they must face in adulthood.

Since I believe it is the responsibility of every adult—parent, teacher, preacher, and professional—to make sure that children and young people hear what we have learned from the lessons of life, hear what we think matters, hear over and over that we love you, that you are never alone, and that you should never believe that life is not worth living or cheap, your own or anybody else's, at home or abroad, I want to share a few lessons with you today to take along as you leave Yale. You can take them or leave them, but you can't say you were never told. Too many of us who are parents have been so busy today making sure our children had all the things we didn't that we may not have shared the things we did have that

Continued on page 176

Continued from page 175
enabled us to survive and succeed.

At Yale, you got your lessons from your teachers first and then got examined on how well you learned them. In life the test and consequences come before the lessons. And in an era of AIDS and potentially lethal drugs, the consequences can be fatal.

Lesson One

Don't feel entitled to anything you don't sweat and struggle for. And help our nation understand that it is not entitled to world leadership based on the past or on what we say rather than how well we perform and meet changing world needs. For those black and other racial minority graduates among you, I want you to remember that you can never take anything for granted in America, even with a Yale degree and even if too many whites still feel "entitled" solely by the accident of birth. And you had better not start now as racial intolerance resurges all over our land. It may be wrapped up in new euphemisms and better etiquette, but as Frederick Douglass warned us earlier, it's the same old snake.

Douglass also reminded all of us that "men may not get all they pay for in this world, but they must certainly pay for all they get."

So I hope you will struggle to achieve. Don't think for a moment that you've got it made with your Yale degree and are entitled to move up the career ladder. It may get you in the door, but it won't get you to the top or keep you there. You've got to work your way up, hard and continuously. Don't be lazy. Do your homework. Pay attention to detail. Take care and pride in your work. Few of us are gifted enough to get by on first drafts. People who are sloppy in little things tend to be sloppy in big things. Be reliable. Take the initiative in creating your own opportunity and don't wait around for other people to discover you or do you a favor. Don't assume a door is closed; push on it. Don't assume if it was closed yesterday, it's closed today. And don't any of you ever stop learning and improving your mind and spirit. If you do, you and America are going to be left behind.

You have come of age in a political era when too many political leaders and voters are looking for a free lunch. As a people, we seem unable or unwilling to juggle difficult competing demands or to make hard choices and sacrifices to rebuild family and community for the good of the nation. Many whites favor racial justice as long as things remain the same. Many voters hate Congress, but love their own Congressman as long as he or she takes care of their special interests. Many husbands are happier to share their wives added income than the housework and child care. Many Americans decry the growing gap between the rich and the poor and middle class and escalating child suffering as long as somebody else's taxes are raised and somebody else's program is cut. We have got to grow beyond our national adolescence!

Lesson Two

Set goals and work quietly and systematically toward them. Too many of us talk big and act small. So often we get bogged down in our ego needs and lose sight of broader community and national goals. It's alright to want to feel important as long as it is not at the expense of *doing* important deeds, even if we don't get the credit. You can get a lot achieved in life if you don't mind doing the work and letting other people get the credit. You know what you do and the Lord knows what you do and that's all that matters.

Lesson Three

Assign yourself. My daddy used to ask us whether the teacher gave us any homework. If we said no, he'd say "well assign yourself." Don't wait around for your boss or your friend or your spouse to direct you to do what you are able to figure out and do for yourself. Don't do just as little as you can to get by as so many Americans are doing today in our political and economic life. If you see a need, don't ask why doesn't somebody do something, ask why don't I do something. Don't wait around to be told what to do. There is nothing more wearing than people who have to be asked or reminded repeatedly to do things. Hard work, initiative, and persistence are still the non-

magic carpets to success for most of us. Help teach the rest of the country how to achieve again by your example.

Lesson Four

Use your political and economic power for the community. Vote and hold those you vote for accountable. Less than half the young people under 25 registered and only 36 percent voted in the 1988 election. Run for political office and enter government service. And don't think that you or your reelection or job are the only point once you do: Strengthening families and communities and protecting American ideals are the point of gaining power. Don't confuse social and political charm with decency or sound policy. It's wonderful to go to the White House or Congress for a chat or a meal, but words and sociability alone will not meet children's or the nation's needs. Political leadership and different budget priorities will. Speak truth to power. And put your own money and leadership behind rhetoric about concern for families and children in your own homes, in your own law firms, and corporations and in whatever areas you decide to pursue.

Lesson Five

Never work just for money. Money alone won't save your soul or build a decent family or help you sleep at night. We are

Continued on page 178

177

Continued from page 177

the richest nation on earth with one of the highest incarceration, drug addiction, and child poverty rates in the world. Don't confuse wealth or fame with character. And don't tolerate or condone moral corruption whether it's found in high places or low places or is white, brown, or black. It is not OK to push or use drugs even if every person in America is doing it. It is not OK to cheat or lie if every Millken, Boesky, North, Secord, or public official does. Be honest. And demand that those who represent you be honest. Don't confuse morality with legality. Dr. King noted that everything Hitler did in Nazi Germany was legal. Don't give anyone the proxy for your conscience. And don't spend every dollar you earn. Save a dime and share a dime.

Lesson Six

Don't be afraid of taking risks or of being criticized. If you don't want to be criticized then don't say anything, do anything, or be anything. Don't be afraid of failing. It's the way you learn to do things right. It doesn't matter how many times you fall down. All that matters is how many times you keep getting up. "It's not failure," former Morehouse College president Dr. Benjamin Mays said, it's "a sin," it's "low aim." And don't wait for everybody to come along to get something done. It's always a few people who get things done and keep things going. This country needs more shepherds and fewer sheep.

Lesson Seven

Take parenting and family life seriously. And insist that those you work for and who represent you do so. As a nation, we mouth family values we do not practice. Seventy nations provide medical care and financial assistance to all pregnant women; we are not one of them. Seventeen industrialized nations have paid maternity/paternity leave programs: we are not one of them and our Yalie President of the United States is threatening to veto an unpaid parental leave bill. Today, over half of mothers of infants are in the labor force and 62 percent of the net growth in the 1990s labor force will be women. We still don't have a safe, affordable, quality child care system. And the men in Congress are still bickering rather than completing action on child care bills passed by both Houses, and the White House, despite President Bush's frequent photo opportunities and promises at child care centers during the 1988 presidential campaign, threatens still another veto.

It is time for the mothers of this nation to tell the men of this nation to get with it and stop the political hypocrisy so that parents can have a real choice about whether to remain at home or choose to work outside the home without worrying about the well-being of their children.

What a dilemma parents, especially women, face today in a society that supports neither the option to care for children at home without falling into poverty or of going into the labor force with adequate, affordable child care. On the 20th anniversary of the admission of women to Yale, I fear these critical issues will not be given the priority they demand until more women are in decision-making roles. Abigail Adams gave the charge in 1779 when she wrote John Adams to:

> Remember all Men would be tyrants if they could. If perticuliar care and attention is not paid to the Ladies we are determined to foment a Rebellion, and will not hold ourselves bound by any laws in which we have no voice, or Representation.

I hope your generation will raise your sons to be fair to other people's daughters and to *share,* not just help with, parenting and family responsibilities. I hope you will help strengthen the American tradition of family by stressing family rituals: prayers if you are religious, and if not, regular family meals and gatherings. Be moral examples for your children. If you cut corners, they will too. If you lie, they will too. If you spend all your money on yourself and tithe no portion it for our colleges, churches, synagogues, and civic causes, they won't either. And if you snicker at racial and gender jokes, another generation will pass on the poison my generation still did not have the will to snuff out.

Lesson Eight

Remember and help America remember that the fellowship of human beings is more important than the fellowship of race and class and gender in a decent, democratic society. Be decent and fair and insist that others be so in your presence. Don't tell, laugh, smile at or acquiesce in racial, ethnic, religious or gender jokes, or any practices intended to demean rather than enhance another human being. Stare them down. Walk away from them. Make them unacceptable in your homes, religious congregations, and clubs. Counter through daily moral consciousness the proliferating voices of racial and ethnic and religious division which are gaining respectability over the land, including college campuses. Let's face up to rather than ignore our ongoing racial problems which are both America's historic and future Achille's heel. White folks did not create black folks. Men did not create women. Christians did not create Jews. So who gives anybody the right to feel entitled to diminish another?

How many more potential Martin Kings, Colin Powells, Frederick Gregorys, Sally Rides, and Barbara McClintocks is our nation going to waste before it wakes up and recognizes that its ability to compete in the new century is as inextricably intertwined with its poor and minority children as with its white and privileged

Continued on page 180

179

Concluded from page 179

ones, with its girls as well as its boys?

Let's not spend more time, whites or blacks, pinning and denying blame rather than remedying the problem. Rabbi Abraham Heschel put it aptly: "We are not all equally guilty but we are all equally responsible" for building a decent and just America.

Lesson Nine

Listen for the sound of the genuine within yourself. "Small," Einstein said, "is the number of them that see with their own eyes and feel with their own hearts." Try to be one of them. The black theologian Howard Thurman told the young ladies of my alma mater, Spelman College, that there is "something in every one of you that waits and listens for the sound of the genuine in yourself which is the only true guide you'll ever have. And if you cannot hear it, you will all of your life spend your days on the ends of strings that somebody else pulls." There are so many noises and pulls in our lives, so many competing demands and signals that many of us never find out who we are. Learn to be quiet enough to hear the sound of the genuine within yourself so that you might then hear it in other people.

Lesson Ten

Be confident that you can make a difference. Don't get overwhelmed. Sometimes I get frantic about all I have to do and spin my wheels. I then recall Carlyle's words that: "Our main business is not to see what lies dimly at a distance, but to do what lies closely at hand." Try to take each day and each task as they come, breaking them down into manageable pieces for action while struggling to see the whole. And don't think you have to "win" immediately or even at all to make a difference. Sometimes it's important to lose for things that matter.

I frequently end speeches with the words of Sojourner Truth, an illiterate slave woman who could neither read nor write but was full of moral energy against slavery and second-class treatment of women. One day during an antislavery speech she was heckled by an old white man. "Old woman, do you think that your talk about slavery does any good? Why I don't care any more for your talk than I do for the bite of a flea." "Perhaps not, but the Lord willing, I'll keep you scratching," she replied.

A lot of people think they have to be big dogs to make a difference. That's not true. You just need to be a flea for justice bent on building a decent America. Enough fleas biting strategically can make even the biggest dog uncomfortable and transform even the biggest nation. Bite so that we can transform America together in the 1990s.

Nathan Hale, facing the firing squad in 1776, said: "I regret that I have only one life to give to my country." You have only one life to live for your country. Live it creatively and well, and ensure that America's ideals are strengthened because you held them high for generations to come.

Questions

1. What political points is Edelman making?

2. How does she connect her life to that of her audience? What does she feel they can learn from her experience?

VIETNAM VETERANS
A Topic That Was Unspeakable

by John F. Ferguson

Minister Ferguson delivered this speech at the Veterans Day Assembly, Juanita High School in Kirkland, Washington, on November 14, 1994. His is a speech of tribute honoring the veterans of the Vietnam War.

I want to begin by thanking you for giving me the privilege of speaking to you this morning. We have come together to honor the military service of American men and women, particularly those who participated in the war in Vietnam.

I'm one of those people. I served in the United States Marine Corps in Vietman in 1967 and 1968. I was a member of the 15th Marine Counterintelligence Team, operating just below the Demilitarized Zone. Our team was a part of small unit combat and intelligence operations, now known as the Phoenix Program.

If you want to honor someone, its beneficial to first understand their experience.

Many people believe they understand the experience of the men and women who served in Vietnam. Unfortunately, that understanding has often been derived from stereotypes.

It is true that about half of those who served in Vietnam experience some psychological and physiological residual of their war experience (e.g., sleep disorders or exaggerated startle reflex).

It is also true that approximately one-third of those who served have some degree of post-traumatic stress disorder. A minority of those so afflicted are homeless. Only a small percentage of Vietnam veterans have ever been arrested or incarcerated for criminal acts.

The truth is, that despite some lingering psychological symptoms, the vast majority of Vietnam veterans have gotten on with their lives. They are productive, functional members of society. In many cases, they have become civic, educational and business leaders in their communities.

The popularized portrayal of Vietnam veterans as lost and disturbed souls, lingering on the edge of violence, is as inaccurate as any group stereotype.

However, saying these things does not deny, or diminish, the intense, often painful reality of our experience.

I would like you to understand that experience, so that you may comprehend the contribution we believe we have made.

Let me attempt to explain.

Published in *Vital Speeches of the Day,* February 1, 1995. Reprinted with permission.

The majority of men who served in Vietnam were only a few years older than most of you. The average age of combat troops in Vietnam was 19. This means that most troops went almost directly from high school into combat.

Nothing can prepare a human being for the reality of war. It isn't anything like war movies or television programs. War is a physically exhausting, terrifying business. It places human beings in situations for which they are intellectually, emotionally and morally unprepared. Modern weapons do not simply kill people, they blow them to pieces. Guerrilla warfare has no front or rear lines. The enemy is often unseen and frequently indistinguishable from the civilian population. Unrestrained violence becomes the means for survival.

Teenagers placed in such an environment returned home old men, having lost their youth and innocence. They returned home with emotional and moral conflicts in need of resolution and closure. Unfortunately, that resolution and closure were unavailable for Vietnam veterans.

In recent years, it has been said that we "lost" the war in Vietnam. That seems to imply that those who fought it were ineffective warriors. Nothing could be further from the truth. Combat troops in Vietnam distinguished themselves with courage, tenacity and skill. On most occasions, they were victorious in battle. The war ended because those who made policy decisions decided it was a political imperative to stop the fighting. That the conflict ended unresolved was not the fault or responsibility of those who fought.

We returned expecting our society would do what it had done for our fathers and uncles returning from World War II. We believed the nation would gratefully honor our service, bringing resolution and closure to the conflicts our wartime experiences had created.

That honoring, resolution, and closure didn't occur. For a variety of reasons, people simply did not want to talk through, think about, or be reminded of Vietnam. America wanted the war to be over, to put a decade of foreign and civil conflict away. Returning veterans felt confused, abandoned and, on occasion, betrayed.

Let me give you an example, with which I hope you'll be able to identify.

The Juanita Rebel football team has had a terrific season. I'd like to introduce

Continued on page 184

Concluded from page 183

you to another winning football team.

That team is the 1962 Neshaminy High School Redskins of Langhorne, Pennsylvania. From the starting offensive 11, the left guard went to West Point. From there he went to command an infantry platoon in Vietnam. The right end went to Annapolis and became a marine officer. In his second tour in Vietnam, he was an infantry company commander. The tailback graduated from college, enlisted in the U.S. Marines and served in a reconnaissance company. The center graduated from college, enlisted in the marines, and served in a counterintelligence team. Yes, that's me! (If it seems as if there were a lot of marines in the group, it was partially due to the fact that several of the football coaches we admired and loved had been marines in World War II and the Korean conflict.)

The seven remaining players went on with their lives. Three of them went to college and on to careers in business. Two of them went into licensed trades. One of them entered a family business. The remaining player became a policeman.

What happened to the four of us who went to Vietnam? The left guard ended up calling in an air strike on his position while being overrun by the Vietcong. He lost most of his platoon. The right end was killed during a batallion sweep against the North Vietnamese army. The tailback was wounded in a firefight. I went to Episcopal seminary to try to sort out the results of having been involved in interrogations of prisoners and assassination operations against Vietcong leaders.

Seven of the starting 11 were untouched by the war. Their lives moved forward as expected. The lives of the three of us who served and survived were dramatically and unexpectedly changed.

In 1982, we gathered for our 20th reunion. The team got together for a few moments to kid and brag, as old athletes are wont to do. When the conversation turned to our friend who died, and to the Vietnam experiences of the three of us who had survived, the seven others quickly left us alone.

It was an amazing experience! It was 13 years since we had been in Vietnam. Yet, Vietnam still remained a topic that was unspeakable.

Near the end of the last century, Rudyard Kipling wrote a poem titled *Tommy*. It describes the experience of a British soldier home from the colonial wars. Let me share a portion of it, because it eloquently describes the experience and feelings of many Vietnam veterans:

> You talk o' better food for us an'
>   schools, an' fires, an' all; but
>   prove it to our face.
> For it's Tommy this an' Tommy
>   that, an' "Chuck him out, the
>   brute!"
> But it's "saviour of 'is country"
>   when the guns begin to shoot;
> An' it's Tommy this an' Tommy
>   that, an' anything you please;

An' Tommy ain't a bloomin fool—
    you bet that Tommy sees!

We were not fools, we did see that our society was not going to give us the honor, resolution, and closure that we needed.

So as individuals, and as groups, we created our own honoring, resolution, and closure. We built a memorial to our fallen comrades in Washington, D.C. We staged welcome-home parades. We created rap groups, counseling centers, and support systems.

Finally and belatedly, the nation roused to honor our service. It was no more than we deserved. We had kept faith with the values our parents, pastors, teachers, and coaches taught us. The nation called, and we went forth into that far away place to face the realities of war with a profound sense of patriotism. We served with honor, pride, and courage. We put our lives on the line in service to our country. We said yes, while others were saying, "Hell no, we won't go!"

Thank you for honoring us, and all the men and women who have answered their country's call. It feels good to be ac-knowledged and valued.

Let me leave you with an idea. If you truly desire to honor Vietnam veterans, don't stop with this assembly. Seek out those who served (perhaps your father, mother, uncle, aunt, teacher, or neighbor). Thank them for their service. Ask them to share their feelings and memories. That will bring them real honor, because in so doing you are telling them you understand and value their experiences and contribution.

Again, from my heart, I thank you for the privilege of speaking to you this morning.

Questions

1. How does Ferguson introduce himself to the audience? Why is this self-introduction so important to his speech?

2. Why does he feel he must explain the truth of the Vietnam experience?

3. What does he want his audience to do?

CHAPTER 10

Four Speeches for Classroom Practice

Learning Outcomes

After studying this chapter, you should be able to:

1 Deliver a speech of self-introduction.

2 Deliver an informative speech.

3 Deliver a personal experience speech.

4 Deliver a persuasive speech.

INTRODUCTION

You have learned the generally accepted theory relating to public speaking and have read models of speeches for special occasions. Now it is time to apply theory to classroom practice. A *suggested* sequence of speeches make up this chapter. Study the requirements for each type of speech, follow the ideas previously suggested, and the results will surprise even the most inexperienced student. Relax. Enjoy yourself and remember that you are acquiring a skill that will be a major asset in your career.

THE SPEECH OF SELF-INTRODUCTION

In many communications skills classes, your first formal speech will be one in which you introduce yourself to other members of the class. There are three major advantages to beginning this way. First, the self-introductory speech serves as an excellent icebreaker, allowing each speaker the opportunity to experience and overcome speech anxiety in a situation where the content of the speech is not a problem to prepare. Second, each class member gets to know the other people in the class. The result is that a clear picture of the audience emerges. This is useful when preparing future speeches. Third, the self-introductory speech is precisely what you will have to do, in one form or another, during your business career.

Format

This first speech should be brief (one to three minutes). Provide the basic biographical information the audience will need such as name, age, your hometown, your class year, and your major. Once the facts are established, you might consider explaining how you chose the college you are attending and your long-term career ambitions. As your speech progresses, give the audience a glimpse of your personal self. Share with them some of your likes and dislikes, how you spend your leisure time, and the things you consider interesting and entertaining. Finally, as with any speech, thank the audience for their attention and move slowly back to your seat.

Model Speech of Self-Introduction

Good afternoon. My name is Mary Gorham. I am 20 years old and my hometown is Mamaroneck, New York, which is a village about 20 miles outside of New York City in Westchester County. Mamaroneck is located on the Long Island Sound and is a suburban community from which many residents commute daily by train to their work in New York.

My major is data processing and I chose Central College because of the up-to-date curriculum it offered and the modern equipment that is available for student use. After graduation, my hope is to get a job with a progressive corporation that has a need for people with my training. Eventually, I plan to go to graduate school in the evenings or on weekends.

One of the major problems I know I will have to face is to balance my career aspirations with my desire to marry and have children. I hope I will be able to sort out my feelings on this question while I am here in college.

In the meantime, when I am not studying I enjoy jogging and playing tennis. Keeping physically fit is important to me as I seem to work better and I am happier when I feel healthy. However, with all those good intentions, I also enjoy parties, concerts, and being with groups of my peers.

My objective in this class is to learn to communicate more effectively and, in particular, to get over my nervousness so that I can speak comfortably to groups.

Thank you for listening to me. I appreciate your attention.

EXERCISE

1

Use the suggestions and the model above to write your own speech of self-introduction. Use the outline below to organize your main points and determine the structure of your speech.

Outline of Speech

Name: _____

Title of speech: _____

Purpose of speech: _____

EXERCISE 1

(continued)

Thesis: _____

Type of audience: _____

Time of speech: _____

I. Introduction

    A. _____

        1. _____

        2. _____

    B. _____

        1. _____

        2. _____

    C. _____

        1. _____

        2. _____

II. Body of Speech

    A. _____

        1. _____

        2. _____

    B. _____

        1. _____

        2. _____

    C. _____

        1. _____

        2. _____

    D. _____

        1. _____

2. _____

III. Conclusion

  A. _____

    1. _____

    2. _____

  B. _____

    1. _____

    2. _____

  C. _____

    1. _____

    2. _____

  D. _____

    1. _____

    2. _____

THE INFORMATIVE SPEECH

The purpose of the informative speech, as the title implies, is to pass on information. The key point is to try to pick a topic that will be new to the audience, either partially or entirely. Find something in your preparation and research that is fresh or interesting. Avoid the "old" topics that the audience has heard before unless you can bring new insights to them. Don't choose a topic that is stale.

If your speech is to be truly informative, it also must be impartial, accurate, and complete. A common problem for student speakers is that their informative speeches often turn out to be persuasive. This can be avoided if you remind yourself that your purpose is to promote understanding of your topic, not to convince your listeners of your own point-of-view.

Audience analysis is crucial to the success of informative speeches. Tailor your material to your listeners. For example, if you are explaining how stress can be overcome by a regular exercise program, you might relate the material to the times when students experience the most stress, for example, exam time. A good informative speech is personally valuable or useful for the audience. Ideally the audience should have a stake in the information given. Instead of giving a speech on meditation, perhaps you could focus it like this: "Meditation: 15 minutes every day will improve your grades!"

Be sure your information is tightly organized. The longer a speech, the more difficult it is to follow. You should make every attempt to see that all parts are clear and that transitions from introductions to conclusions are explicit. Keep in mind the old speech adage: Tell them what you are going to tell them *(Introduction);* tell them *(Body and Discussion);* and then tell them what you have told them *(Conclusion).* Here are examples of the types of remarks that guide the audience from one part of the speech to the next:

> *Introduction:* Have you ever seen someone die? Did you ever feel helpless in an emergency? Would you like to be prepared? Today I will show you the steps to follow when you see an accident or come upon a person who needs emergency aid.
> *Body:* (I will demonstrate on this Red Cross model.) First check the person for a pulse or feel just under his or her nose to determine whether the person is breathing.
> *Conclusion:* As I stated previously, you don't have to feel helpless in an emergency. Again, the steps that we focused on today are: First. . .

Format

The time allotted for informative speeches will vary with each class and each instructor. Five to 10 minutes is a reasonable time period and is dependent on your topic. Time yourself when you rehearse your speech and adjust your material and rate of presentation to fit the suggested time framework.

Remember your task is to inform. You may do this by a simple oral explanation or by "demonstrating" a skill or technique that requires physical movement. A speech on nutrition that shows the audience how to prepare well-balanced breakfasts for improved emotional and physical health is an example of an informative demonstration. Both types (oral explanation or demonstration) can be enhanced by the use of graphics or audiovisuals as discussed earlier.

Once you develop the skill to pass on information clearly in an interesting manner, you will be able to call on that skill again and again throughout your career.

Model Informative Speech

HOW THE HEART WORKS

by Benjamin F. Edwards II

As you read this speech, notice how Edwards uses clear transitions to guide his audience through his explanation and how his visual aid demonstrates his points.

Do you realize, as you are sitting here, that the heart of each of you is beating 70 times per minute, 4,200 times per hour, and over 100,000 times every day? And that, although each time it beats, only this much blood is squeezed out *(Here, 65cc of red liquid is poured into a common drinking glass, to bring in the familiar.)*, your heart pumps over 6,000 quarts of blood every day, and in 19 days, it would pump enough blood to fill this whole room.

But what makes your heart beat? Why is it that it can beat year in and year out without tiring? What will speed it up or slow it down? In the next five minutes, I will try to answer these questions for you. In other words, I'm going to tell you how the heart works. *(Please note in the following discussion that each structure is pointed to on the chart as it is mentioned.)*

First, I would like to give you a brief description of the anatomy of the heart. Here is a picture of the heart as it really looks. As you can see, it is about the size of my fist. Here *(pointing to chart)* is the heart in diagram form. Think of this heart as being my heart. In other words, as I face you, the upper right-hand corner of this heart corresponds to the upper right-hand corner of my heart, the lower left-hand corner of this heart, with the lower left-hand corner of my heart, and so on.

Now, I want you to think of your heart as being a two-story, four-room house. The two upstairs rooms are known as "auricles." They receive the blood. The

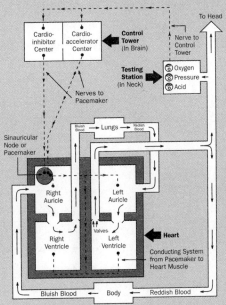

Continued on page 194

Concluded from page 193

two downstairs rooms are known as "ventricles." They pump the blood. To reiterate then, the auricles are receiving stations, the ventricles are pumping stations.

But what makes the heart beat? I want you to compare this sinauricular node, or pacemaker of the heart, to a coxswain. Just as he sits in the back of a shell yelling "stroke, stroke," so does this pacemaker sit in the upper right-hand room, that is the right auricle, and yell "stroke" to the heart. This pacemaker does not actually yell, of course, but it sends out impulses over this conducting system which cause the heart muscle to contract every eight-tenths of a second.

The impulse reaches the auricles first and they contract for one-tenth of a second, and then rest for seven-tenths of a second. Then the impulse reaches the ventricles, causing them to contract immediately after the auricles for three-tenths of a second and rest for five-tenths of a second. Now you can see why the heart can beat indefinitely. Each cycle lasts eight-tenths of a second, and out of this eight-tenths, the auricles are resting seven-tenths and the ventricles are resting five-tenths.

By now you should be able to understand, in general, how the blood circulates. As you can see, the heart is really two different pumps, each consisting of an auricle and a ventricle. Well, the blood returns from the body, here, and enters the right auricle. This blood is bluish, since it has given up its oxygen to the body. From the right auricle, it goes to the right ventricle *(all the time pointing to the chart)* and then out this way to the lungs. In the lungs, it picks up oxygen, then goes back through the left auricle, left ventricle, and back to the body. Get that now? Body, right heart, lungs, left heart, and back to the body.

But what governs the speed of the heart? A normal adult heart beats 70 times per minute, an athlete's heart 40 times per minute, and a child's 125 times per minute. This control tower in your brain is responsible for the speed of your heart. It consists of a cardioinhibitor and a cardioaccelerator center. The cardioinhibitor center sends impulses down this nerve to the coxswain or pacemaker and tells him to send out fewer impulses and thus make the heart go slower. In an opposite manner, the cardioaccelerator center sends impulses down this nerve and tells the pacemaker to speed up the heart.

However, although this control tower governs the speed of your heart, it in turn receives messages from this testing station located in the carotid artery in your neck. The carotid artery is the large blood vessel that carries blood to your head. In this testing station, or carotid sinus as we call it, are cells which are sensitive to changes in pressure, acidity, and oxygen content of your blood. Let me illustrate.

For instance, if the amount of oxygen in your blood tests too low, you will faint immediately, because your brain is not getting enough oxygen. This is prevented by the cells in the testing station, which are sensitive to changes in the oxygen content of your blood. They send messages along this nerve, telling the cardioaccelerator center to work harder and the cardioinhibitor center to let up. The cardioaccelerator center then sends messages down this nerve, as I have explained. The heart goes faster, pumping more blood through the lungs where it, the blood, picks up more oxygen, thus raising the oxygen content of your blood.

In a similar manner, pressure-sensitive cells in your testing station make the heart, when necessary, go faster, thus raising your blood pressure, or slower, thus lowering the blood pressure. Because too high blood pressure might result in a cerebral hemorrhage, or too low blood pressure might result in fainting, you can see that your testing station maintains an optimum pressure between these two extremes.

Again, in much the same manner, acid-sensitive cells cause your heart to beat faster when there is more acid in your blood from exercise.

Thus, you can see that your heart is constantly under various influences, attempting either to speed it up or slow it down. At one time, one of these influences may predominate; at another time, some other influence may predominate. Also, you should now be able to understand why your heart can beat day in and day out, since, as I have explained, the auricles rest seven-eighths of each cycle and the ventricles rest five-eights.

In conclusion, there are three things I would like you to remember. One, auricles receive blood. Two, ventricles pump blood. Three, blood goes from the body to the right side of the heart, to the lungs, to the left side, to the body again. Body, right side, lungs, left side, body. If you can't remember even these three points, please remember that the heart is *not* a one-chambered organ, and it does not look like the ones you see on valentines.

Using the suggestions and the model above, write your own informative speech. Again, use the outline that follows to clearly define your purpose and thesis and to organize your presentation. Remember to use clear, logical transitions to "knit" the speech together.

Follow your instructor's directions for using this outline.

Outline of Speech

Name: _____

Title of speech: _____

Purpose of speech: _____

Thesis: _____

Type of audience: _____

Time of speech: _____

I. Introduction

   A. _____

      1. _____

      2. _____

   B. _____

      1. _____

      2. _____

   C. _____

      1. _____

      2. _____

II. Body of Speech

   A. _____

      1. _____

      2. _____

   B. _____

      1. _____

      2. _____

C. _____

   1. _____

   2. _____

D. _____

   1. _____

   2. _____

III. Conclusion

A. _____

   1. _____

   2. _____

B. _____

   1. _____

   2. _____

C. _____

   1. _____

   2. _____

D. _____

   1. _____

   2. _____

THE PERSONAL EXPERIENCE SPEECH

The personal experience speech could be looked upon as a logical continuation of the self-introduction speech. You are asked to reveal to your audience an experience that had an impact on your life. Ideally, the impact should be significant enough for you to have learned a lesson and for the other members of the class to gather something from your experience.

You are giving part of yourself to your audience. Whether or not you realize it, the whole speech communication process is a giving of yourself to members of your audience. Your credibility will improve with the extent of your sincerity; to reveal yourself, honestly, will actually increase the effect of your message. *Remember,* the audience can tell a "phony" and not being *you* will only increase your anxiety.

Select an experience that is fresh in your mind or that you can recollect well. Perhaps you have learned things from travel, attending schools, playing sports, recovering from an accident, developing a hobby, and the like. Don't think that your life is uneventful or uninteresting. There are many experiences we have all been through with which others could empathize and gather insight, if you search your memory.

Format

You should keep the personal experience speech brief, preferably fewer than five minutes. Since you are familiar with the experience, you will not have to do any research. Prepare the speech like any other speech. Make sure you have a specific thesis in mind and that your audience will understand explicitly your purpose for sharing. A brief outline is sufficient for this effort. Don't try to memorize your speech. Use your outline or brief notes to remind you of the chronological sequence of the events of your story. Try to keep your language informal but not overly conversational.

Again, the important thing to remember is your audience. If you have a good idea about their various interests, hobbies, likes and dislikes, you should have a good understanding of how to compose the speech (You have learned these types of things by listening to the self-introduction speeches of your classmates.) Select a topic that is worthy of instructing or entertaining the audience. As you prepare this speech, ask yourself: Does this narrative have value for most of the students gathered here? Have I covered the basic journalistic questions: Who? What? When? Where? Is the language choice specific and descriptive enough so that the audience can visualize the scenes? Have I been selective enough to omit unnecessary details? Are the transitions from scene to scene smooth?

Model Personal Experience Speech

INCIDENT AT LACEY BRIDGE

by Thomas J. Farrell

The author of this speech describes a brief experience which caused him to reflect on issues of courage and individual identity versus that of a crowd. As his conclusion suggests, his purpose is not only to tell of his own reaction, but to provoke one in his audience as well.

New Year's Day, 1995, is a day that I will never forget. It was a cold, quiet day with the temperature at 1:00 P.M. about 30 degrees. My family and I had driven to a place called Lacey Bridge in our home town of Narragansett, Rhode Island. The bridge ran over a river whose water temperature was later estimated at 32 degrees.

We had come to Lacey Bridge to watch a group of winter swimming fanatics called the "Ice Cubes" begin the New Year by plunging off the bridge into the bitter waters below. I learned later that the "Cubes" were trying to outdo the more experienced "Polar Bears" who welcomed each New Year by charging into the Atlantic surf from a local beach.

A large crowd had gathered at the bridge and many of them clambered down the banks of the river where they could look up at the jumpers. I remember people waving and laughing to each other, wishing each other a "Happy New Year."

A few minutes after one o'clock, a husky young man dressed in sweatshirt and pants jumped up onto the wall of the bridge to announce the Ice Cubes' arrival. He entertained the crowd, joking while he shadowboxed precariously on the ledge of the bridge. A friend passed up a bottle of whisky and a long drink made him dance all the more. Suddenly, he was joined by another figure who climbed somewhat tentatively onto the ledge. He wore a "Cubes" shirt, tattered pants, and a colored Hawaiian lei around his neck—probably a souvenir from a New Year's Eve party.

Without a word, he launched himself into space and landed with a splash in the dark waters below. As soon as he surfaced, the current caught him, pulling him northward under the bridge. He tried to swim to the bank but was pulled in the other direction. I saw him disappear under the bridge and I assumed he would let the current take him to the other side of the bridge where he would climb out.

Continued on page 200

Concluded from page 199

As this was happening, the rest of the Cubes began cannonballing into the water. The crowd whooped with delight as the jumpers landed, surfaced, and were helped ashore by their friends. It was then that I glimpsed the first leaper trying in vain to get out from under the bridge. Other people saw him too and sensed he was in trouble. I vividly remember a lady standing next to me saying, "Aren't we going to do anything? Are we just going to stand here and let that man drown?" In the confusion, all but one of us did nothing.

One man in all that crowd saw his responsibility and acted. Mark Gillooly, a 22-year-old college student, became concerned when he noticed the Hawaiian lei worn by the first leaper come floating out from under Lacey Bridge. He ran down to the bank on the north side just as a man's body emerged, face down in the water.

Gillooly immediately dove into the frigid waters and, holding a limp wrist of the almost dead leaper, he pulled him to shore. The novice Ice Cube was rushed to the hospital, suffering from exposure and asphyxiation. He survived though doctors estimated another minute or more in the water might have been fatal.

Afterward, it was clear that Mark Gillooly had saved the leaper's life with his heroic act. What wasn't as clear, and yet just as certain, was that the same act of courage saved many of us who had stood immobilized on the banks of the river from having to absolve ourselves forever after of the guilt of inaction.

Later, I, along with others, would ask myself some difficult questions. Should I have gone into the icy waters after the helpless swimmer? Should we, a few of us, have formed a human chain to save him? The answers were unclear. The problem about being in a crowd, it seemed, was that individual responsibility became blurred. Fortunately, for both the leaper and all the spectators, one young college student was courageous enough to risk his own life for a fellow man he didn't even know. Think about it for a moment. . . What would you have done?

Thank you.

Using the suggestions and the model above, write your own personal experience speech. As you use the outline to organize your speech, remember to pay particular attention to your conclusion. It should leave the audience able to empathize with you and your experience.

Follow your instructor's directions for using this outline.

Outline of Speech

Name: _____

Title of speech: _____

Purpose of speech: _____

Thesis: _____

Type of audience: _____

Time of speech: _____

I. Introduction

  A. _____

    1. _____

    2. _____

  B. _____

    1. _____

    2. _____

  C. _____

    1. _____

    2. _____

II. Body of Speech

  A. _____

    1. _____

    2. _____

  B. _____

    1. _____

    2. _____

C. _____

    1. _____

    2. _____

D. _____

    1. _____

    2. _____

III. Conclusion

  A. _____

    1. _____

    2. _____

  B. _____

    1. _____

    2. _____

  C. _____

    1. _____

    2. _____

  D. _____

    1. _____

    2. _____

THE PERSUASIVE SPEECH

The most difficult and most challenging speech you will have to deliver is the persuasive speech. Unlike the informative speech, the persuasive speech is not only seeking to give information, but to influence the attitudes, beliefs, and sometimes the behavior of the audience. For example, when President Franklin Delano Roosevelt delivered his famous war address to a joint session of Congress on

December 8, 1941, he not only wanted to change the opinions of many Americans who did not want to become involved in a war in the Pacific, but to increase our military production and commitment of troops in the Pacific. Other situations may call only for additudinal change. Public relations people are constantly engaged in efforts to secure "goodwill" for their clients even though they may not be trying to bring about any specific behavioral change.

You have learned to choose a topic in which you are personally interested and to complete an audience analysis that reveals the values and attitudes that members of the audience are likely to have. These two points are particularly important to the success of a persuasive speech. Choose a topic you feel strongly about and then develop your themes, appeals, and arguments with the needs of your audience in mind. Show them how your position will benefit them directly.

Gordon Allport's classification system of value types might be helpful to you as you try to analyze present and future audiences. Essentially, the system breaks people down into categories according to the values that are of primary importance to individuals. This system will help you focus on the potential types that could be in your audience and this will allow you to fine-tune your message for your audience. Allport's system follows:

1. The Theoretical Person. This type of person is concerned primarily with the empirical, critical, rational, and logical. He or she is necessarily an intellectualist and frequently becomes a *scientist* or a *philosopher.* The chief aim in life of the theoretical person is to order and systematize his or her knowledge.

2. The Economic Person. This type of person is primarily interested in what is useful. His or her interest develops to embrace the practical affairs of the business world—the production, marketing, and consumption of goods, the elaboration of credit, and the accumulation of tangible *wealth.* The economic attitude frequently comes into conflict with other values. Great feats of engineering, scientific management, and "applied psychology" result from the demands that economic people make upon learning.

3. The Aesthetic Person. The aesthetic person sees the highest value in form and harmony. Each single experience is judged from the standpoint of grace, symmetry, or fitness. One need not be a creative artist, but one is an aesthetic person if he or she finds a primary interest in the artistic episodes of life.

4. The Social Person. This type of person could be called the "social welfare person." This person's highest value is *love* of people, whether of one or many, whether conjugal, filial, friendly, or philanthropic. The social person prizes other persons as friends, and is therefore kind, sympathetic, and unselfish. The social person is likely to find theoretical, economic, and aesthetic attitudes as cold and inhuman.

5. The Political Person. The political person is interested primarily in *power*. Because competition and struggle play a large part in all life, many philosophers have seen power as the most universal and most fundamental of motives. There are, however, certain personalities in whom the desire for a *direct* expression of this motive is uppermost, who wish above all else for personal power, influence, and renown.

6. The Religious Person. The highest value for the religious person may be called unity. He or she is mystical, and seeks to comprehend the cosmos as a whole, to relate himself to its embracing totality.[1]

If you can determine the primary value of a particular audience, or if you can focus on several which seem to be manifested within your audience, you can create a more compelling message.

Format

You can be effective as a persuasive speaker if you use the following suggestions:

- Stimulate interest in your topic during the introduction and establish the social, historical, or political context in which the issue is to be discussed. You may reveal your point-of-view at the outset if you feel your audience is sympathetic to your position. If, however, you feel there are members of the audience who will disagree with your position, it may be better to withhold your opinion until the end, after you have presented your reasons. Either way, you still have to support your argument.

- Use an inductive line of reasoning to support your position. This means that you will offer individual pieces of evidence that, when taken as a whole, will lead the open-minded members of the audience to accept your more general conclusion.

- Present evidence that has both quantity and quality. Factual evidence in sufficient quantity that is taken from quality sources is difficult to resist. Quality sources are reputable written sources or people or organizations who are considered experts on your subject. Offer your facts in a logical sequence and keep your most powerful points for last.

- When appropriate, blend in emotional appeals with factual evidence, but avoid being melodramatic or unethical.

- Explain how things will be better if your position is accepted, or describe the negative scenario that accompanies the opposite position.

- Conclude by trying to obtain the desired result. If it is attitudinal change you are after, ask for it. If it is action you want, tell the audience what to do and how to do it. Very often it will be both attitudinal and behavioral change that is your goal. When that occurs, total persuasion has taken place. You have done your job well.

Model Persuasive Speech

TAKE YOUR COLLEGE IN STRIDE

by William G. Carleton

Professor William G. Carleton delivered this address at a meeting of first-year students, mostly WWII veterans, at the University of Florida, Gainesville, on November 25, 1946.

Notice that your class is very different from the original audience. How has the college experience changed? Do you agree with any—or with all—of Carleton's argument? Why or why not? Discussing Carleton's argument will help you understand how to construct your own persuasive argument.

College offers you five great opportunities—professors, contact with fellow students who themselves are the products of winnowing process, laboratories, a library filled with books, and leisure time. And the greatest of these is leisure time.

Is it not strange that the greatest good provided by a university is something intangible—something that cannot be seen, something that cannot be written down in catalogs or reduced to clock

Source: Published in *Vital Speeches of the Day*, December 15, 1946. Reprinted with permission.

hours, credits, degrees? But the leisure time offered you during your university days is the priceless boon. Never again in your life will you have so much time—time to browse, to think, to dream, to discuss, to argue, to question, to create, to construct. Even if you should become a college professor you will never again have so much precious leisure. Beware of those educators who want to put you in a straightjacket and make you account for every minute of your waking hours. Those educators do not want a university; they want an army.

What any professor can give you in any subject is limited—limited by the inability of any man, however great his sense of the vicarious, to impart but a small fraction of his knowledge and experience; limited by the necessarily formal nature of the student-teacher relationship; limited by the professor's own talents and background; limited by cultural and traditional restraints. Even the greatest of teachers are limited, limited by the very clarity of the point of view which brings them to prominence and makes them "great."

Your professor, to be sure, will be able to suggest, to encourage, to help tie up loose ends, to put things together, to point out connections where none seemed to exist before. If he is the sort of person who can do this in an interesting and exciting way, so much the better. If he has developed enough maturity in his own subject to have come to a definite point of view and to have made some original contributions, then you are blessed. And if he can impart his ideas without pomposity and with humor and sparkle, then you are twice blessed.

However, even the most gifted professors can give you little real insight, understanding, ripeness of judgment, or wisdom. These are the results of living, countless contacts with men and events, wide experience, travel, observation, the reading of great books, the doing of great deeds, and thinking and acting in real life situations.

The library, even in this scientific age, is the student's chief source of knowledge. A university library is a truly wonderful place. There you can find almost all the ideas that men in all times and places have thought—the ugly and the beautiful, the foolish and the wise, the grotesque and the sensible, the curious and the useful. There you can relive the life experience of the race—the story, still unfinished, of man's slow groping for civilization.

As sources of ideas, professors simply cannot compete with books. Books can be found to fit almost every need, temper, or interest. Books can be read when you are in the mood; they do not have to be taken in periodic doses. Books are both more personal and more impersonal than professors. Books have an inner confidence which individuals seldom show: they rarely have to be on the defensive. Books can afford to be bold and courageous and exploratory; they do not have to be so careful of boards of trustees, colleagues, and community opinion. Books are infinitely diverse; they run the gamut of human activity. Books can be found to express every point of view; if you want a different point of view you can read a different book. (Incidentally, this is the closest approximation to objectivity you are likely ever to get in humanistic and social studies.) Even your professor is at his best when he writes books and articles;

Continued on page 208

Concluded from page 207

the teaching performance rarely equals the written effort.

Students who come to the university merely to learn a trade will not understand what I have had to say. Neither will those who come merely to earn high grades or deliberately to make Phi Beta Kappa. But the others—those who have come to learn of life in this puzzling and complicated world of ours—will, I think, understand.

Write your own persuasive speech using the following outline. There are many ways to construct this type of speech. However, one easy way to outline the body of the speech is to identify two major supports of your thesis as "A" and "B." Then briefly refer to the opposition and offer a rebuttal in "C." Finally, discuss one last strong support of your own in "D."

Follow your instructor's directions for using this outline.

Outline of Speech

Name: _____

Title of speech: _____

Purpose of speech: _____

Thesis: _____

Type of audience: _____

Time of speech: _____

I. Introduction

    A. _____

        1. _____

        2. _____

    B. _____

        1. _____

        2. _____

    C. _____

        1. _____

        2. _____

II. Body of Speech

    A. _____

        1. _____

        2. _____

    B. _____

        1. _____

        2. _____

C. _____

   1. _____

   2. _____

D. _____

   1. _____

   2. _____

III. Conclusion

A. _____

   1. _____

   2. _____

B. _____

   1. _____

   2. _____

C. _____

   1. _____

   2. _____

D. _____

   1. _____

   2. _____

CONCLUSION

You will find that most presentations you make in your professional career will be either one of these types of speeches or a blend of two or more. In each, anticipating the audience's needs and concerns, organizing your speech clearly and logically, and providing both accurate and interesting information will be vital to your speech's success.

NOTES

1. Allport, Gordon. *The Person in Psychology: Selected Essays.* Boston: Beacon Press, 1968, p. 52.

QUESTIONS FOR REVIEW AND DISCUSSION

1. Which type of speech will you probably have to give during your business career?

2. How long is the typical self-introduction speech?

3. What type of information should be included in your self-introduction?

4. Which two types of speeches do students often confuse? Why?

5. Why is audience analysis crucial to the success of an informative speech?

6. What are two types of informative speeches?

7. What is the purpose of the personal experience speech?

8. What questions should you ask yourself as you prepare the personal experience speech?

9. What is the purpose of the persuasive speech?

10. What are the six categories into which an audience can be broken down?

APPLICATION EXERCISES

1. Spend a half hour or so jotting down biographical information in note form. Then pass the notes to a classmate and ask him or her to circle at least three items that the classmate would like to hear more about in a speech of self-introduction or in a speech of personal experience.

2. Compose a list of at least 10 topics that would be suitable for informative presentations in *your* class. You will have to ask some questions of the class in order to do so.

3. Conduct an audience analysis of the class based on the Allport system. How many people in the class would describe themselves as fitting into one or more of the categories listed?

4. As a class, compose a list of current and controversial issues that would be appropriate for persuasive speeches. Be sure to weed out those that the class feels have been "overdone."

Applying Communication Skills in Business

Beginning Your Job Search

Learning Outcomes

After studying this chapter, you should be able to:

1 List three necessary steps in the job-search process.

2 Locate companies that may be prospective employers.

3 Write a résumé.

4 Write an effective letter of application.

5 Follow up on your letter of application.

INTRODUCTION

How often do you think of your present role as a student as an investment in your future? If you don't think of education as an investment, you should, and if you do, you're on the right track. What you are doing now as a student may be the best investment you will ever make and, like all sound investments, you can expect to receive future dividends. The extent of those dividends is very clear in studies which periodically indicate that men and women who graduate from college earn substantially more money in their lifetime than those who do not graduate. Indeed, there is a higher lifetime increment of earnings for every additional year that you remain in school.

This information is good news and should reassure you that the time, effort, and money that you are investing now are well worth the effort. However, to reap the dividends that you have earned, you first must be successful in getting a job. The difficulty of finding a job will vary with the state of the economy, career preferences, and other personal factors, but the job search is rarely, if ever, easy. Finding a job you will be happy with is a task that must be approached in a systematic and organized way in order to achieve your objective. Take this opportunity to learn how to obtain employment. After all, wouldn't it be foolish to have worked hard on your investment and not be able to take the last step that allows you to collect your earned dividends?

Think of your job search as a process which occurs in three stages. The three stages are: (1) pre-interview activities, (2) the interview, and (3) postinterview activities.

PRE-INTERVIEW ACTIVITIES

Most of the conventional wisdom on preparing for an interview begins with tips about researching potential employers or writing résumés or application letters. These are important suggestions, but a 1994 survey on employment prospects conducted by Donna Yena, director of university planning at Johnson & Wales University, offers additional advice and helpful information. The survey was sent to 300 companies; respondents included John Hancock Financial Services, Prudential Financial Services, Saab Cars USA, Microsystems, CVS Pharmacy, Caldor, Inc., Polaroid Corporation, American Tourister, and many others. The major conclusion of the survey is that to have an edge in finding good jobs, students must gain some experience in their chosen fields. "I prefer candidates with on-the-job training in specific technical areas," stated Debra Gorgens, vice president of Microsystems.

According to the survey, students who do not work while in college and do not plan for the future will have more difficulty finding a job. One recruiter said, "The attitude that I should enjoy my college years and worry about employment later is totally unrealistic."[1] Another suggested that students learn how to speak, write, and get along with people. In other words, the message is to develop your communication skills and to start *now* to prepare for the future, not immediately before or after graduation.

LOCATING EMPLOYERS

The most logical place to start searching for a prospective employer is with your college or school's placement office, if one is available. A placement office attracts companies to campuses for the purpose of hiring students like you. Part of the fees that you pay support this placement office so be sure to use its services.

In addition to attracting potential employers, placement offices often offer information on résumés, application letters, and interviewing techniques. Even if you are not hired through your placement office, you can gain valuable interviewing experiences that will help in subsequent interviews. Indeed, many placement officers will recommend that students sign up for interviews if only for the practice. Interviewing is like tennis because both depend on approach, practice, and hundreds of conditioned responses. More on that later.

If you do not have access to a placement office, you can turn to sources that are available in the reference sections of local libraries. Librarians will help you find books and databases listing names, addresses, and telephone numbers of companies by industry. In addition, you may read the corporate profiles which appear in Dun and Bradstreet's *Million Dollar Directory,* Standard and Poor's *Register of Corporations, Directors and Executives,* and *MacRoe's Blue Book.* Your state publishes indexes to manufacturers, service firms, and retail firms as well as a census of businesses. Perhaps the most readily available source of corporate information is the Phone Book *Yellow Pages.* These are some of the obvious sources to use at the start of your search. There are many more.

Once you have focused on certain companies, you need to learn all that you can about those companies. You can do this by obtaining annual reports, reading industry trade magazines, or talking to people who work for those companies. Find out about the company's present financial status, its future plans, its operating "philosophy," and its products or services. You also should find out how the company's employees feel about working there. You need to have this knowledge so that should an interviewer pose the much-asked question, "Tell me what you know about our company and why you want to work here," you will be able to give a knowledgeable reply and not draw an embarrassed blank.

WRITING THE RÉSUMÉ AND LETTER OF APPLICATION

Once you have targeted some prospective employers, you now have to begin packaging the product you are selling: you. Specifically, you need to write a résumé and a letter of application.

The résumé and letter of application have only one purpose: to get you a personal interview. Together, the two pieces are a kind of advertising piece which, like any advertising, must be persuasive. They must arouse the employer's interest, build a case distinguishing you from other applicants, and motivate the employer to grant you an interview. As such, the résumé and letter of application must be brief, readable, contain all relevant information, and present you in your most positive light. The following is a sample résumé in a format that is appropriate for the student about to venture into the job market (see Figure 11–1).

Note that the sample résumé presents an abbreviated biography which summarizes and highlights the applicant's education, work experience, and distinctive achievement. Should you apply for jobs that require different skills, you might want to change the emphasis of a section to better suit the situation.

Résumés are always accompanied by a letter of application which is intended to reinforce, but not duplicate, the information on the résumé. The letter should be brief (one typed page), and it should be mailed to the individual who makes employment decisions. You can write an effective letter of application if you follow these suggested steps:

- State the purpose of the letter: that you wish to be considered for employment.

Figure 11–1
Sample résumé

SHARON LEBELT
3838 MacKenzie Lane
Metamore, Michigan 48455
(313) 411-8890

CAREER OBJECTIVE: To use my accounting skills in commercial banking to benefit a progressive company.

SUMMARY OF QUALIFICATIONS:
- Work well with people at all levels.
- Thrive in a competitive and challenging environment.
- Adept at developing strong working relationships.

EDUCATION: BACON SCHOOL OF ACCOUNTING
Troy, Michigan 48084
12/94–3/96   Diploma Awarded March 1996

EXPERIENCE:

3/96–Present   S & P SAVINGS AND LOAN ASSOCIATION
Detroit, Michigan 48236
Branch Management Trainee
Responsible for generating customers' account statements, arranging trust funds, and organizing new safe-deposit box system.

2/95–6/95   TROY VOCATIONAL INSTRUCTION & PLACEMENT
Job Placement Agency—Internship
Troy, Michigan 48084
Job Development Representative
Introduced prospective employers to Troy VIP services through outside consultations, phone solicitation, and mass advertising.

10/93–3/94   ONE ON ONE ATHLETIC CLUB
West Bloomfield, Michigan 49077
Tennis Instructor

ACCOMPLISHMENTS:
- Led a simulated corporate profitability program.
- Taught elementary economics for Junior Achievement.

REFERENCES: Available upon request

From Zarna, *The Job Search: Your Guide to Success*, Burr Ridge, IL: Richard D. Irwin, 1994, p. 42. Used with permission.

- Explain what accomplishments and skills you have which will benefit the employer should you be hired.

- Ask for the opportunity to present yourself in person during a personal interview. This is an all-important point that enables you to keep control of your job search. (See the sample letter in Figure 11–2).

If you follow up on your letters of application and résumés as suggested, you will soon have appointments for interviews. Prior to those interviews, your preparation should include reading as much about the companies as possible and determining and practicing responses to the questions that you feel certain you will be asked.

FOLLOWING UP ON THE LETTER OF APPLICATION

You should not try to call people to schedule interviews on Mondays or on Friday afternoons. Instead, place your calls Tuesday through Friday between 9:00 A.M. and 11:00 A.M. Your chances in talking to the person you wish to reach and getting the desired response will thus be increased.

Think of your telephone call as a logical extension of the statement you made at the end of your letter of application—that you would be calling for an appointment. Refer to your letter by giving the date it was written and its purpose. You will get one of three responses: (1) be told you will not be granted an interview, (2) be told to call back at a later date for an interview, or (3) be given an appointment for an interview. All three are desirable responses, even the first one. If a company has no genuine interest in you as a prospective employee, you need to know that, so that you don't waste time, energy, or hope pursuing a dead end. Determine your own fate; find out what you need to know.

CONCLUSION

If possible, try to schedule two interviews each day. Consider this your job until a paying job comes along. Work hard at it, and you will improve your chances to succeed.

Figure 11–2
Sample letter
of application

Your Street
Your City, State, and Zip Code
Date

Acme Products Corporation
Attention Human Resources Department
12345 E. Nine Mile Road
Oak Grove, Missouri 48089

Ladies and Gentlemen:

Please consider this letter an application for a secretarial position with your company. I am aware that Acme is one of the leading manufacturers of automotive tubing used in brake and fuel lines. Working for a respected leader in the automotive industry and being able to contribute my expertise to enhance your office production is the opportunity I have been looking for.

As my enclosed resume states, I have had experience in nearly all facets of office procedures from my full-time training program at Grant School of Business. My areas of expertise include communication skills, word processing, shorthand, Dictaphone transcription, and some accounting.

What you cannot learn from my resume is that I am outgoing, responsible, creative, and hardworking. Ideally, my greatest contribution would be made in a fast-paced, progressive office atmosphere, where I could blend my personality and skills to become part of the office team.

I will contact you within a week to discuss the possibility of meeting with you regarding any present or future secretarial openings at Acme. If you wish to contact me before that time, you may reach me at (313) 431-8787. I look forward to a personal introduction at your earliest convenience.

Sincerely,

Your Name

Enclosure

From Zarna, *The Job Search: Your Guide to Success*, Burr Ridge, IL: Richard D. Irwin, 1994, p. 71. Used with permission.

NOTES

1. Yena, Donna J. *Career Directions: A Special Edition of Johnson & Wales University.* Burr Ridge, IL: Irwin, 1987.

QUESTIONS FOR REVIEW AND DISCUSSION

1. What activities should you complete *prior* to an interview?

2. Where can you begin to locate a potential employer?

3. How can you choose a company that is right for you?

4. What should the letter of application and the résumé accomplish?

5. What type of information should be on a résumé?

6. How is the letter of application different from the résumé?

7. What should you ask for in the letter of application?

8. While you wait to hear from companies, how can you keep yourself involved in the process of seeking employment?

9. How do you follow up on the letter of application?

10. Why is this last step helpful to *you* as well as the employer?

APPLICATION EXERCISES

1. Visit the placement office on your campus and explore the possibilities for future job searches. Ask if companies ever visit the campus to recruit.

2. Research a company in which you are interested and then tailor a letter of application to its needs.

3. Write a résumé that describes your current level of education, job experience, and qualifications. File this résumé away: The process of résumé writing is one that involves constant revising and updating.

CHAPTER 12

The Employment Interview

Learning Outcomes

After studying this chapter, you should be able to:

1 Explain the basic ways to prepare for an interview in order to increase your chance of success.

2 Discuss different strategies that interviewers are likely to use.

3 Deliver effective responses to the questions most commonly asked by interviewers.

4 Explain how to prepare yourself to deal with the question of salary during an interview.

5 Write an effective follow-up letter after an interview.

INTRODUCTION

Each prospective employee hopes to impress the interviewer positively, so that he or she will consider the interviewee for employment. Job hunters are encouraged to learn as much about the interviewing process as possible in order to increase their chances of doing well. That is the purpose of this chapter. However, another way of approaching the topic is to think about the responsibilities that interviewers have and how they generally carry out those responsibilities.

The interviewer's job is to evaluate candidates based on a face-to-face meeting. The interviewer succeeds when the best possible candidate for a job is selected for a job offer. This is often done through a process of elimination based largely on how the candidate responds to a series of structured questions. The often standard questions are designed to reveal as much as possible about the candidate. There are variations on this typical interviewing structure, but it helps to understand the customary approach before you start.

THE INTERVIEW

Employment interviews are stressful experiences that can cause nervousness and anxiety which, if not controlled, can interfere with your ability to do your best during an interview. Knowing this, you need to try to minimize the effects of stress. Get a good night's sleep and exercise regularly when you are job hunting. Feeling healthy and knowing that you look your best can boost your confidence and help to offset stress.

Dress appropriately. For men the most appropriate attire is a suit, dress shirt, dark tie, and dress shoes. Women have more flexibility but a conservative dress or suit in subdued colors is best. Be on time and, when you meet the interviewer, smile warmly, look the interviewer in the eye, and firmly shake his or her hand. Show your enthusiasm, use positive language, express a reasonable confidence in your own abilities, and sell yourself. Relax and enjoy the occasion. Remember that the interviewer is carrying out his or her job and, like you, has certain objectives which you need to know.

THE INTERVIEWER

Corporate interviewers generally share the same objectives. They want to hire qualified applicants who will perform their job well and who will remain with their new employer for a reasonable period of time. To do this, interviewers employ different techniques. In addition to the customary one-on-one interview, some companies require multiple interviews, after which the actual hiring decision is made by a group or committee. Others engage in "stress" interviews while some companies ask the job candidate to participate in social occasions such as lunches, dinners, or other functions. Whatever the interviewing method, similar patterns emerge. Interviewers ask questions and interviewees give responses. Through this process, the interviewer hopes to learn enough about you to help him or her make a decision. True, there is also the opportunity for you to pose questions about the company, but these are less significant to the evaluation process unless you blunder and ask naive questions about vacation time or unrealistic pay levels.

Because this question-and-answer format is so standard, you can prepare for it by anticipating the questions that will be asked and how to respond to them. Understand that the "real" reason for asking a question might not be the same as the actual wording of the question itself but in what your answer reveals about the type of person you are. Study the questions that follow, write answers that are consistent with the person you want to be, and rehearse them. Your goal is not to respond with memorized, canned replies, but to be able to respond confidently, knowing that you have already considered the questions and are comfortable answering them.

COMMON INTERVIEW QUESTIONS

1. Tell me about the college you attended. Did you enjoy it?

2. What were your favorite courses? Why?

3. Did you do the best work of which you were capable in college?

4. What are your career objectives?

5. Do you work well with others?

6. What is your major strength or talent? What is your major weakness?

7. What kinds of computer skills do you have? Are you comfortable with other types of technology?

8. Do you like to travel?

9. Are you willing to move if the job requires it?

10. Do you read as a leisure time activity? Who is your favorite author?

11. Would you describe yourself as a heavy television viewer? What programs do you like?

12. What kind of personality do you have?

13. Do you consider yourself creative?

14. Are you active in any athletic activities?

15. How much money would you like to be making in 10 years?

16. Do you take criticism well?

17. Tell me about yourself.

18. What type of supervisor would you prefer to work for?

19. Why do you want to work for our company?

20. Why should we hire you?

You will be asked some of the above questions or variations of these questions. Count on it. Also, if you are applying for a job in a specific job category, you can expect questions designed to test your knowledge of specific job skills. Be sincere in your replies, but do try and present yourself in the best light. Here are some possible answers to a few of the more difficult questions:

Interviewer: What is your major weakness? *(Question 6)*

Reply: Sometimes I stretch myself too thin by trying to accomplish too many goals at once. However, my experience in college has taught me to manage my time and my priorities effectively.

Interviewer: How much money would you like to be making in 10 years? *(Question 15)*

Reply: I don't know that I can set an exact dollar figure. However, I would like to feel that if I make contributions of value to the company, I would be rewarded fairly so that I could take care of my responsibilities to my family.

Interviewer: What type of supervisor would you prefer to work for? *(Question 18)*

Reply: I prefer to work for a person who is fair, can provide the guidance I will need, and will recognize that I have performed my job well.

Interviewer: Why should we hire you? *(Question 20)*

Reply: You should hire me because I will be an asset to your firm. I am intelligent, have lots of energy, and I am willing to work hard to achieve goals.

THE QUESTION OF SALARY

If you do your pre-interview homework and prepare yourself to answer the predictable questions, the time will come when the delicate issue of salary will be raised. There are two extremes to avoid: (1) don't undersell yourself, and (2) don't price yourself out of consideration by stating an unrealistic salary amount. You will be more effective if you are governed by two questions:

1. What is the general salary range for the job?
2. What amount of money do I need to support myself?

Go into the interview with a salary goal based on the answers to these two questions and also have a lowest acceptable figure in mind.

Inquire about the frequency of salary reviews and the level of increases given. Keep in mind that fringe benefits such as life insurance, health insurance, and pensions have a dollar value and are part of your overall compensation package. If a company wants to hire you, they should offer you a fair wage. If they don't, you probably don't want to work for them anyway.

POSTINTERVIEW ACTIVITIES

Your interview is over. If you have been offered a job, congratulations—you are the exception. Most worthwhile jobs are *not granted* during the first interview. Offers are made after other prospects have been interviewed and consultations have taken place. Therefore, you need to keep busy doing the following things:

- Immediately after an interview, critique your performance. What did you do well and what not so well? How can you be more effective next time? Plan to make the necessary adjustments.

- Go on to your next interview. Until you secure a job, interviewing is your job.

- Most important of all, write a follow-up note to every interviewer that you have met. Thank the person for his or her time, restate your desire for employment, and restate why you would be an asset. Then request a decision in a reasonable period of time. Your letter will refresh the interviewer's memory of you,

Figure 12–1
Sample follow-up letter

```
                              10 Bell Street
                              Miami, Florida
                              June 15, 1996


Mr. Robert Sharpe
Personnel Manager
Carter Company
10 Main Street
Miami, Florida  33101

Dear Mr. Sharpe:

Thank you for the time and attention you gave me today. I enjoyed meeting
you and the people in your office.

Our meeting confirmed my belief that Carter Company is a firm for which
I would be happy to work. I am hopeful that you feel my education and
work experience would make me a welcome addition to your company.

I am eager to get on with my career and hope to hear good news from you
within the next two weeks.

Thank you again.

                              Sincerely,

                              Linda Anderson
```

impress him or her with your thoughtfulness and drive, and might separate you from other prospects who do not take the time to write a follow-up letter. Figure 12–1 is a sample follow-up letter.

Follow the suggestions made in this chapter, and put into effect the other principles of communication that you have learned, and your job hunt will be successful. Good luck.

For additional reading and discussion, read the model interview, "Management-Trainee Employment Interview." It provides excellent examples of typical interview questions and some very effective responses.

MODEL INTERVIEW: MANAGEMENT-TRAINEE EMPLOYMENT INTERVIEW

Mr. Ken Michaels, personnel director for Parker House Restaurants, interviews Sharon Young, recent college graduate, for a management trainee position.

Opening

Michaels: Hi! [*Smiles*] Sharon Young?

Young: Yes.

Michaels: [*Greets applicant with a handshake*] I'm Len Michaels, personnel director for Parker House Restaurants and I'll be interviewing you today for the management trainee position you applied for. Won't you have a seat?

Young: Thank you.

Michaels: [*Asks an ice breaker question*] Did you have any problem finding the office?

Young: No, not really, When I was here before to complete the application form, I asked the secretary if this was where they'd hold the interviews and she said yes. So I didn't have any problems at all.

Michaels: Very good. [*The interviewer now makes a transition to the body of the interview*] What I'd like to do this afternoon is find out something about you—*your* educational and work background. Then I'd like to discuss the qualifications for this job and, finally, I'd be happy to answer any questions that you may have about Parker House in general and the management-trainee position in particular.

Young: Fine, I'm ready to go.

Body

Michaels: As a starting point, could you please tell me what you think you could offer Parker House?

Young: Well, I'm a self-starter and I work well with most types of people. I pick things up very quickly and I have had specific work experience with Burger World, two summers, and two years with the Fisherman's Restaurant. The psychology, communication, accounting, and management courses that

I completed in college should also help me as a manager at Parker House.

Michaels: What were some of your duties at Burger World? [*Interviewer is seeking work experience information*]

Young: The first summer I worked the grill and the fryers, took orders, and worked the register. The second summer I was shift supervisor for the afternoon/evening shift and I cashed out all the registers and made the bank deposits.

Michaels: And your duties at Fisherman's?

Young: The first year I worked in the kitchen preparing dinners and salads. Then one of the hostesses quit and I took over her position and helped Mr. Mann with the daily deposits and the books.

Michaels: That sounds like a pretty varied experience. Did you encounter any problems while you were at Fisherman's?

Young: I'm not sure what you mean by problems. . . Do you mean personal problems or work-related problems? [*The applicant asks for clarification when unsure of the question*]

Michaels: I mean work-related problems.

Young: There were times when reservations got backed up, so you had to ask customers if they would like to have a drink at the bar while they waited for their table to become available. Sometimes one of the kitchen crew wouldn't show for some reason and we'd have to pitch in and help. Things like that . . . nothing serious though.

Michaels: You mentioned Mr. Mann, was he the owner?

Young: Yes, he and his wife owned the restaurant.

Michaels: What did Mr. Mann do about the people who didn't show for work?

Young: If they had a legitimate excuse but did not call before their shift, he gave them a warning. If it happened again—as it did once—he would fire them.

Michaels: I take it you've never fired anyone?

Young: No, I haven't.

Michaels: Would you be able to terminate or fire anyone? [*The interviewer is trying to discover how the applicant would handle this conflict situation*]

Michaels:	[*Pause*] If there were just cause, I guess I could. Does Parker House have a specific policy on this, Mr. Michaels?
Michaels:	We can cover that later in the interview, but Sharon, what I'd like to explore with you for a moment is what your feelings would be if you had to fire someone.
Young:	Sure. [*Pause*] If someone had done something against company policy, like not showing for a shift and not calling, then the employee would warrant termination. If, for example, the person did a sloppy job of cleaning a stove . . . I'd *tell* them and *show* them how it was to be done, and then I'd have them show me how it was to be done. I would explain to them that the sloppy work should not happen again. If it did, then you'd have to let them go.
Michaels:	If a customer complained that his food was not cooked properly how would you handle it? [*Again, another questions which seeks to determine how the applicant would handle a conflict situation*]
Young:	If his food were not done, I'd find out what was not cooked properly. I'd apologize and find out how the customer wanted it cooked. I'd then ask the cook to prepare it to the customer's specifications and I'd make sure to offer another apology after the dinner was returned to the customer. I'd make sure to check back later and find out if everything was satisfactory.
Michaels:	Your résumé lists a two-year degree from Lock City Community College in New York and a BA from Columbus College. [*pause*]
Young:	Right.
Michaels:	What courses do you think would be helpful in managing a Parker House restaurant? [*Interviewer is attempting to discover what educational experiences would be related to this position*]
Young:	The psychology courses would be helpful in understanding customers and employees. The public speaking course helped me to gain confidence in myself and helped me to improve my communication ability. The interpersonal communication course helped me to learn how to resolve conflicts between myself and others and to work with other

people. The management courses would certainly be relevant for organizing, hiring, training, and managing employees. The economics and accounting courses have given me a background for the bookkeeping and the food ordering aspects of the job.

Michaels: Umm, hum, I see. [*Pause*] Any other courses that you could think of that would be helpful?

Young: I took two noncredit food preparation courses at Lock City College, one in dinner preparation and the other in dessert preparation. [*Pause*] When I was a freshman in high school, my mother said I had something to learn about cooking.

Michaels: Does your mother think that you've improved?

Young: Oh yes!! [*Smiles*] She helped me a lot, and those courses and then Fisherman's have given me a pretty good foundation.

Michaels: Is there anything about cooking you really dislike?

Young: Nothing major, but I never did get the hang of lemon meringue pies.

Michaels: [*Smiles and nods*] I take it that you enjoy cooking?

Young: Very much! I like to experiment with foods. But I also enjoy being "out front," meeting people, making them feel comfortable.

Michaels: How would you rate the education you received from Columbus?

Young: Columbus has an excellent business management program and I am glad that my father got transferred. I was a little apprehensive about the move at first and about attending Columbus. However, the academic training and experiences I received from Columbus supported the foundation courses that I took at Lock City College.

I think the grades I earned at both colleges reflect just as much about my capabilities as they do about the schools' educational programs. The teachers, for the most part, were sensitive to student needs, were challenging and motivating, and were realistic and practical in what they taught.

I also got to learn something about myself, who I was, and what I wanted to do with my life. [*pause*] Probably the most important factors of college life are that it helps you to understand yourself and other people and how to get along with and work with other people.

Michaels: [*Smiles*] What about strengths and weaknesses; we all have them. What would you say is your biggest strength?

Young: I like to be organized, to anticipate problems, and how to solve them. And I like working with people.

Michaels: Why do you like to work with people? [*Interviewer probes for more specific information*]

Young: [*Pause*] I can't really put my finger on it, but I worked with a lot of different people in my life. I guess I got this from home. There was always someone at the house—neighbors, friends, relatives, and so forth. In high school and college, I was working with people to solve mutual problems—like on the student senates at Lock City College and Columbus College.

Michaels: What's your biggest weakness?

Young: [*Pause*] I don't like people who are gossips. One of my best friends got hurt by gossip that wasn't true. And I guess I get short tempered with people who constantly slack off; who do just enough to squeak by in doing a job.

Michaels: I see. Excluding age, racial background, and gender characteristics, what types of people do you like to work with most? [*Notice that the interviewer is tacitly telling the applicant that he does not wish to pursue material which might be classified as unlawful according to the Civil Rights Act of 1964*]

Young: I like to work with people who are organized, who try to do a job right the first time rather than having to do it over again. I like to work with people who are willing to "hop" right in and help others if a problem occurs. I guess I prefer to work with people who are *willing* to work with others. It doesn't matter if they are quiet or outgoing, but, like I said, I can work with a lot of different types of people.

Michaels: Let me tell you about this management trainee position and what Parker House can offer *you.*

We start all of our management trainees out with a 12-week, intensive, training orientation. This pamphlet outlines in detail [*smiles and hands applicant the pamphlet*] what the training sessions are all about.

Basically, you will be rotated through all of the basic operations and procedures that all of our restaurants follow: cooking, dishes, register, waitressing, hosting, record and bookkeeping, ordering, scheduling, employee evaluations, and supervision.

During these three months, you are on probationary status and if you do *not* work out you can be terminated. The pay for these three months would be $265 per week. Room and board will be paid for by the company during this three-month orientation, and the day you begin your training you'll be covered by our medical and dental insurance policies.

After the orientation program, you will be assigned to a Parker House restaurant in the greater Columbus area for a period of nine months. What happens during these nine months is explained in another pamphlet. [*Hands the material to the applicant and smiles*]

Essentially, during these nine months you will be a shift supervisor and you will work very closely with the manager of the restaurant—sort of like the "buddy-buddy" system. The manager will reinforce what you learned in the orientation sessions. For these nine months your pay will be elevated to $300 per week.

After one year with the company you will be eligible for a one-week paid vacation. In the second year you *could* be offered an assistant manager position with an area restaurant with a *minimum* pay of $350 per week.

Finally, after the second year you could move up to manager status by bidding on a restaurant—bidding is done by seniority—and this move may involve a relocation on your part.

Well, Sharon, I guess that's the best summary I can offer of our policy for trainees, supervisors, and managers. Is it too much to digest too quickly?

Young: No, Mr. Michaels, it seems to fit together very nicely.

Michaels: I have a lot of information about you, Sharon. Would you have any questions that *you* might want to ask?

Young: During this 12-week orientation, what type of hours would I be working?

Michaels: Sessions start at 8:45 A.M. You'll spend two hours in class and one hour in the kitchen. Then there's a lunch break.

When you return from lunch, there are another two hours of class and a one-hour demonstration. Finally, you have a one-hour classroom summary and then dinner.

Trainees usually spend a couple of hours in the evening preparing for the next day's orientation sessions. The remaining part of the evening is free time as are Saturday afternoons and Sundays.

Young: So, there are classes on Sunday mornings?

Michaels: Classes are held from 10 until noon.

Young: I see. What about shift hours for the nine months following the orientation?

Michaels: Sharon, the schedule would be determined by the restaurant manager. However, you would be working one of the three shifts during those nine months. Most likely you would start on the 11 P.M. to 7 A.M. shift because that would be the shift with the least amount of activity. Then you would be eased slowly into the busier shifts.

Young: What about relocation? You mentioned that it was possible. Where do you have plans for expansion?

Michaels: Within the next two years, we will be adding restaurants in the Virginia, North Carolina, and northern and southern areas of Florida. We also would like to expand in western New York and eastern Ohio.

It is premature to ask, but would you have a preference for a particular area?

Young: Oh, [*pause*] I would not mind western New York. That's where I was born and raised. Florida would be nice—the weather is nice most of the year. [*Long pause*] Would there be any special requirements for clothing?

Michaels: No, not really. The only thing we require of our management trainees, supervisors, and managers is that they dress neatly, wear business attire, and dress conservatively on the job. [*Long pause, the interviewer looks at his watch*] Would there be any further questions that you would have at this time?

Young: [*Having seen the interviewer's clue that the interview was coming to a close*] No, Mr. Michaels, I think that you have answered all the questions that I had. However, I would like to reinforce what I said earlier about my qualifications for this position. [*pause*]

[*Smiles*] I think the varied experiences that I have had in the restaurant business would help me considerably. I also believe that my educational preparation and my ability to comprehend things quickly would give me a solid foundation for the management trainee position. These two factors and my ability to work well with people should make me a strong candidate. [*Pauses and smiles*]

Closing

Michaels: It's been a pleasure meeting with you today, Sharon, and discussing your qualifications for the position. As you know we haven't finished our personal interviews with all of our candidates, but I am sure that we will have made our decisions by late Monday of next week. I will be contacting you by phone on Tuesday morning and let you know our decision at that time.

In the meantime, if you have any questions, please don't hesitate to call me at the number on my business card. [*Hands candidate his business card*]

Young: I appreciate your time, Mr. Michaels, and the opportunity to discuss my career goals with you. I'll be home on Tuesday morning to accept your call personally. Thanks again. [*Candidate extends her hand and shakes the interviewer's hand*]

Michaels: Take care, Sharon, and have a good evening.

Source: Reprinted with permission of Paul Seland, Niagara County Community College and Scott Foresman and Company.

CONCLUSION

Interviewing skills get better with practice. Knowing this, make an effort to see if your career placement office conducts workshops with mock seminars. It may be that you can enroll in a professional development course for the same purpose. If these two options are not available, gather two or more friends together and try asking and answering the questions in this chapter. It will help and can also be enjoyable. Finally, when the time arrives for you to look for full-time employment, sign up for as many interviews as possible.

QUESTIONS FOR REVIEW AND DISCUSSION

1. How can you minimize the stress of an interview?

2. Why is appearance so important in an interview?

3. What are the different types of interviews you can expect to encounter?

4. How can you prepare for the question-and-answer interview?

5. What is the purpose of an interview from an employer's viewpoint?

6. How can you prepare for a question regarding salary?

7. What are three postinterview activities?

8. What can the follow-up letter accomplish?

9. Why might an interviewer ask you to describe your biggest weakness?

10. What are the different types of interviews you can expect to encounter?

APPLICATION EXERCISES

1. Research and describe the type of position for which you hope to apply upon graduation.

2. Working with another person, conduct a mock interview using the job description above and questions from this chapter. Critique each other's performance.

3. Working in groups of four, conduct team interviews with three people interviewing one. Be sure to set up a realistic situation: Begin the interview with the interviewee walking in the room and shaking hands, and so forth.

4. Write a sample follow-up letter, again using the information from question 1.

5. As a group, discuss possible answers to common interview questions.

Dynamics of Corporate Communications

Learning Outcomes

After studying this chapter, you should be able to:

❶ Define and discuss the concepts of "corporate culture" and the "grapevine."

❷ Provide definitions for the business terms discussed under the heading, "The Language of Business."

❸ Explain the things a person must do to conduct an effective meeting.

❹ Use the telephone as an effective tool for business communication.

INTRODUCTION

College and university students often talk about preparing to go out into the "real world," implying that life as a student is not the same as the life that will follow. This is true because the culture or "way of life" of a student is very different from any other phase of life. Student life is so distinctive that most first-year students experience some degree of difficulty adjusting to it. The same challenge of adjustment holds true for the college graduate who heads out into the business world. It makes sense for students to begin learning as much as they can about the corporate world so many of them will be entering.

THE CORPORATION: A NEW WAY OF LIFE

An older couple we know travel each year to a foreign country. Prior to each trip, their preparation follows much the same pattern. They read extensively about the culture of the country they are about to visit, trying to learn as much *beforehand* as they possibly can about that culture. They study the country's history, its heroes, value systems, customs, practices, and language. In this way, they guard against culture shock and ensure that their visit will be successful. Their preparation makes good, practical sense.

In a similar way, those of you who are ready to enter the world of business also need to engage in preparation because most corporations have their own cultures and their own way of life. In their book, *The Rites and Rituals of Corporate Life,* Terrence E. Deal and Allan A. Kennedy point out that businesses are living organizations whose real existence is in the hearts and minds of its employees. They contend that the culture that the employees create affects practically everything from who gets promoted and what decisions are made, to how employees dress and conduct their day-to-day business.[1] If this is so, then you need to learn as much as possible about a company's culture *before* and *after* you become part of it. This holds equally true whether you are beginning your first job in business or later, when you may be planning a switch to greener pastures.

In short, you need to find out all you can about your company's culture. Is the company's philosophy liberal or conservative? What services and/or products do they market? What are the beliefs and values that they hold important? How much freedom and creativity do they allow their employees? Who are their "heroes" and are employees expected to imitate them? What are their customs and rituals? What standards of behavior are expected of employees? These are some of the aspects of corporate culture that you need to examine.

Prospective employees can learn about a company's culture from a few different sources. Find out what the company says about itself in its annual reports, press releases, and advertising. Talk to employees of the company, when possible. Use the interview to learn more. Ask questions. Generally, a conscious effort in these sources will reveal much of what you need to know. Once you have been hired, however, you need to learn even more about the new culture in other ways.

The best advice for a newly arrived employee is to observe quietly and listen a lot. Learn from the "natives." They have been there longer than you and generally have much to offer. A word of caution is necessary: Beware of disgruntled employees who, instead of working to improve the things that need improving, suffer from negativism and wish to pass their discontent on to others. Look to those with positive messages who are tapped into the lines of corporate communication. Make your own assessment of the corporate culture and decide whether you can be happy working and living in it. Don't let others do that for you.

Grapevines

Once established in your new job, it is inevitable that you will tune into the company "grapevine" or informal channel of communication. Grapevines are much like cultural universals in that every company and industry seems to have one. Communication is much more active on the grapevine when the regular lines of communication have stopped functioning.

As a new employee, you need to listen to the grapevine even though it is the least desirable way of exchanging information. Vanessa Dean Arnold of Management World claims that, "Some studies indicate the grapevine to be 80 to 85 percent accurate, with inaccuracies in the form of incompleteness rather than wrong information." The problem is that the missing 15 to 20 percent of the message might be vital to a full understanding of the message.

The advice is simple. Use good judgment when you evaluate news from the grapevine. Ask yourself who is transmitting messages and what are their motives? Be suspect of the person who always carries bad news or who is constantly critical of fellow employees or company policies. The grapevine is part of corporate culture and, like all other parts of that culture, you need to come to understand it for what it is.

THE LANGUAGE OF BUSINESS

As any world traveler will attest, the foremost barrier to communication is one's inability to understand the language of people from another culture. Individuals who take the time beforehand to learn the language of the new culture they are visiting have a distinct advantage over people who do not. They are immediately accepted on a different level than the people who arrive unprepared, fumbling and awkward in their efforts to understand and to make themselves understood.

In a similar way, those of you who are preparing for careers in business are like the travelers to a new land. Business is a new way of life and it has its own vocabulary. You can give yourself an advantage by learning the terms that are part of business history and are used in everyday give-and-take transactions.

The list that follows is not intended to be a complete vocabulary. That will come in time as it does to all individuals who stay in a new land. Think of these terms as ones that are commonly used in the culture you are preparing to enter. If you learn them, the transition to business will be smoother, with fewer awkward moments and less culture shock. You will be able to participate fully in communication immediately without feeling like a stranger from another place who does not understand what he or she reads or hears.

Antitrust laws. A series of laws, starting with the Sherman Act of 1890, passed by the federal government to forbid attempts by business firms to develop monopolies or restrain trade; that is, to eliminate competition through mergers and other kinds of combinations.

Aptitude tests. Used to determine a person's probability of success in a selected job.

Arbitration. Outside neutral parties assist in resolving conflict between labor and management or their disputing parties. The arbitrator is given the authority to act as a judge in making a fair decision. If both disputing parties agree beforehand to accept the arbitrator's decision, the arbitration is considered "binding."

Balance sheet. The accounting statement that summarizes the relationship of *assets* (the left side of the balance sheet), on the one hand, and the claims against those assets—the *liabilities*—by creditors or owners (the right side of the balance sheet), on the other.

Bear market. A market for securities in which prices are falling and buyers are showing little interest in buying.

Board of directors. A group of individuals given the power by law and by vote of stockholders to manage a corporation.

Board of Governors. The governing body of the Federal Reserve System, with seven members appointed by the president of the United States to serve single, 14-year terms.

Bull market. A market for securities in which prices are rising and buyers are interested in purchasing securities.

Capital. Buildings, machinery, tools, equipment, materials, and money that a business must have to operate; sometimes used to describe the amount of ownership in a business.

Centralized. The type of situation in which decision-making authority is concentrated at the upper levels of the organization.

Chain of command. Means by which authority flows from top to bottom in the organization.

Collective bargaining. The process of negotiating a labor agreement between management and labor representatives.

Computer hardware. The machinery of computers.

Computer languages. A collection of numbers or computer words that the computer is able to understand. Different languages may be required for different purposes.

Computer software. Ideas, systems, programs, and methods required to run computer machinery or hardware.

Corporation. An artificial body that is endowed by law to act with most of the rights, powers, and obligations of natural persons—among them the rights to own property, incur debts, and be sued for damages.

Delegation. The process of making specific work assignments to individuals within the organization and providing them with the right or power to perform these functions.

Downsizing. The reduction in the number of employees by a company for the purpose of cutting costs and increasing profits.

Dow Jones Stock Averages. An index of stock prices published since 1884 and comprising 65 leading stocks, of which 30 are industrial stocks (DJIA), 20 are transportation company stocks, and 15 are public utility stocks.

Entrepreneur. A person who undertakes to start and conduct an enterprise or business.

Equity. The value remaining in business or property in excess of any liability or mortgage.

Federal Reserve System. Legislation passed in 1913 established a system of 12 district Federal Reserve banks, whose operations are under the control of the Federal Reserve Board. The principal function of the district Federal Reserve banks is to make loans to commercial banks that are members of the system. The district banks also influence the money supply by the purchase and sale of government bonds.

Income statement. A financial statement summarizing sales and subtracting expenses incurred in a period of time to arrive at a profit or loss for the period; often called a profit and loss statement or a statement of income.

Inventory. A list of all finished goods in stock, goods in the process of manufacture, and the raw materials used, made annually by a business concern.

Job description. Summarizes the purpose, principal duties, and responsibilities of a job.

Labor agreement. A contract between management and a union specifying terms and conditions of employment.

Line of credit. An arrangement made by a company or an individual with a bank, giving the company or individual the right to borrow funds as needed up to a certain amount.

List price. The price printed on the package or on a price list.

Management. The process of planning, organizing, influencing, and controlling to accomplish organizational goals through the coordinated use of human and material resources.

Management by objectives (MBO). A systematic and organized approach that allows management to attain maximum results from available resources by focusing on specific, individual goals.

Merit rating system. A system for evaluating employees for possible promotion or salary increases on the basis of their performance, productivity, or merit.

Merger. Two companies join together to form a new company.

Nepotism. The practice of hiring one's own relatives to work in the organization.

Net worth. The value of an owner's property after all claims of creditors have been deducted.

Partnership. A form of business ownership in which two or more persons own the business.

Policies. A predetermined general course or guide established to provide direction in decision making.

Prime rate. The interest rate commercial banks charge to their best customers with an unquestioned credit rating; usually the lowest rate charged by such banks for short-term business loans.

Product life cycle. The idea that products are introduced, grow in sales and profitability, reach maturity, and then decline in sales and profitability.

Proprietorship. A business owned and controlled by one person.

Quality circles. Groups of people working together who meet regularly to discuss work-related problems and solutions.

Reengineering. Companies reorganize their management structure in order to operate more efficiently.

Small Business Administration (SBA). The federal agency that provides financial, managerial, and procurement assistance to small businesses.

Span of management. The limit to the number of employees a manager can effectively supervise.

Specialization. Employees concentrate their efforts on one particular activity or subject.

Strategic planning. The determination of how the organizational objectives will be achieved. Primarily accomplished by top-level management.

Team building. A conscious effort to develop effective work groups throughout the organization.

Theory X. Traditional philosophy of human nature. Suggests that motivation of employees requires managers to coerce, control, or threaten employees in order to achieve maximum results.

Theory Y. A theory of human nature that provides an alternative to Theory X, suggesting instead that people are capable of being responsible and mature and should be treated accordingly. Theory Y management often allows employees to participate in decision making.

Top management. Referred to by titles such as president, chief executive officer, vice president, or executive director. Responsible for providing the overall direction of the firm.

Usury laws. Laws limiting the amount of interest a lender may charge a borrower for money.

Zero base budgeting. Requires management to take a fresh look at all programs and activities each year rather than merely building on last year's budget.

THE BUSINESS MEETING: SMALL GROUP COMMUNICATION

A major part of business communication takes place in meetings where you must interact with others in small groups. The authors of

Corporate Cultures, Terrence E. Deal and Allan A. Kennedy, contend that the most important management ritual continues to be the formal meeting. All companies have them, but their form varies widely in terms of the number held, the seating, table shape, who sits where, number and composition of attendees, and the actual conduct of the meeting.[2] Dorothy Sarnoff, author of *Make the Most of Your Best,* quotes a study of managerial work time done by Professor Henry Mintzberg of McGill University which shows that executives spend an average of 69 percent of their work life in meetings of one sort or another. She also quotes a survey in which executives rank meetings as the fourth biggest timewaster—the first three were time on the telephone, drop-in visitors, and ineffective delegation.[3] Because of the time devoted to meetings and the potential for them to be wasteful, you need to study the nature of meetings from both the point of view of one who conducts meetings and one who is a participant.

Whether you are a chairperson of or are simply conducting a meeting, the best way to ensure productive interchange is to prepare an agenda and send copies of it to all the participants prior to the meeting. This not only gives people notice of what will be discussed, but gives them the opportunity to formulate their ideas ahead of time. If you are in charge, start the meeting on time and tell the group how long the meeting will be and how much time is allotted to each topic. Encourage contributions from all present, but keep the discussion limited to the topics listed on the agenda. The biggest single obstacle to the successful conduct of a meeting is the tendency of speakers to wander off the topic to discuss irrelevant topics. Anyone who has ever participated in meetings knows that. It is the responsibility of the person in charge to stick to the agenda and to cut off long-winded speakers. End the meeting on time by summarizing what was said and what actions will result from the meeting. Finally, arrange for all participants to receive a copy of the minutes of the meeting and notify them of future meetings.

New employees normally attend meetings rather than conduct them. If this is to be your first role, follow these suggestions. When you receive an agenda, prepare your thoughts in advance; jot down notes which will serve as a reminder during the meeting. Don't be bashful. Say what you have to say, but be brief and stick to the point. Listen carefully to what others have to say, and keep your emotions under control. If all the participants conduct themselves accordingly, the sharing of ideas in group meetings can be a productive process from which both individuals and organizations can benefit.

TEN TIPS ON TELEPHONE TECHNIQUES

A great deal of business is conducted over the phone. One reason is that it is relatively inexpensive—the average expense of an industrial *in-person* sales call is over $204 per call. The average business letter costs more than $10 to produce. Telephone contacts also possess the advantage of information shared instantly. In addition, the lack of the face-to-face contact of the telephone has already been remedied by telecommunication technology allowing a visual dimension. You can learn to use the telephone if you follow these tips.

- Use the telephone when subjects require immediate attention and when the subjects lend themselves to a brief phone discussion. Leave more detailed issues which do not have the same urgency to their more appropriate forum, written correspondence or face-to-face meetings.

- As part of the overall organization of your workday, plan to make most of your phone calls at the same time. Research indicates that the majority of business phone calls are not completed on the first attempt. As indicated in Chapter 12, you can increase your chances of completing your calls by calling in the mornings from Tuesday to Friday. Do not place your calls on Monday mornings or near the end of a workday unless absolutely essential.

- Before you place an important call, jot down the items you wish to discuss in the order you wish to talk about them. This habit eliminates memory lapses and the need for further calls, which are more expensive and may be embarrassing or irritating.

- Identify yourself and the person whom you are calling immediately. For example, "Hello, this is George Patterson from Manville Steel. May I speak with Ruth Page?"

- Inquire about the timing of your call and then get to the point. "Ruth, do you have a few minutes to discuss the content of the training session you proposed last week?"

- Be a good listener. Apply all of the principles of active listening discussed earlier in this text. If necessary, take notes during the conversation.

- Be brief and initiate the end of the call before the other party does. You have no way of knowing how busy the other person is and how much of an interruption your call has made. Be considerate. It will be appreciated.

- When you are taking phone messages for others, write down all the facts and put a date and time of day on the note before you deliver it.

- Be courteous to all callers and return their calls at a time convenient to them. If a person persists in not returning your calls, write a business letter containing the message and keep a copy for your files.

- Regulate the use of the phone so that it does not interfere with your work schedule. Use it efficiently for the situations for which it is best suited and it will serve you well during your career.

CONCLUSION

One of the best ways to soften the "culture shock" that accompanies many first full-time jobs is to experience corporate cultures during your student years. Look for internships, practicums, summer employment, or community service learning opportunities that will give you early insights into how corporate cultures really work.

NOTES

1. Deal, Terrence E. and Allan A. Kennedy. *Corporate Cultures: The Rites and Rituals of Corporate Life.* Reading, MA: Addison-Wesley, 1982, p. 4.

2. Ibid.

3. Sarnoff, Dorothy. *Make the Most of Your Best.* New York: Holt, Rinehart, and Winston, 1983, p. 78.

QUESTIONS FOR REVIEW AND DISCUSSION

1. What is the "corporate culture" and what aspects of business can it affect?

2. Where can you learn about a company's culture?

3. How can an employee use the grapevine productively?

4. In which types of companies are the grapevines most active?

5. Why is it useful to learn your business vocabulary?

6. How much time does the average executive spend in meetings?

7. What is the biggest obstacle to successfully conducted meetings?

8. What steps can the person conducting a meeting take to be effective?

9. What steps can the person *attending* the meeting take to increase its effectiveness?

10. Describe at least four telephone tips that will help you to use telephone communications more effectively.

APPLICATION EXERCISES

1. Choose a local company that you can easily gain information about and write a brief description of its corporate culture.

2. List and define at least five terms not listed here which are the language of *your* future business.

3. Working in small groups of four to six, try problem solving. Choose a current social or campus issue. Choose a leader of the group, who should run the meeting according to the principles discussed in the chapter. When the group arrives at a unanimous decision, present its findings to the class.

4. Write a paragraph describing your most recent unsatisfactory telephone exchange. What went wrong and why? What could have been handled differently?

5. Working with a partner, conduct a telephone conversation based on one of the scenarios you described in question 4. Try to eliminate the problems you identified and create a more productive exchange.

FOR ADDITIONAL READING AND DISCUSSION

SELL YOUR CEO!
Winning the Corporate Image Battle in the 90s

by John J. McGrath

John J. Mcgrath, director of marketing and management communications, Argonne National Laboratory, delivered this speech to The Corridor Group, Chicago, Illinois, March 21, 1995. Though you may not be a CEO, his analysis offers guidance for marketing yourself and your company.

There are many excellent speakers in the United States. There also are many business executives. Apparently, the policy is not to intermingle the two.

Those are the words of Norman Augustine, chairman and CEO of Martin Marietta Corporation. I've known Norm Augustine for more than a decade. He is that rarest of creatures—an American chief executive who speaks common English, and speaks it well . . . even in public. When you consider that he's also a brilliant engineer, it's all the more remarkable because engineers (like doctors and lawyers) seemingly must shed the ability to speak common English in order to be licensed to practice.

The same might be said for CEOs. True, most CEOs earned their positions. True, they tend to be bright and fairly decisive. But in public, well . . .

OK, so what?

Why should we care? Why should CEOs care? If they turn a respectable profit, so what if they aren't especially charming and persuasive at the Rotary Club meeting . . . if they can be persuaded to attend at all!

Here are two reasons why we should care:

1. Organizations, like people, are not islands. Their ability to function, to succeed, to turn that profit, is directly affected by other organizations and groups at their boundaries. Like individual pieces of glass in a stained-glass window, each is both constrained and supported by its neighbors. For one to grow, for one to even move, its neighbors must cooperate.

2. Organizations don't speak. They can't. Nor can they attend that Rotary

Published in *Vital Speeches of the Day,* May 1, 1995.
Reprinted with permission

Continued on page 252

Continued from page 251

Club meeting. Only people can do that. So, the image projected by the individual tends to become in the audience's mind the image of the organization that person represents. And if that individual happens to be the CEO, the depth to which that image is impressed grows markedly.

So, the CEO's public image is the organization in the audience's mind. And strategic audiences, which we can call "boundary publics," directly influence the organization's ability to succeed.

Then why go at all?

After all, there's obvious risk in this image-transference business. Wouldn't it be better to avoid all risk and hide in the corporate office? Perhaps. *If* you, the communications executive, and your CEO were the only people interested in crafting an image for your organization. But you're not.

Many others would like to handle that task for you. And if you don't? Audiences, like nature, abhor a vacuum, so the image of your organization that is impressed upon them will be an image created by others. Who? The government, for one. Your unions, for another. Mike Wallace and his troops, maybe. Your competitors, perhaps. And how about those pesky environmentalists trained at the knee of Ralph Nader and Saul Alinsky?

It's a long list.

Recent history abounds with organizations that abdicated their roles as self-image shapers, only to find others more than willing to undertake the task. Exxon and the *Exxon Valdez* oil spill leap to mind. William Small, writing in *Public Relations Review,* put it this way:

> No company ever spent more to repair the damages of an industrial accident. None worked harder to marshal an army (and navy) to fight the damages to the environment. No corporation had to cover so much territory to repair the results. And probably no other company ever got a more damaging portrayal in the media.

Exxon's postspill actions did not cause an image problem; the way it communicated those actions did, coupled with the virtual invisibility of top company management. So, Exxon's public image was shaped by the State of Alaska, the U.S. Coast Guard, a legion of reporters, and the many environmental groups who never met a large organization they didn't hate.

But is all this communication and image making really the CEO's job? Can't we hire, say, an actor to do it? Or delegate the job to a glib young executive?

International management and organization-design expert Henry Mintzberg says every CEO has three essential duties: (1) direct supervision, (2) development of the organization's strategy, and (3) management of the organization's boundary conditions—its relations with its external environment.

Literature relating to the first two duties is voluminous. Literature relating to the third is scattered and occasionally contradictory. No one in the communications profession should be surprised about that. We encounter this daily. What's more, too many top managers view what Mintzberg terms an essential duty as an incidental chore to be avoided whenever possible.

We can agree, I think, that top management's responsibility at and beyond the organization's boundaries is largely a communication responsibility. However, no commonly accepted model exists for decision, execution, and assessment of communication opportunities. Within even some of the largest and most venerable organizations, the process used is haphazard and inconsistent at best, and nonexistent at worse. Decisions frequently are made at the middle-management level, and sometimes lower, by persons acting with neither strategic guidance nor a "big-picture" perspective on the organization's situation and external environment.

After the Supreme Court extended First Amendment free-speech protection to corporations in cases including *First National Bank* v. *Belotti* in 1978 and *Consolidated Edison* v. *New York Public Service Commission* in 1980, noted constitutional-law expert Constance Vibbert wrote:

> The Court created the possibility for corporations to assume a large role in society, and corporations quickly are grasping this opportunity. More and more corporations view their public

speech as more than a promotional mechanism for products and services, but also as a social responsibility.

Professor Vibbert was optimistic. She's talking about the *right* to speak. That's decidedly different from the *will* and the *skill* to speak clearly, consistently, and in one voice. Though opponents of corporate free speech make much of the magnitude of an organization's resources compared with those of the individual, the history of organizational external communications in the United States demonstrates that money, manpower, and intentions do not assure success.

Two years ago, I was in Nashville speaking to a business group. One of my fellow speakers was a bright senior executive who obviously had prepared very hard for her speech. Too hard. No doubt at her direction, the company whipped up several handouts, a video, and slides for the talk. She and several assistants came well armed with statistics. Numbers. Dull, droning numbers illustrated by many tedious charts.

What happened? The audience, which had been sympathetic initially, moved from interest to apathy to outright hostility. Fortunately, her speech followed rather than preceded mine—the way she left that audience, Mother Teresa and the Vienna Boys Choir couldn't have won them back. Despite her company's

Continued on page 254

Continued from page 253

money, manpower, and good intentions, she failed because she didn't have a clear objective for her talk, because she hadn't identified with her audience, and because she didn't know how to use her information to persuade and entertain.

By the way, with her talk over and the audience looking for rope and a suitable tree, her assistants came up and told her what a marvelous job she had done! If she believed those sycophants, she'll repeat the disaster next time. And she just might believe them. Most senior executives think they do a good job in public. Sometimes it's pure ego. In many cases it's because they're surrounded by yes-men who believe telling the boss he's wonderful is career enhancing. Sadly, they're sometimes right.

But what kind of a career can the organization itself expect if it's unknowingly alienating one or more of those boundary publics we've been discussing. Mintzberg defines them as those who control or otherwise have power over the organization (such as its owners, government agencies, unions, and pressure groups), publics which influence the organization's fate.

Oddly, even though its future and fate may be at stake, an organization's communications with those influencers (when it occurs at all) may not be linked to the organization's strategic objectives. Sounds incredible, doesn't it? Yet, not long ago the Wyatt Company published a survey of communications professionals. Just 58.1 percent of them agreed that their organization's communication objectives are linked to business objectives, and 83.3 percent reported that their organizations conduct no formal review of return on communications investment!

Ronald Reagan knew better. We can learn much from him about effective CEO communication with boundary publics. For one thing, Reagan always understood *who* he was talking to, *why* he was doing it, and *what* both he and they wanted.

Reagan seems to have learned much from Aristotle, who some say Reagan knew personally. Aristotle believed the chief purpose of public oratory is persuasion, defined as:

> a conscious attempt by one individual to change the attitudes, belief, or behavior of another individual or group of individuals through the transmission of some message.

Aristotle sorted such persuasive oratory into three types:

1. Forensic or judicial (to prove the justice or injustice of an act).
2. Deliberative (to motivate an audience to act).
3. Ceremonial.

He then listed three methods of persuasion:

1. Logos (the appeal to reason).

2. Pathos (the appeal to emotion).

3. Ethos (the appeal to character).

Aristotle published his theories in 360 B.C. I've been in this business for a while and I still haven't found anyone with more communications insight than that ancient Greek.

OK then, it's essential that the CEO establish and reinforce the organization's image in public. It's essential that the CEO know why he or she is out there: to persuade the audience to do something. And it's essential to know how to persuade. But we need something else to make that CEO a great communicator. Something that President Reagan also had: terrific marketing.

For guidance on what constitutes "terrific marketing," let's look at the folks who depend on it to pay their bills—professional speakers. Among their guidelines for success, they include:

1. *Mission-focus*—know who you are, what you have to offer, and what you hope to achieve.

2. *Target marketing*—identify your target audiences and then stick to the target.

3. *Audience orientation*—know who your audience is and what that audience wants.

4. *Common-ground baseline*—know what common-ground you and your audience share, then base your presentation firmly on that turf. (There's always some common ground with a boundary public. You'll find it *at* the boundary.)

Many pros say it's hard to overstress the importance of being market driven. View each target public as a client. By doing the research, looking at the trends, collecting clippings from the trade journals, talking to the experts, and so forth, you focus on selling what the client wants to buy.

And all the effort is, of course, focused on target audiences. Which leads to the question: Who are those boundary publics and which should be targeted? Each organization has a different answer to that question, so I won't attempt a global answer here. But I will tell you this: Left to their own devices, top management always will choose the friendliest audiences.

In 1992 and 1993, I studied 24 organizations of varying size in the United States and Canada, identifying which boundary groups senior managers talk with professionally when they're away from their desks. Results? Senior managers spend about 60 percent of that time talking at meetings of industry and trade associations and professional societies. They devote another 18 percent to events their own organization sponsors; about 14 percent to local, regional, and national civic groups; 6 percent is spent

Continued on page 256

Continued from page 255

with consumer groups; and just 2 percent is spent on all other activities, including conversations with government officials and legislators.

All of which means our top managers are spending more than three-quarters of their external "talking time" talking to each other—peers at company, industry and professional gatherings. Relatively few resources are dedicated to communicating with broader communities which arguably exert a much greater influence on the organization's operating arena and future.

Tackling broader and perhaps tougher audiences may not make for relaxing evenings for the CEO, but it may be the best tactic for the long-term success of the organization. And marketing becomes much more important when we persuade the CEO to venture outside the warm, fuzzy environment of an industry association meeting.

There are those who contend that marketing the CEO is a semimystical art, best done by wizards in the moonlight. But I don't think so. I think it's good, old, basic product marketing. The only trick is viewing the CEO as a product. Which of course, in this context, he or she is. (I have, however, found it best not to tell the CEO that's how you're approaching it.)

Unfortunately, we tend to begin this product-marketing task with a not-too-appealing product. You may wish you had an award-winning actor to represent you in public, but chances are you have a CEO who mumbles in monotone acronyms and hates every minute of it. That isn't because of a shortcoming within the CEO. It's due to a shortcoming in the organizational system which produces CEOs. As these executives rose through the organizational ranks, one lesson was constant: Superiors speak for the organization in public; you don't. Typically, they received no training and no "out-of-town tryouts."

Chances are your CEO's personality already mirrors that of the organization, or it mirrors hers or his. But marketing means we need to cause them to look, act, and speak the part in public, too.

Our advertising brothers know that audiences identify best with people they perceive to be just like them. Reaching that identification demands a thorough demographic understanding of the audiences, to include age, gender mix, occupation, political tendencies, average education, interests, pertinent jargon, and their wants and needs. Wants-and-needs are vital because the first question in every listener's mind is: What's in this for me? By knowing what the average member of that audience wants, our CEO can make key points in the context of how those points, if acted upon by the audience, help the group achieve its goals. There is no more effective way to make a point, no better way to persuade.

What factor is most often overlooked in marketing the CEO?

Hands down, it's that public appearances always involve *two* levels of communication with the audience—the one for which the CEO has a script and the silent one which he or she projects to the audience. The latter is nonverbal communication and, unlike the formal presentation, it commences when the CEO enters the event and continues all the time he or she is there.

Nonverbal communication is the transfer of information without the use of words, and includes facial expressions, head movements, body positions and acts, tones of voice, clothing, and even odor. It can be as powerful as verbal communication. Indeed, it often is *more* powerful because people need not be conscious of sending or receiving a message to communicate nonverbally.

Gestures are perhaps the most consciously recognized nonverbal form; they come easily to some people, and not so easily to others. CEOs also communicate nonverbally by what they wear and by whether they appear comfortable at the event.

Nonverbal messages express emotion and attitude; they can reinforce, diminish or counter the impact of concurrent verbal messages. Some researchers contend that specific nonverbal acts have specific meanings. You may be familiar with Julius Fast's book *Body Language* and many similar works. But these experts do not always assign the same meanings to the same acts.

What happens if the verbal and nonverbal messages conflict? Audiences almost always dismiss the verbal in favor of the nonverbal. It's that important!

There's a famous but little-discussed example of that. You've probably seen film of President John Kennedy's speech in front of the Berlin Wall. Next time you see it, watch closely what happens when Kennedy says, "Ich bin ein Berliner!" Sure, the audience goes wild, but there's a brief pause between the remark and the reaction.

Why that pause? Well, some researchers and linguists argue that what Kennedy really was saying as the audience would perceive it was: "I am a jelly doughnut."

You see, residents of Berlin don't call themselves "Berliners." Indeed, the only thing they do call a "Berliner" is a jelly-filled pastry. No matter what the words actually meant, however, the audience briefly paused and then cheered enthusiastically. Thus Kennedy's intent was communicated clearly by his actions and demeanor. That pause was the time it took the audience to recognize a conflict between verbal and nonverbal messages, then select and react to the nonverbal. The nonverbal "symbolic speech" he delivered overshadowed the literal text he read!

Had Kennedy ever returned to Berlin, he probably would have gotten it right the next time. Because every effective

Continued on page 258

Continued from page 257

CEO marketing effort features continuous improvement. Learning from each appearance, and fine-tuning so that the next one always is better than the last.

To be productive, evaluation must occur on two levels. The first is the instant event, examining impact achieved versus impact intended and forecast. The second and more important level is the degree to which the total communications plan was furthered.

Most external appearances by senior management are not evaluated. Of those that are, many are evaluated subjectively: Did the audience applaud, did the speaker return to the office happy, did someone praise him or her at the event? Such subjective judgments are of little use. Moreover, the judgments tend to change as the people involved change. The process becomes haphazard and unreliable. Objective evaluation is uncommon for several reasons:

- Pre-event goals frequently are too vague to permit effective postevent evaluation on any but subjective terms.

- Measurement and evaluation often are additional expenses deemed to be avoidable.

- Some managements are not interested in objective evaluation.

- Some communications managers fear such evaluation.

Yet objective evaluation is essential to a well-managed, continually fine-tuned program, and return on investment cannot be calculated without it.

The key to objective evaluation after the event is objective goal setting before it. The more precise the goal, the faster and more efficient the measurement and evaluation. This basically involves answering two questions before the event: "Specifically *what* do we intend to achieve?" and "*How will we know* that we have achieved it?" Or put another way: "In what way do we predict the primary audience will behave differently after the event than before it?" The answers must be a realistic, quantifiable measure of projected postevent behavioral changes in the primary audience. Armed with that yardstick, we later can measure the relative success of the appearance. Evaluation then follows measurement, and revision follows evaluation.

Over time, this measure-and-improve process creates a database useful in isolating significant variables in current appearances under evaluation. In short, this is a building process in which evaluation becomes more efficient and more accurate over time. If measurement and evaluation suggest revision, any revision should achieve one of three goals:

1. Improve the consistency, quality, pertinence and impact of the message.

2. Heighten exposure to our target

audience (and decrease exposure to nontarget audiences).

3. Expend fewer organizational resources to achieve 1 and 2.

Achieve *consistency* first. No matter what the program's strategic goal or goals are, its overriding tactical goal should be consistency of message. All initial program revisions should be aimed at achieving that. It is the first mark of quality. Only after the organization is delivering consistent messages—no matter the presenter and no matter the audience—can it profitably move to higher levels of quality and pertinence. ("Consistency" here means absence of conflict, not sameness. For example, the CEO should not be telling those New York stock analysts of projected record profits while the director of labor relations is pleading red ink in negotiations with a union.)

Improving the quality and pertinence of the message usually involves doing a better job of telling the story in the audience's language, with "language" including the visual as well as the verbal. Measurement frequently indicates that a key point to the speaker, one he or she believes was made effectively, either was lost upon or misinterpreted by the audience. As is sometimes said of America and England, the U.S. general public and the U.S. business community are two "nations" separated by a common language—each assumes the other understands the intent of its words (or pictures), but that is not always so.

An audience will always presume their definitions apply, not yours.

Because we're seeking continuous improvement with minimum necessary risk, CEO marketing plans should embrace test marketing as a tool. Most don't.

Wherever possible, messages revised in form or substance should be test-marketed to an appropriate audience before the CEO or other senior executive employs them at high-value forums. Such tests may involve focus groups or, preferably, an "out-of-town" audience and a less prestigious forum, with the speaker someone other than the senior executive. Such secondary forums may not be handy when a CEO marketing plan is in its initial phase but, after a moderate period of development, forum choices from among multiple "value" levels will be possible.

I'll close with two vital "nevers": Never lie . . . and never condescend.

CEOs and their companies should always tell the truth. The only ethically acceptable alternative is silence, and silence is an abdication to your foes. Happily, telling the truth is both the *right* thing to do and the *smart* thing to do. You may pay a short-term price, but you'll reap a greater long-term reward. Joe Kordick, one of the executive team that brought Ford back from the brink of disaster in the early '80s, calls it "doing well by doing good."

Continued on page 260

Concluded from page 259

The second vital never: Never condescend.

No matter the value-level of forum and audience, no speaker should ever talk down to an audience. It alienates the crowd and always works against you.

There's a story about two 19th-century British leaders as told by a Victorian matron. She supposedly said:

> When I talk to Mr. Gladstone, I feel *he's* the most intelligent man in the world. But when I talk to Mr. Disraeli, I feel *I'm* the most intelligent woman in the world.

American business today includes very few Disraelis. And not all that many Norm Augustines. So they always stand out.

Yours can too.

Questions

1. According to McGrath, why is the "marketing" of the CEO so crucial to today's company?

2. What suggestions does he offer to management wishing to improve their communication skills?

3. Does any of McGrath's advice strike you as usable in your current stage of life? How?

Using New Communications Technology in Business

Learning Outcomes

After studying this chapter, you should be able to:

❶ List the benefits and concerns associated with mobile car phones.

❷ Explain how voice mail can be an effective supplement to personal telephone communication.

❸ Describe the appropriate use for fax machines in business communications.

❹ Define electronic mail and explain how computer users communicate with this medium.

❺ Recognize the advantages of conference calls.

INTRODUCTION

Today more sophisticated information technology is creating a faster flow of information in the information channel. This is referred to as the "collapsing of the information float." New technology not only speeds up the flow of information, but often changes the very nature and type of communication that takes place. Interactive television is a clear example of this kind of revolutionary change.

Similar transformations have been occurring in the workplace, dramatically altering patterns of business communication. Some of the more significant technological developments are mobile calls, voice mail, fax machines, electronic mail (E-mail), and conference calls. Employees who wish to keep current must familiarize themselves with each of the new communication tools, so that they may use each appropriately and to best advantage.

MOBILE CALLS

Cellular telephone technology has developed rapidly in recent years. This remarkable combination of telephone and radio technology has dramatically changed the way that business people use their travel and leisure time. Telephones are now commonly available in the coach and first-class sections on commercial aircraft. Boaters and golfers are no longer cut off from business communication, and the person on the street can dial clients from portable, handheld telephones. While these breakthroughs are important, the most significant change has been the widespread use of the mobile car phone. Today, companies and individuals must consider the role that mobile car phones can play in increasing productivity.

Advantages of Mobile Car Telephones

The arguments for mobile car phones are direct and convincing. Proponents of car phones quote business management experts who claim that the secret to success is improving personal productivity. Productivity is directly connected to how we utilize our time, and car phones allow us to transform previously unproductive time into productive time.

Some studies estimate that people who drive to work can gain as much as two hours each working day, a 25 percent increase in potentially productive time. This gain in time benefits not only professional people, but also sales, delivery, and service people. Time wasted driving and parking simply to find pay phones can be converted to more profitable activities. The cliché that "time is money" nonetheless holds true and becomes a strong argument for mobile car phones.

Cost and Safety

Once the benefits of mobile car phones are acknowledged, consideration and attention need to be given to the questions of cost and safety. As business investments, car phones are not for everyone. To justify the cost of the equipment, there must be clear evidence that having a mobile phone will permit an individual to be sufficiently more productive. This will vary by company and individual, but ultimately it requires an individual to estimate what his or her time is worth. Once that is determined, a direct comparison can be made with the cost of the car phone to see if the expense is justified.

Finally, businesspeople planning to use mobile car phones must take precautions to ensure that the telephone transaction doesn't jeopardize the primary activity of driving safely. Common sense is the best guide, but it also helps to drive more slowly when making calls, to keep calls brief, and to dial only when stopped for lights or when traffic is minimal.

VOICE MAIL

Technology is changing telephone communication inside offices as well as outside. Major telephone companies now offer many different services that businesses can select for their employees. One of the most useful services is voice mail, a telephone answering service that stores messages and uses a signal to alert employees that a message is waiting in the voice mailbox. Employees are able to erase the message from the voice mail's computer system after hearing the message, or they can retain it for future reference.

Properly used, voice mail can be a communications asset. Ideally, voice mail activates when all phone systems are busy or no one is in the office to answer calls personally. Callers can still leave messages with important content or simply ask that their call be returned.

Problems occur when voice mail is overused or misused. Callers quickly become frustrated when their efforts to make a personal business contact are met only with recorded messages. Effective communicators realize this and try to minimize the use of voice mail, realizing it is intended to be a *supplement,* not a replacement for live personal communication.

FAX MACHINES

The fax machine is perhaps the clearest example of a technological tool that is in step with the times. During the early 1990s, fax machines appeared everywhere; no business was complete without one. Even individuals who could not afford their own machine could send and receive fax messages from their local business centers for a fee. Fax machines extend the collapse of the information float even further and satisfy a public impatient to exchange business information.

Fax machines have this broad appeal because they allow users to transmit printed pictures of written copy or graphics immediately to a second party with a receiving fax machine. "Fax it to me" has become a standard part of today's business jargon.

As is the case with all the new technological communications supplements, fax machines must be used appropriately. When time can be saved by faxing important information or urgently needed written records, faxing is the method to choose. Too often however, fax machines are used for commonplace communications for which there is no pressing need. Such material is better sent through interoffice or regular mails. In all cases, the sender should choose the most suitable and cost-efficient medium of communication. While fax machines are a major advancement, they are not intended to replace the more traditional forms of communication such as business letters or telephone calls.

ELECTRONIC MAIL

One of the fastest growing forms of communication is electronic mail, or E-mail, a system in which senders type messages on computer screens. The messages are sent via data circuits run by major commercial networks such as CompuServe or America Online. Users of these services can now connect with one another through the Internet, the computer-linking service that allows users on one system to communicate with users on other systems. The number of users is increasing rapidly.

Both E-mail and fax machine communications are written messages and require different skills than oral communication. However, they share some characteristics with oral communication. For example, privacy cannot always be guaranteed, a fact which must be considered.

The major limitation of E-mail is that it can only be used when both parties have access to a computer and know how to use E-mail.

CONFERENCE CALLS

Some new technology offers businesses substantial savings and increased efficiency. Conference calling, which allows three or more persons at different locations (across the country or across the world) to talk on the same telephone connection, is an example of this type of technology. Whether the conference call is arranged with the assistance of an operator or with specially installed equipment, it can be a major improvement in business communication when conducted properly.

To be successful, conference calls must be directed by one person, just as any successful meeting needs a leader or chairperson. He or she should state what is to be discussed during the call and be sure that all parties have their chance to talk. To be productive, all participants should have advance notice of the conference call, so that they can properly prepare and gather information. Conference calls can save considerable time and expense, allowing group decisions to be made without requiring all parties to come together from different locales.

CONCLUSION

No technology can take the place of effective interpersonal communication skills. However, there is no question that new communication tools can enhance our ability to be quality communicators. This can only happen, however, if we learn to use technology properly. We must also understand that the new technologies can offer disadvantages if they are misused.

QUESTIONS FOR REVIEW AND DISCUSSION

1. What are three of the more significant technologies currently transforming business communication?

2. What are the benefits of car phones?

3. What are the disadvantages of car phones?

4. What are the advantages of voice mail?

5. What are some of the problems with voice mail?

6. Has the fax machine eliminated other forms of business communication? Which remain?

7. What is E-mail?

8. What are the limitations of E-mail?

9. What are the advantages of conference calls?

10. What steps can you take to ensure a successful conference call?

APPLICATION EXERCISES

1. Conduct a survey of car phone users to determine car phone usefulness.

2. If your school or work has a voice mail system, write a brief critique of its effectiveness. Have you found it to be useful? How does it change *your* communication?

3. Which communication option would you choose to communicate the following? Don't forget the traditional letter or phone call also are options.

   a. Laying off an employee.

   b. Congratulating an employee on a project well done.

   c. Announcing the date and time of a future meeting.

   d. Requesting a copy of a colleague's report.

   e. Last-minute notification that an office is closing for the day.

   f. Making an important decision based on input from several colleagues from different locations.

FOR ADDITIONAL READING AND DISCUSSION

CLOSING THE GAP BETWEEN BUSINESS AND TECHNOLOGY
Success in the 1990s

by John Parker

This speech was delivered by John Parker, senior vice president and chief information officer, Sea-Land Service, Inc., at the Nolan Norton Institute, Tarpon Springs, Florida, February 7, 1991. Parker describes the changing nature of business communication and emphasizes that the key to success is to use communication technology effectively.

We've made a switch. Alex (Mandl, chief executive officer of Sea-Land) is unable to attend today. But since we were invited to talk about information technology (IT) in the 1990s—who better to fill in than the top techie?

To those who share my responsibilities as leaders of technology groups in your respective companies, be assured I am a long-serving, long-suffering member of the technology fraternity who remembers being awed by the announcement of the IBM 1401 about 30 years ago.

To those of you with nontechnical responsibilities, I'll try to keep my talk today in English.

Published in *Vital Speeches of the Day,* May 15, 1991.
Reprinted with permission

In fact, I want to take a tour of life on *both* sides of the gulf of technology. That's the expanse bordered on one side by managers thinking, "I wish these technoids would get their heads out of their terminals and learn what I really need." And on the other by technoid types thinking, "I could bump market share by five points if these management types would try to think a little bit beyond next quarter and grasp the vision of what information technology could really do."

How many meetings have we all attended in which one side is talking share points, ROI, and sustained competitive advantage and the other is talking relational databases, distributive processing and expert systems?

Nose to nose . . . but miles apart from really joining forces to get the business where it needs to go.

Welcome to the information revolution—1991.

But this is the decade when closing the gap between the business and its information technology support will separate the winners from the losers.

Continued on page 268

Continued from page 267

It's the decade where we are going to come to grips with the single most important measure of information technology's impact on a business enterprise.

ACCESS.

By access, I mean *all* the elements: the technologies, the relationships, and the applications that must come together if IT is to live up to its promise of a mechanism to transform the business.

Even though IT's applications are as unique as the companies it serves, we can still distill the essence of access down to two points.

First, how it happens.

And second, who has it.

The first step on the path to creating access is to understand how the company is wired.

I'm not talking about circuits; that's the easy part. I'm talking about the ways the information flows through a company, the wiring, and what it does along the way. It's an understanding of the pressure points of a company and how it fits into its competitive environments. The unique and distinctive competencies that can be leveraged. The critical points where you win or lose advantage. The points where performance and change count the most.

Many companies in attempting to use technology for strategic gain have skipped this first step of full self-understanding. And they've paid the price. For all the spectacular successes with IT, there have also been some world class flameouts that cost money and careers.

The hardware and software execution was often flawless. But the results were towers of technology that nobody wanted to to live in or they were isolated systems that were powerful, but far too easily duplicated.

These innovators actually suffered a competitive disadvantage by bearing a heavy development cost burden, which their competitors then happily copied at a fraction of the cost.

Others were able to pinpoint a distinctive competence in their firm. And they had tremendous success in leveraging it with information technology.

Usually these success stories boil down to "computer-aided something"—computer-aided manufacturing, computer-aided marketing, computer-aided distribution, computer-aided portfolio management, etc. But the problem for many of them is that after they hit one home run, they never hit another.

That says one of two things to me. Either their firms were so one dimensional that they only had one distinctive competence or, more likely, their one-shot success was as much a matter of luck as a feat of strategic foresight.

When you fully understand the wiring of the company—and you begin to leverage that understanding with the power of technology—you are heading for home base. The computer aided enterprise is an enterprise with not just one distinctive competence, but many.

An enterprise that is gaining the most powerful sustainable advantage of all: to learn faster than the competition. We'll be seeing more and more of this kind of enterprise. They will be lean, agile, and lightning fast. With luck, a few may even be based in this country.

They won't be measured as much by what they have, or where they are, or what they sell as by the power of their access to information and the rate at which they can evolve to seize new opportunities and meet new threats.

As access spreads, it is changing a lot of rules about how businesses are organized. There are some interesting biological parallels here. As life evolves, more complex forms develop. And at the top of the chain are life forms with the most complex nervous systems. Their competitive advantage is their ability to process information.

One could argue that the 1920s, Alfred P. Sloan, General Motors model of division decentralization was necessary because the corporate organizations of that bygone era had undeveloped nervous systems.

As technology has enriched and expanded the corporate nervous system, more complex forms have developed. Like matrix organizations, global line of business concepts, strategic alliances, and network organizations. They're now at the top of the Darwinian chain.

One of the most important kinds of

access is the kind given to customers. Now, it's becoming synonymous with control. The customer wants to be able to not only get at information but also be able to work with that information. They want it to give them options. They want to take control of those pieces of your business that impact theirs. And more and more frequently they are willing to give you the same kind of access inside their organization to make the relationship work.

It adds a whole new dimension to distributive information power. Once, that meant distributing information resources inside the organization. Now it means distributing information resources outside. Look at one of the hot-button selling points in telecommunications. Companies like MCI and AT&T aren't really competing on price any more.

They're now competing on issues like network control. They're selling virtual networking, which gives the customer the ability to see, change, and even fix traffic flowing through a logical subset of the real physical network.

And consider the evolution of electronic data interchange. EDI is defined as replacing paper exchange with electronic exchange. In a lot of businesses, the exchange of paper goes back hundreds of years. In my business, the original entrepreneurs were the Phoenicians. They used clay tablets, wooden styli, and a

Continued on page 270

269

Continued from page 269

cruciform alphabet for their pre-EDI exchanges. And even though the first generation of EDI is transforming business to business communications, It is still exchanging the same basic information that the Phoenicians did 4,000 years ago.

Let me now move from what I've been talking about a step or two closer to the real, everyday world. At least the one encountered by a global transportation company bouncing back from some tough times.

But before I tell you how Sea-Land is trying to harness information technology, I'll need to tell why. In 1956, a trucking executive named Malcolm McClean shipped goods in a metal container from Port Newark, New Jersey, to Houston, Texas. It started the age of containerization, which today is the heart of the shipping business.

In a lot of ways the emergence of containerization has enabled the global economy. It still boggles the mind that it makes economic sense to ship bottled water from the middle of France to Duluth, Minnesota. Or even more startling that it is cheaper to collect waste newsprint in the United States and ship it 3,000 miles to Europe than it is to collect newsprint in Europe for recycling. The fact that shipments can now move for pennies per ton mile has opened markets and resources in an explosion of international trade.

For two decades, Sea-Land had this industry. We defined the standards and always outdistanced the competition. But like a lot of companies that enjoy that kind of dominance, we were due for a fall. And we took ours in the early 80s. We were big, maybe a little arrogant. But worst of all, we were slow to change.

We started getting hammered from all sides. A strong dollar hurt our cost structure, just as the market was becoming crowded with too many companies with too many ships. Foreign competitors starting showing up, many of them were being subsidized by their governments and their first priority wasn't making a return on investment of the kind demanded by Wall Street.

Next thing we knew we were in a scuffle with a raider, and almost got sold off for our spare parts, as some of you may recall from the book *Barbarians at the Gate*. Then in 1986, we were acquired by CSX, which ran one of the biggest railroads in the United States. The acquisition brought stability, new resources, and opportunities, but it didn't make things any easier in the market.

We knew we had to get closer to our customers, offer them more than the other guy. And we had to offer it faster and with more flexibility. So, we made two important moves.

First, we pushed responsibility from our Edison, New Jersey, headquarters out to our regional offices. By breaking down the hierarchy, we felt we could break down barriers to fast action for our customers. We did it carefully, after a lot of study, and as humanely as possible. But the bottom line is, we went into reorganization with a 12 level table of organization and came out with only 7, max.

Second, we redefined our mission. We set our sights on being more than a company that moves goods across water. We set out to be a point-to-point transportation and distribution company, one that literally offers door-to-door service worldwide.

Time and your patience won't let me take you on a global tour of the information infrastructure that is the foundation of this new model. But I can give you the highlights.

The backbone is a network of terrestrial and satellite circuits that links five continents. It's a web that literally embraces the globe. All controlled by an international system of data centers with on-line customer help centers that roll from continent to continent . . . never sleeping . . . following the sun. The volume of information flowing through the network is staggering. Every day, almost a million messages cross the network between Sea-Land and our customers. We're spending considerable time and money to leverage the power of this global network with the right software applications.

Our Sea-Trac system was the first real-time PC-based transportation software anywhere. A major share of our largest customer firms, who account for 15 percent of volume around the world, use it

exclusively. It gives them on-line booking and tracking, and offers sailing schedules and customs information.

We also custom-design systems for selected industries. Our Sea-Lect system is specially made for perishables. Another system, called Cheers, is tailored to the needs of the wine and spirit industries. Other customer workstation solutions are under development.

One of our newest technologies—in fact we're still testing it—is equipment tracking with passive radio tags. The tags can trigger electronic readers on cranes, in container warehousing yards, and other critical locations to automatically record shipment progress. It's a big investment, but it's promising. It can take cargo tracking to a new level of speed and accuracy.

Our systems are also steadily taking paper out of the service equation. With our rail partners today, we're already 100 percent paperless in location tracking. And we were the first shipping company to go paperless with U.S. Customs for all ports and all inland destinations.

We're not there yet with our trucking partners. But we will be soon. Because we're demanding it. We've recently opened negotiations with trucking firms that we will only do business with those companies that could connect with us electronically.

These paperless operations signal a very important step. Even with computers

Continued on page 272

Concluded from page 271

on every desk, as long as paper is the product of the process, we're still doing things pretty much the way they were done in the past. We won't really make our own critical break with the Phoenicians until the exchange of information is totally electronic. There is no reason why paper—even computer-generated paper—can't be eliminated.

Sea-Land's information technologies are clearly helping us do a better job in serving our customers. But they're also helping us to a better job in serving ourselves. They have made us much faster in reacting to market and world events. And they let us see those events taking shape much further out on the horizon.

For example, we now electronically track order patterns around the world. And those patterns told us 10 months ago that a recession—and probably a bad one—was on the way. We had time to make the necessary adjustments and we just finished the most successful year we ever had. A number of people in the office—only half in jest—suggested that maybe we should start a commodities futures business. Our information flow around the world is becoming so sensitive that we seem to spot some changes before many economists do.

I'll turn now from our technologies to our people. You're probably bracing yourselves for a barrage of clichés about people being our most important asset. Relax. I'll skip the clichés. But I do want to make some very important points about how people—the technology people and the people we serve—fit together in our system.

Our people must go in knowing the business and knowing how technology can help it. They have to understand where access will really make a difference, before they can tell a client how to create it.

Having a global network in place also lets us build relationships through office technologies like E-mail and videoconferencing. Sea-Land had an internal telex system when global E-mail was introduced in 1989.

To give you an idea how fast E-mail has caught on, take a quick look at the chart behind me. And that was before one of our internal quality committee recommended that every Sea-Land employee should have access to E-mail. Now at Sea-Land, if you're not on the system, you're out of the deal stream. Information goes right past you. When you can't get on the system for some reason, you start to go through a sort of information withdrawal. A feeling that you're a step behind what everyone else knows.

We're also reaching outside the company by connecting our E-mail network to public telex and fax services. And we can now E-mail to ships at sea and exchange messages, through satellite service to other companies.

We're still building our videoconferencing system which rides on an international data circuit. So far, we have 11 Sea-Land and CSX sites hooked in. We're using new generation technology that lets us broadcast right from a standard conference room without an elaborate studio setup, using voice-activated cameras that switch the active broadcast sites electronically.

That's a very quick tour of information technology at Sea-Land. I hope I have made the point clearly: that fast, easy and effective access to information will drive our organization through the 90s and beyond. It is changing how we define the business.

Already today and even more so in the future, Sea-Land is an information network on which we hang transportation assets such as ships, trucks, trains, warehouses, depots, and offices. How those assets will be arranged on the system 10 years from now—or even the look of the system itself—is impossible to predict. Who knows what left turns and leaps technology will throw at us? And who knows where political, economic, or social change will strike? Who knows when Sea-Land or a competitor will come up with something that will upset the competitive balance?

Today's global market holds far too many variables—and they change too rapidly—to say with any real certainty: This is how it's going to be from here on.

But we *can* say with certainty that IT will be at the core of the world's strongest players. It will create some big winners in this decade just as it has in the last. They will be companies that understand the wiring of the business, and they will have injected the right technologies at the right points.

They will have spread access to technology up, down, and across the organization. And they will have carefully prepared people to lead and to use that technology.

They will be lean, flexible and fast. They will sense changes in their markets early, and they will have the agility to react in time to make a difference.

They will be able to do that because when change comes—and we know it will—response will not happen as it has in the past, by opening or closing divisions or making other massive physical or organizational changes.

Information technology access means:

They will not *reorganize* their companies.

They will *reprogram* it.

Thank you very much.

And good luck in this most exciting decade ahead.

Questions

1. What is *information technology?*

2. According to Parker, how has "technology enriched the corporate nervous sytem"?

3. How is *your* field, or the one you aspire to, changing as the result of the information revolution?

Index

Patterns; *see* Organizational patterns

Peale, Norman Vincent, 142

Personal experience speeches, 197–198

format, 198

model, 199–200

outline, 201–202

Personality, 81

development of, 9–10

habits and, 12–13

self-evaluation of, 9, 10, 11, 12

self-image and, 11, 12

socialization and, 10–12

Personal space, 63, 65

Persuasive speeches

format, 204–205

outline, 209–210

purpose of, 202–203

topic, 203

value types and, 203–204

Policies, 245

Political person; *see* Value types

Post-industrial society, 6

Posture, 65

Power of Positive Thinking, The (Peale), 142

Presentation, speeches of

expectations for, 159

formula, 159

model, 160

outline, 161–162

Presidential speeches, 146

Prime rate, 245

Product life cycle, 245

Proprietorship, 245

Public Speaking and Other Coronary Threats (Isaacson), 151–153

Q

Qualities of Success, The (Lidstad), 107–112

Quality circles, 245

Quotes, 115

R

Redundancy, 116

Reengineering, 245

Rehearsing, 122, 141, 143–144

Relaxation Response, The (Benson), 141

Religious person; *see* Value types

Research for speeches, 99–100

Résumé, 216

sample, 219

Rhetorical questions, 121

Rites and Rituals of Corporate Life, The (Deal and Kennedy), 240

Robinson, James Harvey, 141